The Odyssey of the Soul

The Odyssey of the Soul

Experiments on the Edge of Consciousness

Translated from the French by

Franck LABAT

Franck LABAT

ISBN: 978-2-9595447-0-5

To my wife Karen
and my children Tom and Tina,
with all my love.

FOREWORD

As we had never met in person, I wasn't sure what to expect from Franck Labat when he first offered to host a workshop in the French countryside with his group of non-English speaking participants. In November 2007, the person I encountered was a young and enthusiastic explorer of the nonphysical realms. I was impressed not only with his professional organizational skills but his determination in seeking the truth of our reality.

Over the years, his light has not dimmed. From that first workshop in Valence, to those that followed, to our frequent exchange of ideas and thoughts today, he has only increased his commitment to exploring our energetic existence.

Franck has a strong background in Acupuncture. His first book "Comprendre l'Acupuncture" (Understanding Acupuncture) was published in August 2012 and is an impressive work on its own. It gives him a unique perspective as he weaves together the dynamics of energy flow in the body to having a self-controlled experience in the nonphysical.

And so it seemed only natural to follow up with his work on out-of-body travel and this has come to fruition with his latest publication "The Odyssey of the Soul." In this work, he has captured the essence and excitement of the out-of-body experience. Throughout these pages, his dedication to the study of consciousness is clearly illustrated. With his own experiences interspersed with his insights and clear, simple instructions, you can feel his passion.

Franck has incorporated many elements such as Mudras, energy activation, sleep patterns, and more that encourage the reader to develop a customized practice designed to achieve whatever spiritual goals are on the horizon. And he backs it up with his own adventures of conscious exploration.

Whether you are a beginner seeking a spiritual pathway or a seasoned out-of-body explorer you will be sure to find helpful suggestions, techniques, and a variety of possibilities that you may never have considered. He will encourage you to take a look at many aspects of your practice, whether it be your astrological sign, your psychological traits, and even what time of day you are best suited for this endeavor.

Since our first meeting so many years ago, we have been sharing our methods, results, roadblocks, and research. He has been a valuable source of support and inspiration, not only for his followers in Europe but also for many of those seekers of conscious exploration that find value in collaborating within online communities.

On the following pages you may discover the start of an exciting journey into your own conscious awareness or unexpectedly identify the missing element in your current practice. I highly recommend "Odyssey of the Soul" to all explorers of consciousness. Be open to whatever happens and enjoy the ride!

William Buhlman

PREFACE

I grew up in an ordinary little village north of Valence, nestled in the charming Drome region of France. My childhood—cradled by the tranquility of this place—was marked by an extraordinary event in the summer of 1982, when I was just 10 years old. The intensity of this singular experience is engraved in my memory with astonishing precision, leaving an indelible imprint on my perception of the world.

As I slowly awoke, I gradually regained awareness of my surroundings and began to perceive the reassuring familiarity of the morning sounds of my home. However, an unusual sensation took hold of me, as if a numbness had invaded every inch of my body. Slight tingling ran over the entire surface of my skin, and I felt as if I were paralyzed. Panic set in as I found myself unable to move. Suddenly, an electric current seemed to flow through me and I felt myself floating above my bed, drifting gently through the air just a few inches from my physical vehicle. Then my body slid down my left side in a horizontal position, following a quarter-circle trajectory in which my feet represented the axis of rotation and my head the extremity describing this circular path—a bit like a compass, with the tip at my heels and the lead at the top of my skull.

My body moved gently, slightly in line with this movement as it floated in the air, and then stopped dead in my position at 90° to the starting point. Totally a spectator of this experience, I remained aware of my surroundings, hearing the noises of the house, but I felt powerless to act—like a mummy, unable to open my eyes or move to determine my position in space. My attempts to move were fruitless. My only option was to watch and let things happen. Finding myself suspended above the ground and outside my bed, the fear of falling suddenly seized me. This reflex reaction caused my "subtle body" to start moving in the opposite direction, gently bringing me back to my starting position in bed. The sensation of lightness and paralysis gradually faded, allowing me to open my eyes again and regain contact with my physical body. I was disorientated; this experience—though disturbing—was an undeniable reality for me, not the fruit of a dream.

Over time, two other similar events punctuated my nights.

One evening after going to bed, I got up and went into the living room. Glancing out of the window, I noticed small gleams of color behind the transparent white curtain. I stepped forward and—pulling aside the veil in front of the glass—I marveled at a shower of different-colored light. I found myself standing on the balcony in the middle of the night, watching as big drops of red, then yellow, white, and green fell from the sky. It was magnificent, magical; I felt good, as if they were bringing me sweetness and love. Then the experience stopped and I resumed my sleep.

Another night I found myself outside in the courtyard of my house; it was dark and I was playing on the concrete path between the little gate and the front door. I'd watch the stars in the sky and then go back to playing. The next day, I decided to share this intriguing experience with my mother, hoping perhaps to get some answers or clarification on what had happened. However, her reaction was far from what I had anticipated. From the outset, she categorically rejected the very idea of my going out at night, arguing that it was simply impossible for me to venture out at such a late hour. Her reasons were as categorical as her convictions: on the one hand, she firmly maintained that she would never have allowed me to wander about at that hour, and on the other she asserted with certainty that the house was double-locked, thus ruling out any possibility of an involuntary nocturnal escapade.

After that, I never told anyone what happened to me; I kept it to myself for many years but I thought about it regularly until one day many years later, I got the answer to my questions.

It was in 2004, when I was interested in esotericism in general, that I discovered books on what was called "astral travel." As a member of an esoteric internet group of enthusiasts, I had been advised to read Robert Monroe's "Journey Out of The Body." Monroe was an American former businessman who initially experienced a series of spontaneous out-of-body experiences. He later learned to master this ability to the point of reproducing it at will. From that day on, he devoted his entire life to the subject, going so far as to set up a research institute in Virginia known today as the Monroe Institute.

I was so fascinated by this book that I read it in just a few days. After that first reading, I felt the need to know more. It was like a need to be satisfied. As if I had something important to discover.

I was just starting to come to grips with the internet, so I decided to try to find some more interesting books on the subject. By chance, I came across William Buhlman's book "Adventures Beyond the Body." The cover inspired me, but I didn't know what to expect. I'd heard of well-known authors like Yram, Monroe, Rampa, etc., but never Buhlman. Two days later, the book arrived at my house and as soon as I opened it, I was captivated. It was when I read the first chapter of this book that I finally understood what I had experienced as a child. His description of the sensations of separation—what William calls the vibrational state—and his account of his first experiences, all took me back a few years, and I felt a kind of relief at finally being able to put into words what had remained an enigma all that time. The excerpt from his journal that started me on my journey is as follows:

"Journal Entry, December 7, 1992

I enter the vibrational state and float approximately two feet above my body. Determined to experience my finer vibratory body, I say, "I experience my higher body." After a brief sensation of motion, I'm floating in a different form. I feel calm and energized and sense a smoother internal energy. Inwardly, I know I've shifted to my inner energy-body. But I feel out of sync and my vision is hazy, so I demand complete clarity of awareness, "Clarity now!" Immediately my thoughts are clear. I feel extremely light and overflowing with energy. At that moment, my goal flashes in my mind: "I wish to visit another system." Instantly, I'm moving through a dark void at incredible speed. At first I'm startled by the speed, but I relax and adapt to the new sensations. Within seconds I'm floating in space. I look down at myself and see that there is little to see: my form has no arms or legs; I'm like a spherical form of conscious energy. For some reason, I'm not surprised—it seems completely natural that arms and legs are unnecessary in whatever state I'm in. I slowly rotate and focus on the spectacular sights around me. In awe, I stare at things I've never even imagined before. Clusters of lights are everywhere, thousands of them, like Christmas lights strung across the heavens. I feel as if I'm floating in an ocean of lights…"

- ***William Buhlman - Adventures Beyond the Body****: How to Experience Out-of-Body Travel: Proving Your Immortality Through Out-of-Body Travel - HarperCollins.*

After being enlightened by this revelation, I made the firm decision to put into practice the valuable advice and techniques taught in his book, with the aim of bringing about my very first deliberate out-of-body experience.

Every evening before drifting off to sleep, every time I woke up in the middle of the night, and even at every opportunity for a nap, I tirelessly repeated my affirmation, "Now I'm out of my body!" sometimes accompanied by a mental visualization. With perseverance and determination, I stuck to this routine even when doubt began to creep in.

For almost three weeks, I continued this assiduous practice without faltering, despite the moments of discouragement that became more and more numerous. And then, just as hope seemed to be dwindling, just as my efforts seemed doomed to failure, I was finally rewarded with a transcendent experience on July 21, 2005, the story of which I relate later in the book.

After such a profound experience, it's impossible to simply relegate it to the past and forget it. As Robert Monroe so rightly pointed out, once you've opened the door to the exploration of altered consciousness, the quest becomes a lifelong commitment. It's a journey punctuated by ups and downs, of course, but once you've had a taste of it, it's hard to resist the call to return, to continue practicing and evolving. It's a journey that demands constant devotion, a perpetual search for understanding and inner growth. It's a fascinating spiritual quest. I went on, met people, took workshops, wrote several journals, and started this book. Here, I gather my experiences and reflections. And even if there are many of us who share the same opinion—at least on most subjects—and even if my reflections are the conclusion of discussions I've had with several people following my personal experiences, all this concerns me alone. So please don't believe me…find your own answers.

My wish is simply to share with you some interesting elements both practical and theoretical, but above all to give you the desire and the keys to experience it for yourself. This work doesn't read like a novel; you can go straight to the chapter that inspires you. I've called it "The Odyssey of the Soul" because it's about the continuum of consciousness. When we seek to induce out-of-body experiences voluntarily, we have to practice various exercises such as meditation, visualization, self-hypnosis, dream analysis, lucid dreaming and so on. So, we navigate the ocean of different planes of consciousness—a bit like the frequency cursor on a radio, we pass through different stages of altered states of consciousness.

Dear reader, I hope you'll find in this book even a single element that can add a stone to the edifice of your spiritual quest.

Franck Labat

THE ODYSSEY OF THE SOUL

TABLE OF CONTENTS

PART ONE

THEORY

TRIBUTE TO WILLIAM BUHLMAN

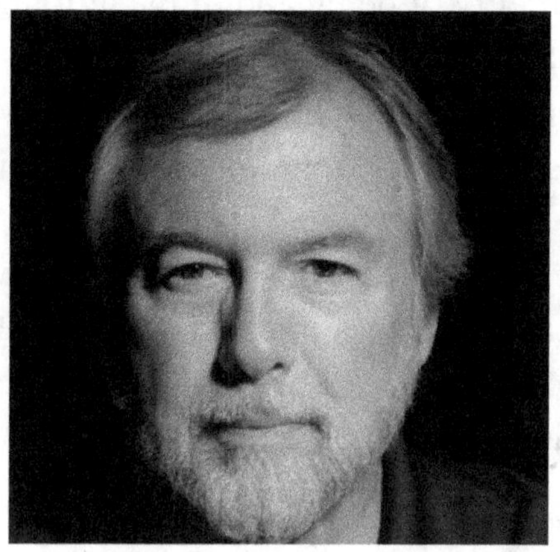

This book is a special tribute to my friend **William Buhlman**, an American author renowned for his significant contributions to the field of out-of-body experiences, illustrated in particular by his best-selling books "Adventures Beyond the Body" and "The Secret of the Soul." With over forty years of practice and research, Bill has established himself as a leading figure in the study of expanded states of consciousness.

His quest began in 1972, when he was still a student. An anecdote shared by a friend, describing his experience of floating above his own body, awakened in William an insatiable curiosity for the phenomenon. At a time when information was scarce, he embarked on a personal quest, gradually discovering techniques and writings that would forge his path in this unexplored field. After three weeks of assiduous practice, he experienced his first out-of-body experience, marking the beginning of a series of explorations that led him to question the nature of existence and spirituality.

Like Robert Monroe, over the years William has established

himself as an explorer of these invisible territories, overcoming his own apprehensions and pushing back the boundaries of knowledge on the subject. His personal discoveries convinced him of the multidimensional reality of being and of the unfoundedness of the fears traditionally associated with these experiences. It took him two decades to share his knowledge in "Adventures Beyond the Body," a book that compiles an extract from his journal, a scientific analysis of the phenomena encountered, and accessible techniques so that anyone can try the experience. Subsequently, he developed a vast survey, collecting numerous testimonies to constitute an in-depth study of out-of-body experiences, work that would culminate in the publication of "The Secret of the Soul."

After a rewarding career punctuated by international workshops and many years of collaboration with the Monroe Institute in Virginia, William has retired. He has written six books that have been translated into several languages, and numerous guided meditations that are available on CD or download. He leaves behind a valuable legacy for researchers and enthusiasts of expanded states of consciousness. He remains active, however, making himself available on his Facebook group and running two online workshops.

Workshops with William Buhlman:

Each year, William organized two-day workshops in Europe (France and Italy) as well as intensive week-long courses at the Monroe Institute in Virginia (USA). These workshops were mainly experiential and began with a series of hypnotic conditioning techniques. A wide range of out-of-body methods were explored, including such renowned techniques as hypnosis, the target technique, chakra and energy-body development, the rope technique, and sound-frequency induction, among others described in the books "Adventures Beyond the Body" and "The Secret of the Soul."

William generously shared his personal experience with

participants while encouraging everyone to form their own opinions through experimentation. The main goal of these workshops was to provide the tools needed to induce this fascinating experience. With over forty years of out-of-body experience behind him, William imparted a wealth of essential information. He also addressed the fundamental questions that everyone asks (dangers, death, creative thinking, etc.), providing clear answers devoid of esoteric folklore.

For further information, please visit William's website: www.astralinfo.org

Our meeting:

In 2004, I had the privilege of discovering William's works, in particular "Adventures Beyond the Body," a reading that had a profound effect on me and remains today an essential reference for me. At the time, I dared to try my luck by sending him an e-mail requesting a signed book, knowing that my chances were slim. To my surprise, not only did he reply, but he also sent me two of his books free of charge, in French. At the time, William was living in Shanghai, and I still treasure the parcel containing these precious books.

To express my gratitude, I decided to create a website for him in French, and then in Spanish. At the time, William wasn't very well known in France, which I found extremely regrettable, and I promised myself I'd do everything I could to remedy the situation. In 2007, I had the honor of organizing his first workshop in France. Despite my misgivings, I decided to go ahead, aware of the unique opportunity this event offered to the French. I had to find a location, accommodation, and a translator, as well as promote the event to attract enough participants. In the end, everything went very smoothly, and shortly afterwards I found myself at Lyon airport, waiting for William to arrive at Terminal 2. When I saw him from a distance, I felt an excitement mixed with the unreality of the situation, like that experienced when meeting a celebrity.

His friendly hug reassured me, and we left for Valence. On the highway, William burst out laughing when he noticed how small our French cars were compared to the imposing American ones, which marked the beginning of our budding complicity. My wife introduced him to French cuisine, and we shared some memorable moments together. I remember that on the first evening of the course as I was driving home, I expressed my sincere disappointment with the meal offered by the center. Indeed, the people in charge of the training place were offering vegetarian-inspired cuisine of mediocre quality. Not knowing me well enough yet, William didn't dare express his opinion on the subject. However, after discussing the matter openly, I noticed that he was pleased to see that our opinions concurred and that I was not a strictly vegan person, but one devoted only to a lifestyle based on love and simplicity. When we arrived, I brought out bread, sausage, pâté, cheese, and a bottle of good French red wine. We shared a memorable moment, alternating our good French products with moments of laughter. After this discussion, I felt that our relationship was gaining in authenticity.

Over the years, we've kept up this friendship. When William came back to us, my wife Karen and I took him to Paris. Then we were invited to his home in Baltimore with Susan, his wife. And a few years later in 2017, Bill invited me to the Monroe Institute for a week's intensive workshop, for which he was the instructor. Though William has retired, I continue to contribute to raising his profile by taking care of things like the Facebook group; I've also written several articles for French magazines, been invited to interviews, created videos, as well as other services. To this day, he remains one of the world's most recognized experts, and in France, he's a must.

Without "Adventures Beyond the Body," I would not be where I am today. I would like to express my deep gratitude to

William for the significant impact he has had on my life.

William and I at the Monroe Institute in 2017

It's impossible to talk about William without thinking of Susan, his wife. As the saying goes, "Behind every great man is a great woman." Indeed, to be the companion of a world-renowned expert in the field of out-of-body experiences requires profound openness and acceptance. In addition to being William's wife, Susan Buhlman is an experienced palliative-care professional. As a certified end-of-life doula, her vocation is to bring comfort to those going through the final moments of their lives. William and Susan have co-written a particularly remarkable book on preparing for death, offering a profound and comforting perspective on this universal passage. For those interested, the title is "Higher Self Now!"

Intensive workshop with William Buhlman
at the Monroe Institute in Virginia

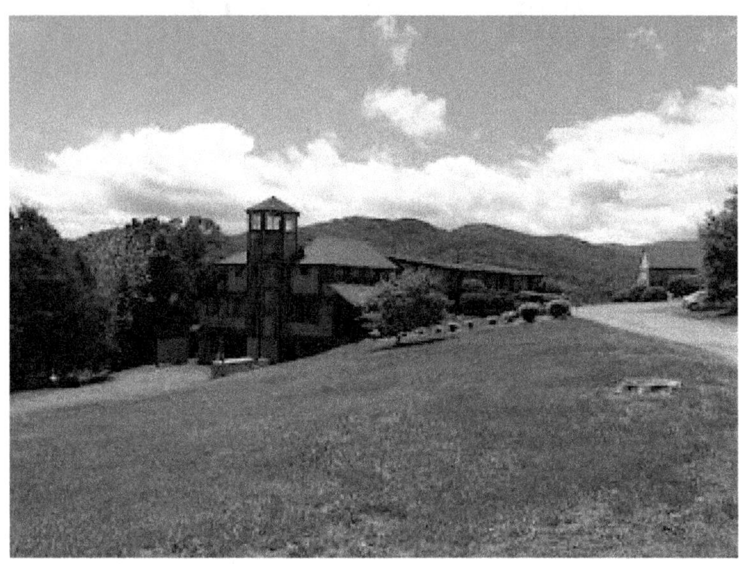

The Monroe Institute

I was privileged to be invited by William to participate in his intensive course at the Monroe Institute in May 2017. This establishment is truly exceptional and enjoys a worldwide reputation among specialists and enthusiasts of altered states of consciousness. Indeed, It is one of the only places in the world where scientific researchers conduct studies into out-of-body phenomena, lucid dreaming, and more. The institute also offers training courses open to anyone wishing to learn and practice different techniques under ideal conditions. Various teachers—all eminent personalities, renowned authors, and researchers—take turns teaching a variety of subjects.

The Monroe Institute (TMI) was founded in 1971 by Robert

Monroe, a successful businessman. At the time, Monroe was interested in accelerated learning methods using sleep and sound frequencies. It's by testing one of these frequencies at home that he experienced the out-of-body experience, an experience that had a profound effect on his life. After several such experiences, Monroe initially thought he was suffering from a neurological disease, but no medical diagnosis confirmed his fears.

While researching, Robert Monroe discovered that information on this phenomenon was scarce at the time. Determined to find out more, he decided to investigate further and develop methods to teach others about the practice. To this end, he collaborated with two physics engineers, Tom Campbell and Dennis Mennerich, with whom he worked intensively for almost a year to successfully induce out-of-body experiences in a controlled manner.

Thanks to their hard work, they developed a method of recounting the experience live by speaking into a microphone placed close to their mouths. This enabled them to study the reality of the experience and to give each other meeting "places." Alongside this training, Campbell and Mennerich also explored different frequencies to induce states of consciousness such as meditation and deep relaxation. Their collaboration with Monroe led to the creation of the famous Hemi-Sync sounds and the beginning of the Monroe Institute.

The institute is in the Blue Ridge Mountains—the eastern part of the Appalachian Mountains—just thirty minutes from the Charlottesville airport in Virginia. Nestled deep in the mountains in the heart of soothing nature, it's a magical place conducive to spiritual development.

On arrival, we are immediately welcomed by a member of the TMI staff who takes us to our room. This is very important, as this is no ordinary room: it's actually a CHEC Unit (Controlled Holistic Environmental Chamber Unit). It's a room with two cabins—in other words, for two participants—in which you'll find your bed, high-fidelity headphones, speakers, and buttons controlling lights of various colors. A curtain allows us to isolate ourselves in this box, which will serve as a practice area as well as a bed to sleep in at night. This building contains many CHEC Units.

A CHEC Unit

There are three main buildings on the estate: the one housing the CHEC units with bathrooms and toilets, a lounge, a classroom, a kitchenette, and a cafeteria. It's all very comfortable, very cozy, a bit like being at home. You can help yourself to drinks and food as and when you like. Large sofas adorn the lounge, and we often came in during breaks to chat with each other. Another adjacent building houses a large lecture and conference room below, with offices and a store above. A little further on is a third house, which turns out to be the research laboratory with highly sophisticated equipment.

The whole complex is set in magnificent grounds featuring an enormous rock crystal from Brazil, which beyond its impressive appearance, serves as a meeting place for some out-of-body experiences.

The Monroe Institute's crystal

The workshop was an intensive six-day venue, rich in both theory and—above all—practice. Day and night, we explored various methods. William gave us the gift of his personal experience, his in-depth reflections, and his precious advice. It was a rare privilege to benefit from his forty years of experience, and his advice proved invaluable. His passion—as vivid as ever—was reflected the depth of his explorations into subtle dimensions, even after many years. We acquired new knowledge unavailable in academic texts. Our practical sessions were held in our CHEC units under William's enlightened direction from his control tower. This unique installation housed the controls for manipulating hemi-sync soundtracks, adding his voice in real time, and supervising all CHEC units. Hemi-sync melodies integrated into the exercises greatly facilitated access to the targeted states of consciousness. The effectiveness of this technology enabled us—after just a few days of intensive training—to induce physical sleep while maintaining an awake state of consciousness, all without resorting to the Monroe Institute's CDs.

As William has retired, this type of workshop is no longer available nor are there any OBE training courses such as those he taught. There is, however, the famous Gateway course— the cornerstone of the Monroe Institute—developed by Robert Monroe and his engineers. This course is designed to facilitate access to this kind of unique experience.

William during a teaching session at TMI

In conclusion, I'd like to emphasize the singularity and energetic power of this remarkable place. To leave these blue mountains is to be profoundly transformed by an extraordinary experience. What particularly struck me was the diversity of the participants: a surgeon, an emergency doctor, a priest, a medium, and a radio host, to name but a few. Despite our different backgrounds, a sense of unity bound us together as if we were one family. This connection didn't fade with time; on the contrary, we kept in touch.

I strongly encourage you to live this experience if you have the opportunity. Even without William as a trainer, the place continues to offer enriching and transformative programs. Don't let this opportunity pass you by; you won't regret it. However, William continues to perpetuate his teaching through online courses. These courses are extremely well produced, with access to brand-new material and guided mediation using the hemi-sync technology. For more information, visit www.astralinfo.org.

Experience I had at the Monroe Institute on May 15, 2017:

"In the afternoon we experimented with the rope technique. After entering a deep state of relaxation guided by William and the support of hemi-sync music, we had to imagine a rope dangling from the ceiling. Using our imaginary hands, we were to visualize ourselves lifting off into the air holding onto this tether, to induce an out-of-body exit.

I don't know why, but I imagined myself being carried upwards by this rope. I then felt myself pass through the ceiling of my CHEC unit to find myself above the Monroe Institute. I could clearly see the building and its surroundings. The image was very clear and stable. I took the opportunity to attempt a trip to France to see my wife, children, and parents and then return to the Monroe Institute. At the end of the exercise, I was confused. I'd really experienced an out-of-body experience above the institute, but afterwards, when I went to visit my loved ones, I felt as if I'd fallen back into a sort of daydream. Whatever the nature of this experience, it was the one that left the strongest impression on me during my stay at TMI."

Monroe Institute contact details:

- https://monroeinstitute.org

Monroe Institute
365 Roberts Mountain Road
Faber, Virginia 22938 USA
Phone:
Toll-free (866) 881-3440
(434) 361-1500
Email: **Info@monroeinstitute.org**

INTRODUCTION

Each of us possesses unseen, untapped abilities that modern science is only beginning to comprehend. Controlled out-of-body experiences open the door to a new era of human development and exploration; however, it's up to us to explore the reality of this for ourselves—or to remain prisoners of our physical limits.

- William Buhlman

There are a lot of books about the out-of-body experience (OBE) and many of them have striking similarities. They often define the phenomenon, describe techniques that for the most part are hardly new, and offer explanations that have already been given many times over in other works. From time to time, a few tales of experience are shared; sometimes they're embellished, but these are often the exception rather than the rule.

Except for a handful of serious works that are now considered indispensable classics, a non-exhaustive list of which is provided in the appendix, serious researchers in search of knowledge and practice often find it difficult to quench their insatiable thirst for answers to their many questions. It's a daunting challenge to disentangle the true from the false, to find reliable sources, and to access authentic knowledge in a field where subjectivity and mystery reign supreme. Most people interested in the subject buy books, scour the internet, read forums, and try techniques without success.

The profusion of exercises of all kinds confuses everyone. Only successful or even invented experiences are reported. But what is it really like? Why does it seem so easy for some and so unattainable for others?

That's why I wanted to write this book.

As an ordinary person without exceptional gifts, juggling a busy career and a busy family life, I am fully aware that this book will probably not find its place among the essential works in this field. Nevertheless, my greatest desire is to humbly share my personal experience of lucid dreaming and out-of-body experiences: the difficulties encountered, the failures, the disappointments, the doubts, the fears, but also the perseverance and the successes. These extraordinary experiences have to be earned, but they are well worth the effort because they are transformative.

Today, we have far more information than we did a few years ago. The subject of out-of-body experiences has become less mysterious and has lost much of its taboo character. Although the USA remains in the lead with an open and welcoming approach to this field, we are seeing a growing interest in France compared to a decade ago. And yet we have authors who were among the pioneers in this field, such as the 19th-century Marcel Louis Forhan—known by his pseudonym Yram, and Charles Lancelin, also from the same period.

Then the New Age movement got involved, taking up the arguments of theosophy, notably with the notion of the seven planes and terms such as "astral," "astral travel," etc., which have since become part of everyday language. To preserve a secret or indoctrinated by some belief system, some groups or individuals have spread false information about the possible dangers of this practice.

Other individuals claiming to be spiritually advanced have once again contributed to the propagation of totally erroneous information, distorting the reality of out-of-body experiences. I don't claim to hold the absolute truth, but it's essential not to blindly accept the stories presented to us and to explore for ourselves to find the answers to our own questions.

Today, the French literary landscape lacks serious authors and teachers in this field. I'd like to take this opportunity to pay tribute to a late friend and instructor of mine, whose name was Akhena. She was one of a handful of rare individuals who provide quality teaching in France.

Technology has also been put to good use in the USA, as witnessed by the Hemi-Sync process developed by the Monroe Institute.

The challenge with this kind of experience is to approach the practice with an unbiased mind. By this I mean to approach it with as little conditioning as possible, without taking events at face value, and with the awareness that all experience in both life and out-of-body take place through the filters of our mind.

This is precisely where things get complicated. It's a mistake to impose one's vision as the Truth. In my opinion, a good author and experimenter is one who asks himself questions with each experiment. One who shares his thoughts, knowing that they are very personal and may be wrong. And above all, one who is open to other answers, confronting them with his own.

We are so small compared to the Creation, and what we perceive, we do so with our five physical senses, i.e., in an extremely limited way. Some experiences are so profound that they're beyond words, they can't be described, and that's when we become aware of our limits.

It seems to me—and this is only my opinion—that as long as the notions of form, space, and time exist, then we are in a limited reality, conducive to illusory projections. The quest of human consciousness should therefore be to go beyond all concepts.

Once out of the body, we find ourselves in a dimension that is highly sensitive to thought, whether conscious or unconscious. We therefore need to approach our experiences and encounters with caution. That's why some authors have written fictional stories about their out-of-body journeys, thinking they reflected reality when in fact they were only describing their own perceptions.

I'm not denigrating this type of story, however, as any out-of-body experience is of great benefit to our own spiritual evolution. But it must remain intimate and personal, because what we experience is in line with our level of evolution at a given moment. We all have to go through various stages of evolution in order to move forward; they are like steps leading us towards progressive spiritual maturation. We must learn from each experience, use it to go further, and never stop there thinking we've reached the end of the journey.

I insist on paying close attention to the phenomena we encounter during a session beyond our body of flesh, and not falling into the trap of illusion.

CHAPTER 1

OUT-OF-BODY EXPERIENCES

Definition and Personal Journal

Out-of-body experience is a pathway to understanding who we really are. It shows us that our consciousness is not limited by our physical body but can explore dimensions far beyond what we imagine.

- Robert Monroe

I don't consider myself an expert but rather an explorer of the mysteries of existence, driven by a relentless quest to understand the mysteries of life. Birth itself is an extraordinary phenomenon. Have you ever wondered where we were before we were born? So many years have passed, so many historical events have taken place, and what about us? What were we doing all this time? Did we exist? Perhaps not, in which case we were essentially dead before we were born. However, if we start from the principle of the immortality of consciousness, the concept of reincarnation invites us to reflect on the different lives we've had, the choices of rebirths we've had to make, and the significance of these "repetitions."

Then, after our birth, a film of our life is projected. What is our role here on earth? Why such a short time in this physical reality? Why so many trials? What's terrible these days is that people are turning away from the mystery of existence in favor of material comfort. Routine parasitizes our consciousness with the sound of a lullaby, blinding and deafening us on the raft that carries us across the river of life to our deathbed.

As we breathe our last breath while watching the film of our lives, our regrets emerge from the realization of our actions.

So why be born if we're going to die? Nothing lasts; all the elements making up this physical universe are doomed to disappear one day or another. And you too, dear reader, will eventually die. You have to face up to this reality if you want to give value to your life. Do you really think we can avoid all these questions by taking refuge in futile pleasures? Work, money, comfort, vacations, etc…we have no choice but to honor our obligations and suffer the distractions of life, but we can do so with our eyes open and our consciousness awake.

There are different ways of finding the answers to these questions, and altered-consciousness experiences are one of them. They enable us to *know*—not *believe*—that our spiritual essence is immortal. Death has nothing to do with us; it's a matter for our physical body, the mere vehicle of our consciousness.

My first self-induced experience

In 2004, after reading William Buhlman's book "Adventures Beyond the Body," I decided to practice the exercises suggested, and more specifically the method of affirmations. Every night and at every nap, I repeated the phrase, "Now, I'm out of body!"

Three weeks later on September 23, 2004, I went to bed with the determination to get out of my body and repeat to myself the affirmation "Now, I'm out of body!" while relaxing, until I fall asleep. I'm awakened around 4 a.m. by my daughter crying. After getting up with great difficulty because I was so tired, I went back to bed repeating my favorite affirmation to myself again. Around 5 a.m., I was awakened by huge vibrations and a roaring noise in my ears. The power of the phenomenon knocked the wind out of me, and I didn't have the reflex to apply a technique to get out of my body. I was disappointed to have missed this opportunity, but very happy to have experienced what the famous vibrations. This experience made me realize how true this book was and how serious its content was. That day was the starting point for all my adventures beyond physical reality. In the months that followed, I experienced vibratory phenomena on several occasions without ever managing to induce a total exit.

It wasn't until July 21, 2005, in a moment of relaxation, that I finally managed my first voluntary out-of-body exit. That evening, tired from my day, I hadn't done any exercise.

Journal entry, July 21, 2005

"I was dreaming that I was trapped in some kind of steel cage with bars when my dream adventure was suddenly interrupted by strong vibrations that woke me up. I then became aware that I was in my bedroom, lying motionless on my bed, and I immediately had the reflex to get out of my body. I don't know why—perhaps because of practicing so much—without thinking I moved my consciousness out of my physical body—which was asleep—starting with my head. It was as if I was rushing headlong into it, and then the rest followed. The first sensations were weightlessness and a deep silence. I found myself at the foot of my bed facing the wall, and my immediate reaction was to turn around and look at my body. There it was; I could perceive the dark shape of a body sleeping peacefully. I then thought of climbing up to the roof to see the sky, and I saw myself crossing the ceiling and the rafters before reaching my destination. I searched the firmament and the surrounding area, but my vision was blurred and I couldn't perceive any colors. Everything was in black and white. This might seem logical, given that it was nighttime, but I was expecting a brighter, more luminous environment. Although I said out loud, as William Buhlman recommended, "Clarity now!" not only did no sound come out of my mouth but there was no improvement in my perception either. I went back to my room and remembered, for no reason at all, the time my wife had told me she'd passed a white shadow in the hallway at night. As soon as I thought about it, I saw myself rushing towards it, and then I was back in my body in a flash; it was 5.30 a.m. and I had vibrations behind my neck and a strong internal sensation of rocking from left to right. I wanted to take advantage of being in the right state to try again, but the

excitement and disorientation put an end to the trip."

This date will remain in my life as an upheaval, a radical change in my beliefs and an understanding of our true nature. I had direct, personal proof that consciousness exists independently of the physical body, which is also proof of the existence of life after death. I felt an intense euphoria, overwhelmed by thousands of questions.

A new adventure had begun.

My experiences

During the writing of this book, I questioned the relevance of sharing my own experiences. This choice illustrates my role as an explorer of subtle dimensions rather than as a simple narrator. The literary world already abounds with accounts of "astral travel," and it was not my intention simply to add another tale to this collection. After all, it's easy for a gifted writer to invent a captivating story, with no one able to dispute its veracity. On the other hand, an out-of-body experience is intrinsically personal and cannot be considered universal.

That's why I subscribe to William Buhlman's perspective, which favors the dissemination of knowledge and tools that enable each reader to undertake his or her own explorations. Because, in the end, that's what really matters. Telling a multitude of subtle adventures can only enrich the reader by offering a moment of escape and a perspective that remains fundamentally my own.

I'm about to unveil a collection of astral projection experiences that have punctuated my journey over the last few years. The stories I've selected are those that have made a profound impression on me, not for their spectacular appearance, but for their significance and impact on my understanding of this extraordinary phenomenon. My aim is to arouse your curiosity and encourage you to explore, while emphasizing that the concepts discussed in this book are the fruit of rigorous personal practice.

The first attempts at astral projection are often engraved in the memory, the result of weeks or even months of persevering practice punctuated by successes and failures. The emergence of warning signs—such as sensations of intense vibrations—marks a turning point, revealing the tangible reality of these experiences. While these first astral sorties may lack the brilliance of more advanced adventures, they are nonetheless fundamental. They represent a moment of profound transformation, a true rite of passage. As Robert Monroe pointed out, once the door is open, it never fully closes. It's the inauguration of a never-ending inner journey, forever transforming our perception of the world and ourselves.

In my first few months of stammering, I had many episodes such as the following little experiment:

Journal entry, October 3, 2004

I take advantage of a nap to begin a relaxation session while repeating my affirmation to myself. Then, tired out, I fall asleep. I'm awakened a few minutes later by strong vibrations and the sensation of rolling over myself. I tried to get out using Robert Monroe's method, i.e., by imagining rolling on my side, but the fact that I wanted to try it put an end to the experiment. The problem here was a lack of concentration.

Various phenomena that can be experienced

During your explorations of altered states of consciousness, you may encounter a variety of strange and fascinating phenomena, signs of an impending out-of-body experience. Here, I share the most common manifestations to prepare you to welcome them without surprise. Understanding and mastering these phenomena is equivalent to mastering the experience itself. In sharing this knowledge, my aim is to dispel the fears borne of ignorance, for it is these apprehensions that represent the greatest obstacles to our nonphysical adventures. This section of the book is devoted to some of my personal experiences, focusing mainly on two phenomena: astral sight and astral noise.

Astral sight, or the ability to "see" through closed eyelids, manifests itself when we are about to leave our physical body. It seems then that our "astral" eyes can perceive our immediate surroundings and sometimes even beyond. This ability enables us to observe distant scenes as if our physical limitations were no longer an obstacle.

As for "astral noises," these are noises perceived at the threshold of the experience during the initial vibratory state. These sounds can be as simple as voices or as intense as detonations sometimes so startling as to interrupt the journey prematurely. Personally, I'm inclined to think that these sound manifestations are the product of our brains during the hypnagogic state, like the borderline between wakefulness and sleep where we can experience fleeting visions or hear sounds without an identifiable source. This is how I interpret these phenomena, because once fully projected out of the body, I have never been able to identify any physical origin for these sounds such as entities whose voices I might have heard.

Journal entry, June 18, 2006

I woke up without moving last night, in an ideal state of consciousness for a projection—what Robert Monroe called "mind awake, body asleep."

As usual, I immediately began reciting my affirmation. The black veil in front of my closed eyelids slowly dissipated as I concentrated on the experience. I could perceive my bedroom window and my bedside table very clearly but in black and white, as my room was plunged into darkness. When my concentration waned, the black fog gradually came back to obstruct my vision. For the first time, I experienced what is known as "astral sight," i.e., vision through closed eyelids. It's an experience that belongs to the vibratory state, the moment preceding an out-of-body exit.

Journal entry, October 26, 2006

Following a nighttime awakening, I took the opportunity to make a few affirmations before falling asleep. A little later in the night I was startled awake by a gunshot near my left ear.

According to the information I've found on this phenomenon, it's a noise emitted when the subtle body separates from the physical body. Personally, I'm more inclined to think of it as a hypnagogic sound. When we're on the borderline between wakefulness and sleep, we naturally become sensitive to visual and sometimes auditory hallucinations. We perceive images and occasionally hear a voice, music, or noise. This type of manifestation is interesting because it tells us that we are in the ideal state of consciousness, also called the vibratory state, to induce an experience. It's at this point that you need to use your exit technique, because at this point, the separation has begun. I regained consciousness as I was leaving my physical body and being startled by the noise put an end to the experience.

Journal entry, March 1ᵉʳ 2007

Last night, I had barely been in bed for five minutes when I heard a man shouting in my ears. He uttered a swear word that I couldn't write down here. There was so much echo that it sounded like he was using a microphone plugged into an amplifier. Having experienced this kind of phenomenon before, I knew at once that it was a hypnagogic sound. However, this was the first time I'd heard such a loud and clear voice, so much so that it startled me, and I looked around to see if everyone was asleep. What surprised me most of all was that I'd just gone to bed and was fully conscious when it happened, as I'm usually on the borderline between wakefulness and sleep.

Journal entry, June 3, 2017

Since my return from the Monroe Institute, I've been practicing almost every day during a short nap between 12:30 and 1:30 p.m.

Lying on my bed and listening to the "Into the Deep" CD developed by the Monroe Institute, I perform the relaxation William taught us (imagining floating in a comfortable cloud combined with a countdown from seven to one). And then I start repeating my affirmation "Now I'm out of the body and on my way to the crystal!" At the end of the workshop, we were challenged to come home and project ourselves onto the giant rock crystal hoisted up in the middle of the park where participants used to walk. That's why I modified my affirmation. Suddenly, I feel something like a soft cloud surrounding me. All my tensions gradually dissipate. I feel good, calm, and safe. Then, through my closed eyelids, I perceive a kind of mauve fog. The center of the fog gradually dissipates, giving me a brief, clear glimpse of the Monroe Institute crystal. Then it gently closes, and the image disappears. The experience ends with an internal rocking sensation that lasts a few seconds. As always, I try to take advantage of the situation to induce an out-of-body exit by amplifying the vibratory state, but to no avail.

Experiences of contact with entities or the deceased

From the moment you begin to experience things outside our physical reality, you can expect to encounter other entities, and even deceased people. Whether they're deceased or not, their nature is identical to yours: they're souls, just like you. What's more, it's important to remember that we're different out-of-body, so things that would seem completely bizarre in the physical realm don't shock us in the slightest. An encounter in the afterlife isn't frightening at all. We tend to be apprehensive of what we don't know, which is perfectly normal. We create a whole world for ourselves, a distorted representation of something that ultimately seems natural. Let's not forget that we're not physical beings having a spiritual experience; we are first and foremost spiritual beings having an experience in the physical dimension. As a result, when we leave our bodies, we return home. The place from which we were born.

Personally, I have the sensation with every out-of-body experience that I'm truly me, that I've found myself again. These contacts are opportunities, a chance to live them, especially when it's to find loved ones we've lost. I understand that at first we may be afraid of this, but remember that these disembodied entities are no more powerful than you are; they are consciousness just like you. If you read the writings of various authors on this subject, you'll discover that they have all lived this type of experience to the point of being transformed by it. It enriches and transforms you in a significant way. I sincerely hope that you will experience such a revelation.

Journal entry, September 19, 2005

I woke up at 6 a.m. and went back to sleep around 6:30 a.m. I then found myself in a very real dream in which I was lying down. A few seconds later I became aware that I was making short out-of-body exits, i.e., exiting about eight inches from my body and then re-entering, repeatedly.

I was lying on my stomach and felt like I was penetrating my mattress several times, until at one point my knees touched the tile floor. Then I felt the cold of the floor. After this little series of repeated experiences, my chest came out completely and I was able to observe a person beside my bed; the image wasn't very clear, but it was a friendly presence. It was like a shadow whose contours I could describe with precision; there was no doubt that it was indeed a presence, watching but reassuring. Then I regained consciousness in my bed and as always, felt vibrations throughout my body as I re-entered my physical form. Who was this person? I never found out, but I was convinced I knew her.

Journal entry, January 24, 2007

Last night, I found myself somewhere between dream and awake, in an altered state of consciousness that I often experience where I'm holding a conversation with people in my bedroom. I see the place as it is, with the light on but with an extra protagonist. I have experienced and still experience these situations quite regularly. I'm sitting up in bed while my physical body is asleep, stretched out behind me, with a clear vision of the surroundings. The room is lit up, but the scene is taking place in the middle of the night. I was in a spontaneous projection chatting with my son when my maternal grandfather somehow appeared, walking on my duvet and saying something I can't remember. It was then that I noticed a change in my degree of consciousness, because usually in this kind of experience I don't notice anything abnormal. Here, I was surprised to see him because I was aware that he was no longer part of this world. He was talking to me when I interrupted his monologue to tell him how happy I was to see him again. He smiled and came over to me; I wrapped my arms around him and felt so much happiness and love. Then he disappeared and I started to cry. Throughout the experience, I also noticed a presence to my left. It was then that I gently regained consciousness in my physical body, accompanied by vibrations that are now familiar to me as well as the sound of an engine in my ears. I savored this moment for a long time, simply happy with what had just happened, without feeling the need to do anything else.

Journal entry, February 11, 2018:

I woke up around 3:30 in the morning. Then I went back to sleep, repeating with determination my affirmation, "Out of body now!" Without going through the vibratory phase, I found myself in a small, dark room, a kind of spaceship interior with indigo-blue metal walls and I could perceive electrical cables and switches. White, dimly lit neon lights were embedded in the corners of the ceiling. Then I closed my eyes; I was sitting on a gray metal chaise lounge and could feel four caring people around me. I opened my eyes and saw three men and a little girl. One of them came up behind me, tipped me backwards and took my head in his hands. I then picked up words in my mind, as if by telepathy: "If you want to have out-of-body experiences, then you have to unlock this!

He pressed hard with both thumbs on my forehead, at the level of the third eye, so hard that I could feel the pain, but I was confident and relaxed despite everything. Vibrations began to run lightly through my body. The man did it a second time, pressing even harder, and once again I felt pain, when suddenly the black veil behind my eyelids dissipated, giving way to a blue light that grew brighter and brighter.

I then spontaneously found myself lying on the seats of an airplane. It was very surprising, a bit like waking up from a heavy sleep. I was in a row of three seats, lying full length.

I had trouble waking up. I managed to stand up and open one eye, but had great difficulty opening my other eye. Then I fell back, lying on the seat. This was unusual for me, as I'm usually the type to wake and get up quickly.

I had the sensation of being in another person's body. Finally, I managed to stand up and open my eyes completely. I could see all the details very clearly; it was extremely realistic. The people around me were putting on their jackets, as if we were about to arrive at our destination. Then, suddenly, I was back in my body. It was around 5:30 a.m., vibrations were running through my body and I was in great shape. Afterwards, I hardly slept at all.

<u>*Journal entry, July 24, 2018*</u>

It's been eleven days since my mom passed away, and it's been a very difficult time for me. Of course, I miss her and would like to see her again. So, I've resumed my practice as best I can in the hope of communicating with her. At around 2:30 a.m., following a nocturnal awakening, I began to repeat my usual affirmation with determination until I fell asleep. I'm in the middle of a dream when vibrations bring me back to consciousness. I feel that characteristic fresh breeze on my face but it's as if I'm stuck in my physical body, unable to get out. I force myself with a lot of willpower until I manage to extricate myself. I find that I'm levitating in my bedroom and start flying around the room, circling the ceiling. It's daylight and my peripheral vision is a little blurred, but I can see my surroundings just fine. I shout, "Mom!" several times, visualizing her face in the hope of contacting her. Nothing happens. I feel that the experience is coming to an end and I have great difficulty maintaining my concentration and the duration of this state. I suddenly lose consciousness and wake up lying in bed, bathed in a fading vibratory ocean.

Journal entry, June 28, 2019

I found myself in a park and, to my surprise, my mother, who died almost a year ago, was standing there, facing me, in the middle of the path. She was wearing bright, light-colored clothes. She looked serene, but I noticed that she was wearing a bandage on the left side of her throat. I was both surprised by this unexpected encounter and so happy to see her again. I went over to her and took her in my arms. Her eyes were beautiful, but she was staring straight ahead, staring into space, a bit like a robot. She seemed lost; it was strange.

I hadn't heard from her since she passed away. I'd heard that some of the deceased were taken after their death into a kind of care center after having suffered physical damage during their lifetime. That would also explain why I haven't been able to get in touch with her all this year. That night in the park, it was as if I'd been given the honor of being able to pick her up on her way out of the care center. I suddenly returned to my body and in full vibratory state as always, I saw the scene again, my emotions torn between joy and confusion.

My most unusual contact experience

Now I will relate an experience that's a little different, and I'm classifying it as a contact because that's what happened, not with an entity but with another person: Akhena.

Akhena, now deceased, was a leading figure in the world of out-of-body experiences in France. She offered training at her home in Marseille or by correspondence with CDs and contact by phone or email. I started with her distance-learning course out of curiosity, to find out about her techniques, and it was there that one night during an out-of-body experience that I met her. I'd never seen her before in photos or anywhere else, and it was the first time I'd had this kind of experience.

Journal entry, January 25, 2008

For the past three weeks, I've been taking a correspondence course on out-of-body experiences with Akhena. I've been practicing the exercises she proposes on CD every day, and we've been in regular contact by e-mail and telephone. Last night, I applied the course guidelines. Affirmations are one of the techniques proposed. I fell asleep in the middle of my practice and without any vibratory transition, I found myself in a room with a very clear vision of the place. There's a white sofa next to a bay window and a lady is sitting on it. It's Akhena! I've never seen her physically or in pictures, but deep down I know it's her. She's dressed in white—a woman with graying hair, of a certain age but exuding a certain youthfulness. We exchange a few words that I do not remember. Then I decide to change location and try to fly away. I feel strong vibrations, but I'm stuck in this room. It's impossible to get out of here. Then I return to my body.

In the morning, I sent an e-mail to Akhena to tell her about my adventure. To my great surprise, she replied that she had experienced the same thing and thus confirmed—based on her over forty years' experience in this field—that we had met in a subtle reality. Out-of-body communication is a rare phenomenon, difficult to induce voluntarily, and this one was a real highlight for me.

Two years later, I decided to sign up for a two-day workshop she was organizing in Lavera, a village near Marseille, to meet her in person. No sooner had we seen each other than we recognized each other. One evening, we were alone, chatting about that famous experience. Everything matched. The colors, the clothes, etc.

There was no doubt about what happened. In fact, Akhena included this story in her book "Sorties Hors-Du-Corps - Manuel Pratique." She changed my first name to "François" in her manuscript to preserve my anonymity. Then she asked my permission to use my real identity before being published, and I agreed. Unfortunately, she died before the change was made and the book was published as is.

Continuum experiences

I'll come back to this notion of the "continuum of consciousness" later in the book, but to summarize, it corresponds to the notion of the multi-dimensionality of being. We are both in this physical world and in all existing dimensions simultaneously, while our consciousness focuses on a specific reality. So, there's no real separation of body and mind when we have an out-of-body experience; it's a shift of consciousness on this continuum, like changing the frequency of a radio. Instead, we speak of an expansion of consciousness. But since consciousness needs a vehicle to experience each dimension, it really does feel as if we've moved away from our physical body, without actually being separated. It's a sensation that's difficult to explain, and one that needs to be experienced. I'll come back to this point in the next chapter, but I'd like to share a few experiences that illustrate this notion.

Journal entry, February 22, 2006

Following a nocturnal awakening, I was concentrating on my usual affirmations as I drifted off to sleep, when suddenly I had the feeling of being in two bodies at once. It was as if I had separated from my body and was floating a few inches away from my physical form and facing it. I could feel my ribcage breathing, but in a different way. In other words, I was aware of my breathing but at the same time watching my body breathe as an outside observer. It was as if there was another person's rib cage facing me, the two chests in contact. The only difference was that I could clearly perceive inhalation and exhalation, as if my physical and nonphysical lungs were overlapping without getting in each other's way. It's hard to describe; the experience was certainly strange but not at all unpleasant. It could be that I became aware of the situation just as my subtle body began to exude slightly. According to many authors and experiencers, this is a process of energetic revitalization common to everyone that occurs every night.

Journal entry, July 11, 2016

After waking up at night still lying on my back, I took advantage of this favorable moment to repeat my affirmation. Two or three minutes later, something unusual happened to me that I'm still struggling to explain. I felt my physical body turn to the right, the position I usually take to fall asleep. I felt the movement while I was still consciously on my back. I found myself lying in my subtle body; my physical body had turned over on its own. So, I was out of my body the whole time. Then I returned to my physical body.

It's interesting to note that despite the externalization of the spirit, because it's close to the physical body, one feels as if they're in both bodies at the same time. I've never seen a silver cord, but I've often had the experience of feeling a connection with the physical body while on an astral journey.

Existence of a magnetic field

Experienced people have observed a zone close to the physical body that tends to blur vision and draw us towards our body like a magnet. This force field has a radius of around fifteen feet. I relate here one of my experiences on this subject. I could share others, but they wouldn't add anything new.

Journal entry, April 28, 2006

I had several thought-provoking little experiences last night. It began with what is known as a "false awakening," the experience of dreaming that you are emerging from sleep. It's a phenomenon that often occurs when we practice psychic projection exercises daily.

After I've gone to bed and am half asleep, I repeat my favorite affirmation as usual. Then I open one eye and, seeing the time, realize I'm late for work. I got up in a hurry to get ready when suddenly I woke up again, but in a second dream. At this point I say to myself, "Well, I've just been the victim of a false awakening!" However, despite this observation, I didn't immediately realize that I was still in a dream environment. During this period of practice, I'm finding it hard to become lucid, despite the obvious signals I'm being offered, which raises a lot of questions for me.

Then finally, I was awakened by strong vibrations and an intense ringing in my ears. I took the opportunity to immediately try an out-of-body experience. True to my routine, I did a head-first push-up, and at that moment, I was out of my body. Once out, I found myself in a very dark environment where I couldn't see or hear anything. So, I decided to leave my room, trying to get through the wall to the outside of the house.

I found myself back in my hallway and to my surprise it was impossible to cross the partition leading outside. At this time, my vision became clear again; I could finally see my hall, but in a grayish way. It was during this experience that I became aware of the existence of a kind of magnetic field around the physical body that had the side-effect of blurring subtle perceptions such as sight or hearing. I'd heard about it without paying much attention, but this time I had proof. This explains why during certain experiences when we are too close to our vehicle of flesh, we very often experience vision problems. Then, for no reason at all I tried to see if I could move my physical left leg, and not only did I do so, but I also suddenly felt my whole human form. I didn't experience the re-entry; perhaps I lost consciousness for a short while. Some people call this effect a "blackout." I've noticed that during an outing, we sometimes have uncontrolled reactions whose cause remains an enigma. Why did I want to move my left leg? After this episode I fell asleep to have another false awakening. I've been prone to this type of phenomenon for some time now, and it's a common occurrence among many OBE practitioners.

That night taught me two important things: to do projection exercises while half-asleep is very effective; and above all, the existence of magnetic fields makes it imperative to move away from the physical body quickly, as William often says, if we don't want to put an end to our adventure.

Various experiences

I'd like to share with you several experiments I've carried out that I think are interesting. I've considered them unclassifiable because they don't really stand out, but they do contain information that may help beginners.

Journal entry, October 6, 2005

I fell asleep repeating my affirmations and then I woke up at around 4 a.m. I take advantage of this nocturnal awakening to reiterate my phrase again, when suddenly I realize that I'm practicing foolishly, without enough motivation. So, I put an end to the exercise and put a hand on my heart (cardiac chakra), trying to bring up emotions, thinking of people close to me or pleasant situations. I find it hard to feel anything. Because my first sleep cycle has left me half asleep, my emotions have trouble surfacing. After a few minutes, I finally feel an inner strength, a desire to experiment. I begin my practice again, saying to myself "I want to have a beautiful out-of-body experience!" Then I repeated to myself, "Now I'm out of body!" with a firm intention to make it happen right away. This time, the intention was so strong that I had a bit of trouble falling asleep. I was awakened at around 6:30 a.m. by strong vibrations. My first reflex is to push myself forward, to extract myself from my fleshy form. Then the vibrations stopped and I felt dizzy, as if I were spinning around. I couldn't see anything yet my eyes seemed to be open. The event only lasts a few seconds and then I regain consciousness of my physical body, feeling vibrations once again. I tried to amplify them to voluntarily induce a new experience but was unable to do so. This out-of-body experience was very brief but instructive. Last night, I understood the importance of desire and willpower. It's important to prioritize quality of practice over quantity by working on intention. As I reread my journal, I also realized that practicing after waking up at night is an ideal time for me.

Journal entry, November 10, 2006

I wake up around 5 a.m., too tired to practice any method, so I decide to get up and have a drink to come to my senses. Ten minutes later, I go back to bed and start repeating my affirmation combined with a visualization. Seeing that it was already 6 a.m. and that I had to get up at 7 a.m., I turned on my side and drifted off to sleep. I wake up slowly, without moving, with a slowly rotating fan blade in my frontal field of vision, my eyes closed. I perceive it as a shadow with the light flashing between each pass of the blade. Out of curiosity, I try to increase its speed. I immediately feel and perceive the speed increasing. Almost immediately I find myself shaken by enormous vibrations throughout my body and loud ringing in my ears. My subtle vision then works for a few seconds, just long enough to perceive the bedroom window through my closed eyelids. My heart starts beating rapidly, as I wasn't expecting such a strong reaction. Knowing what's going on, I try to control the situation by calming down and maintaining the few vibrations I can still feel. I try again to increase the vibratory state, but it's at this point that my alarm goes off—it's 7 a.m.

<u>*Note:*</u>

- This is the first time I've triggered vibrations of this magnitude from the waking state.

- I wasn't in a state of half-sleep, I was wide awake and I hadn't moved; I was quite relaxed. I think that concentrating on something and creating an internal movement must have triggered the vibrations.

- I don't know whether this fan image (in shadow form and therefore not a clear image) was hypnagogic or a simple visualization.

<u>*Journal entry, July 25, 2014*</u>

Last night, following a night awakening around 4 a.m., I did what's known as a "wake back to bed" (WBTB). This simply means getting up in the middle of the night to regain some consciousness, having a drink or whatever, then going back to bed to start your practice (see the chapter on techniques). Once I'm lying down, I relax as much as possible before mentally repeating my favorite phrase, "I'm out of body and I experience my higher self now!" I find it hard to fall asleep but that's normal; I put a kind of stress on myself to influence my subconscious. Usually when I do it this way, I get results. Once I've imprinted the intention on my mind, I can let go and fall asleep.

Then I fall asleep and regain consciousness directly outside my body without having undergone the usual vibratory phase. I'm in a gray environment and can't see where I am, but I can feel that I'm flying and I can feel fresh air on my face. I ask out loud, "Clarity now!" and my vision becomes clearer and clearer; I can see a starry sky all around me.

Right now, on a Facebook group devoted to out-of-body experiences, we've set ourselves a challenge: to get to the Statue of Liberty via an OBE. Remembering this, I ask to go to this place I know from physical experience. I feel myself being taken somewhere but without being able to see anything. I stop moving and change my goal, wanting to visit William in Baltimore, and again I start moving quickly but still in the dark. I then lose consciousness and find myself in a dream, lying in bed in a modern bedroom. Karen is sleeping next to me when our daughter Tina arrives and climbs onto the bed. She's a baby, but in reality, she's 12. My wife asks Tina, "What's the matter, darling? Have you had a fright?" and I tell her, "But look, it's a baby." She doesn't seem to understand so I insist: "Our daughter is 12, she has long hair and talks, but this is a baby; it's an illusion, we're in a dream!" Then I went back to sleep, tired and putting an end to the experiment.

<u>*Journal entry, June 8, 2015*</u>

For the past month and a half, I've been trying to get back into the regular practice of out-of-body techniques. I'm finding it difficult to concentrate due to a high level of fatigue. This is disrupting my motivation, but I'm persevering and my desire is to move on to a higher stage of exploration.

Last night, I got up around 4:30 a.m. Once back in bed, I had a little more trouble falling asleep than usual so I took the opportunity to try to relax while remaining conscious. I decided to use two affirmations for a change: "I remain conscious while my body is asleep!" and, "I'm out of body now!"

I didn't repeat my sentences many times. Eventually, I drifted off to sleep only to be awakened half an hour later by strong vibrations. Surprised by this unexpected awakening, I first enjoyed the vibrations and tried to amplify them, then I let myself be lulled by them. My whole body was vibrating. I took the opportunity to assert my desire to go out, but it didn't work. A little exasperated, I tried to force my way out. I was lying flat on my bed while my physical body was asleep on its side. I leaned on my subtle hands and mimicked doing push-ups to induce the exit. I pulled myself out with difficulty, a few inches above my physical body, struggling against what felt like a force trying to pull me back in. I tried several times to no avail and fell back asleep.

I woke up again around 5 a.m. with the desire to try an astral projection again. So I relaxed my body and repeated a few affirmations before drifting off to sleep again. I slowly regained consciousness, feeling good and refreshed as it was warm in the room. I gradually opened my eyes to find that I was lying under my bed. The tiles were cool, and I realized that my laptop was on the floor next to me, so I got up and put it on the armchair. A silver sheet covered it, which surprised me because it's not the case in reality. The bedroom light was on above our sink, so I went to turn it off.

Fatigue overwhelmed me; I walked with difficulty, finally reached the switch and pressed it. Turning towards my bed to go back to sleep, I realized that the light was still on! So, I pressed the switch again when suddenly I saw my hand going through the button!

I then realized that I was out of my body. So I decided to rise into the air, not without some difficulty as I was finding it hard to control my movements. Positioned close to the wall, I could observe its texture up close—it's always amazing to look at the details in this situation. I raised my arms to the ceiling and said aloud, "I want to experience my higher self!" There was a brief movement, then nothing, I was back in front of the wall.

Glancing in the direction of the bed, I could perceive my sleeping wife. Thrust forward as if attracted by a magnet, I saw myself crossing the mattress, then my wife's body and finally the bedroom wall. I found myself in a dark environment. I tried affirmations again to get out of there, but nothing worked. I woke up around 5:30 a.m. feeling sensations of vibration and energy throughout my body.

Given the hour, I decided to try another experiment. I was rudely awakened a few minutes later by my wife Karen, who was banging me on the back with her knee. I assumed she was moving in her sleep. Wanting to see what time it was, I reached for my phone but the screen was blocked by a game I couldn't turn off. I could press all the buttons but nothing worked. I suddenly woke up and realized that I'd been the victim of a false awakening. It was around 5:45 a.m., and because I was planning to get up at 6:30 a.m., I had time to try something again, taking advantage of this prolific night.

Now I am in a dream, moving through a large dreamlike warehouse. I pass a gorilla wearing an orange jacket who apparently works there. He slaps my hand to say hello, which makes me suspect I'm dreaming. Doubts challenge me, but I'm not totally aware of them.

The scenery changes; I'm in a hamlet and the old farmhouse there is my home. I play with my dog, run a little farther and then turn back to go home. As I go along, I don't recognize the scenery I've just left behind. Finally, I arrive in a village alley accompanied by three young boys and become lucid as I realize that the place is different.

Standing in front of some posters stuck on the wall, I start looking at my right hand, the one I'm currently using to do reality tests. My vision is perfect, my hand looks normal; I stare at it to see if it starts to melt but nothing happens. I find this curious because my hand usually melts, indicating that I'm lucid dreaming. I then try to press my thumb into my palm, but again to no avail. Turning back to my dream friends, I see a knife, grab it quickly and start pointing at my compatriots one after the other with the tip of the blade saying, "I don't need you, I don't need you, and I don't need you!"

Alone, I make my way to a bar with a nautical decor, a bit like an old pirate saloon. After entering and crossing the hall, I take the exit on the other side and land in the village square. This is a place of medieval architecture. A few young people are engaged in a rather enchanting dance performance. My lucidity remains stable, and the environment is extremely realistic.

I jump onto a low wall. Realizing that I'm wearing a T-shirt, I say to myself "Why not put on a tuxedo?" So soon said, so soon done—here I am, in the blink of an eye, dressed in a suit and adorned with a beautiful cape. I take the time to observe the fabric, to touch it.

Then I decide to take off. I had a bit of trouble getting off the ground but finally managed to head for the sky. I perceive a few small vibrations but I'm unable to transform my lucid dream into an out-of-body experience. I regain consciousness a little before the alarm goes off. The night was very fruitful and instructive.

Journal entry, June 4, 2017

I woke up at around 3 a.m. and once I'd gone back to bed, I relaxed and repeated a few affirmations to motivate myself. I said "I must have an out-of-body experience," with determination; then I began to repeat my favorite phrases firmly: "Now I have an out-of-body experience!" "Now I'm out of body" and "Out of body now!" as I visualized myself writing them on a whiteboard.

I found myself at the Monroe Institute, but it was different; the place was like a private home with the living room where in reality there are sofas near the classroom. I could see the large crystal through the windows.

I was a guest at the home of Robert Monroe and his wife Nancy, sleeping on the sofa in their living room. In the middle of the night, a man arrived and he, Robert, and Nancy went into the adjacent room. Nancy came to get some drinks from the buffet next to the sofa where I was sleeping. I didn't want to move but the light in the living room was bothering me. Nancy then returned to join her husband and their guest. I heard them talking about me and my attempts at out-of-body experiences. Then I woke up in the morning, got up and told myself it was time to go home. On the way home, I met a black woman and her toddler who wanted to see if I'd changed the wallpaper on my IPhone.

I lost consciousness in that OBE and suddenly found myself in a dream. I was in a room with friends; there were other people and children. Everyone was dressed like it was the 1970s. I saw shelves with toys from my childhood. Seeing these old toys caught my attention and I concentrated on them. Like every other time I fix my attention on an object in a dream, I became lucid. I could touch the green wooden shelves—everything was so real!

I immediately took advantage of this opportunity to try to induce an OBE and repeatedly asked for mindfulness. Each time I repeated, "Consciousness now!" the environment gradually brightened while the ceiling seemed to be getting closer, lowering inexorably until I passed through it. I found myself in a dark place, as if in some kind of black void, and lost consciousness.

Then I had a regular dream. I was in the garden of my current home. It was warm, the sun was soft, and the glow was yellowish, not unlike days when a summer thunderstorm is expected. I could feel a warm, gentle wind. I enjoyed the moment. I could hear my wife from the kitchen asking me what I wanted to drink. But I didn't want to give in to distraction, I just wanted to enjoy this moment of happiness. And that's when I became lucid. I wished for one thing: to fly. Without waiting, I rose into the air, quietly, higher and higher, until I reached the edge of my property. I floated above the trees, observing the magnificent landscape before me. It's amazing how lucid dreams can seem so real. Then I heard a little voice calling out to me "Daddy, Daddy!"

So I flew back to my house and hovered above the roof; I could see my daughter Tina below. She was about three years old (she was 15 at the time) and walking with a cane.

She said, "I'd love to fly like you!" I replied, "First of all, you don't need your cane, it's an illusion." And she threw her cane to the ground. I was fascinated by this interaction with a dreamlike character. Then I said, "Now jump a little!" And she started jumping; she was fun to watch. I said, "Let go, surrender, trust and fly above the grass" and she managed to float above the grass. Then I lost consciousness.

<u>*Journal entry, August 3, 2017*</u>

Awakened at around 3:30 by my dog, I repeated my affirmation once I'd gone back to bed. As soon as the opportunity arises, I carry out my exercises because it's by persisting that you get results. I found myself out of my body in a brownish-colored room without having undergone the vibratory phase, something that rarely happens to me. I decided to fly through one of the walls to get out. I take off like a bird into the sky, my face caressed by a fresh breeze. As always, it's an exhilarating experience that I manage to maintain for quite some time. I fly over mountains where I can see snow-capped peaks. The whole scene is bathed in the colors of the early morning, illuminated by the sun rising in the distance. As the adventure comes to an end on its own, I return to my physical body, lulled by the familiar vibrations. It's a moment I particularly appreciate, and I try to make this phenomenon last in order to induce a new projection. Mentally, I repeat an affirmation: "Get out of my body now," but nothing happens. I then renew my request by saying, "To the door! Now!" but again nothing happens. In a final attempt, I decide to visualize a room in my house, again without success.

Suddenly, I hear voices all around me. Different people are speaking but I can't perceive what they're saying. Eventually, I fell asleep only to be awakened a few minutes later by strong vibrations. It was a very pleasant sensation to feel all this energy circulating through my body. Right now, I can hear my wife talking to my son and daughter. I can hear the sound of footsteps, which gradually disappears along with the vibrations. I get out of bed; it's daylight. A little out of phase, I wonder what time it is. I glance at my watch, then my phone and my alarm clock, but they all give me a different time. Without transition, I regain consciousness in my bed and realize that I've just been the victim of a false awaking.

Out-of-body experiences induced by lucid dreaming

One of the simplest ways to induce an out-of-body experience is through lucid dreaming. For those unfamiliar with this type of dreaming, it's simply a matter of becoming aware—through the practice of specific exercises—that you're dreaming. It's a fascinating experience and allows you to appreciate the difference between the dream environment and the astral environment. Later in the book, I explain the techniques and how to convert a lucid dream into an out-of-body experience. In the meantime, here are some journal entries describing my experiences converting lucid dreams to OBEs.

Journal entry, March 13, 2007

Some books claim that hypnosis can be a valuable aid to astral projection so I decided to give it a try. I set out to find a hypnotherapist near me who was both competent and open-minded enough to accept my request. It was finally through the ARKEH (ARCHE in French - Academy for Research and Knowledge in Ericksonian Hypnosis) website that I was able to find the therapist I was looking for. And after several e-mail exchanges we agreed on an appointment.

Here's the story of what happened:

Tuesday, March 13, 2007, 1:15 p.m., I arrive at the hypnotist's house with some trepidation, as it's the first time I've had this kind of experience. The house is in a small alley in downtown Valence. When the door opened, I was pleasantly surprised to discover that it opened onto a vast, lush garden adorned with trees and dotted with bright flowers, all bathed in the golden light of a magnificent spring sun. As I walked through the door, I was already in a different world.

I was greeted by a pleasant-looking lady with a gentle voice and followed her up to the second floor into the room set aside for the work we were about to do. I immediately noticed the two diplomas in evidence, one for her training in Ericksonian hypnosis and the other for her training in sophrology. She sat me down in a very comfortable armchair, which was already conducive to relaxation. The first half-hour was devoted to a succession of questions: why exactly had I come to see her, why did I want to induce out-of-body experiences, why did I persist in in trying to induce them, what could it bring me, was there a link with some event in my youth, what was my goal, etc. She asked these questions in order to understand my request and also the person I was. Having read books on hypnosis, I also know that this first stage marks the beginning of a change in the patient's state of consciousness.

The hypnosis session began as I stared at a bright spot in front of me. As the soft music and the therapist's words lulled me, my vision changed; sometimes the brightness was much clearer, sometimes the image split. My eyelids blinked more and more, finally closing for good. From that moment on, the hypnotist guided me through the whole experience, relaxing me as much as possible then using visualization to take me deeper and deeper into the trance state. I was very conscious, and it even seemed to me that I wasn't relaxed enough. Sometimes I let go, sometimes I didn't follow what she was saying. I even feared I'd miss the experience because my concentration was too weak. Nevertheless, I gradually entered the trance state. From time to time, I used my technique of diving to the bottom of the sea instead of going down the stairs as described by the practitioner. Finally, to make sure my unconscious was listening, she asked it to give her a sign. Nothing happened. I told myself I wasn't relaxed enough. She then asked again, when suddenly and despite myself, my eyelashes began to flutter very quickly. The therapist thanked my unconscious for letting her know it was available. At the time, this involuntary reaction gave me the impression that my unconscious was a distinct part of me, a bit like another entity or a second personality. It was quite surprising, even disturbing. So, I had indeed arrived in a state of deep relaxation without really realizing it.

Many REMs (rapid eye movements) occurred for a short time until I lost my bearings. I felt like I was floating without really knowing where I was. Then came the impression that my hands had turned over, palms up, when in fact they were resting on my legs. At this point, I wanted to test a shift of consciousness in the body, but I wasn't successful. Let's just say that it was easy for me to imagine myself in this or that place in the room, that's all. At this stage of the session, the practitioner set up what's known as an "anchor." That is, she placed her hand on my forearm and asked my unconscious mind to reproduce this deep trance when I made the same gesture. In this way, I'll be able to use this principle to enter this altered state of consciousness more easily and more quickly, either to practice self-hypnosis, the preparatory phase of an outing, or for other experiences like meditation, for example. Next, the therapist began to say out loud the suggestions we had previously defined together. These involved asking my unconscious part to open the door to out-of-body experiences whenever I asked. She also asked that in the seven days following this session, the unconscious would share with me—through dreams—the answers to the questions I had been asking myself. Before concluding, the practitioner went over the anchoring process again to ensure that it was properly in place. Then she brought me back to a normal state of consciousness. I returned abruptly to the ordinary world, which left me feeling out of phase when I opened my eyes. I was surprised to find that I had gone very deep into a trance even though I was totally conscious throughout the experience. When I left the house, I felt completely out of touch with everything around me. I felt like I was on cloud nine, and the word that best describes what I felt would be detachment. I've experienced this sensation when I've just finished an hour's meditation with a Buddhist group but this time it was much stronger, as if I'd done five hours of meditation in a row. It lasted all afternoon, so much so that in the evening before going home, I went to the local supermarket—a place I usually avoid—because I needed to come back down to earth.

This session gave me a lot of tools for my practice afterwards. Four days later, here's the little experiment I did:

<u>*Journal entry March 17, 2007*</u>

I woke up around 5 a.m., positioned myself in my bed and began a mixture of techniques. I passively visualized myself strolling down my hallway while repeating my affirmation, " I'm out of body now!" I soon fell asleep and had an interesting dream: I was asleep in the back of a moving car; it was dark and in front were two people I knew. Then a curious thing happened: it was as if my psychic vision had been triggered. Behind my closed eyelids, I could clearly see a can of Schweppes resting on the rear parcel shelf. I concentrated on this image for a long time and noticed a great deal of detail, colors, and textures, all of which were extremely clear. It occurred to me that I was dreaming. Concentrating on my image to maintain my lucidity, I could hear my friends chatting without paying any attention to their conversation. So, I thought I'd take advantage of the situation to induce an out-of-body experience. I mentally repeated my affirmation, "Now I'm out of my body!" and felt vibrations so strong that my body was shaken violently, causing creaking noises in the back seat. I tried to imagine being sucked upwards, but to no avail. I finally decided to stand up as I would physically do. I then had the sensation of slowly emerging from my human form, and turning towards it I saw my physical body and face gradually disappearing. As I sat in the back seat of the car, I realized that I had physically stood up and missed my projection. Then, spontaneously, I found myself sitting around a table with my friends in the presence of a clairvoyant who was using a method of prediction utilizing silver rings. I was touching the spear of a small white statue of Joan of Arc when the clairvoyant told me not to touch anything and that I had to make a promise to myself. I then committed myself to out-of-body experiences.

<u>Comments</u>: The dream was extremely realistic; my senses were working at 100%, as if I were in another life. I remember textures, colors, sensations, etc. I was so shaken by the vibrations that they could only be real. What's more, the sensation of exiting makes me think I've induced a real out-of-body experience in a subtle, thought-sensitive environment. It's possible that this is what's known as "oneiric projection," i.e., an OBE in a dream bubble.

<u>Journal entry, July 27, 2007</u>

Last night I was extremely tired so I went to bed early, at around 9:30 p.m. I fell into a deep sleep in a matter of seconds and woke up at around 2 a.m. I took the opportunity to go for a drink of water, then went back to bed worrying that I wouldn't be able to sleep again. Tossing and turning, I finally decided to do some "NEW" (New Energy Ways by Robert Bruce) and then meditation, concentrating on my breathing. Finally feeling drowsy, I began my usual affirmations; but deep down I wanted to induce a lucid dream, as at the moment I'm reading a lot on the subject. I'm also researching the relationship between neurotransmitters and lucid dreaming (and indirectly with out-of-body experiences, of course).

Which explains the experience that followed:

I'm dreaming that I'm in a bedroom trying to fall asleep, but I'm disturbed by yellow and white lights projected onto my window blind. I close my eyelids to rest when suddenly I'm shaken awake by my mother. I open my eyes and realize to my surprise that it's daytime. Bewildered, I ask her what time it is, to which she replies "10:30 a.m.!" I can't believe how quickly I fell asleep and how short the night was. I head for the bathroom and arrive at the sink to see a denture sitting on the edge. I'm amazed to see this device here. Focusing on this unusual object makes me immediately aware that I'm dreaming. I reinforce the lucid awareness by saying aloud, "Now

I'm lucid!" It's the first time I've been able to observe a dream environment with such clear awareness and the feeling of being firmly anchored in this new reality. It's both strange and fascinating to find oneself in a universe as real as everyday reality while knowing that you're dreaming. The first idea that comes to mind is, of course, to try to induce an out-of-body experience. I raise my arms above my head, just like Superman, and try to reach the ceiling. Slowly I take off upwards; the sensation of flying is fantastic. I take the opportunity to watch my mother watching me. These dreamlike characters are amazing! It's the first time I've watched a dream for so long. I tell myself it's amazing what the unconscious can create. As I reach the ceiling, my body pivots and slowly penetrates it until it stops at my waist. I find myself trapped in the ceiling, which despite its density doesn't prevent me from seeing the room below. I look back up at my mother, who's watching me, and gesture to her that all's well. I pull myself together, determined to get out, and with a final effort I say out loud, "I'm getting out of my body now!" This time my ascent resumes in earnest, and I feel as if I'm passing through an interminable wall. My speed increases, the vibrations get stronger and stronger, everything around me is gray, and finally my run comes to an end with the sensation of being released into a strange environment. The place seems like an arid planet with an atmosphere reminiscent of the Moon. My consciousness is very clear, but my vision is a little blurred. I'm flying in a sort of huge hangar looking down at the metal beams everywhere. It's exhilarating to hover—the first time I've been able to enjoy the sensation for so long. I feel a fresh breeze caressing my face; I hear a whistling sound comparable to that made when driving a car with the window ajar. My vision becomes clear in the center and blurred on the sides and I wonder—given the dull atmosphere—if I'm not in what some call "the lower astral." So I decide to leave this place and ascend to the sky. Then I had an idea to carry out an experiment I'd always wanted to try: to experience my higher self, as explained in William Buhlman's book. Three times I say, "I am now experiencing my higher self!" But nothing happened. On the contrary, this put an end to my adventure and I was instantly reintegrated into my body at

4:05 a.m. It's the first time I've had such a clear and long experience. I had the impression of being able to handle the different situations well and I was able to observe many details. It was an extremely enriching experience in many ways. For a long time, I'd wanted to induce an astral projection from a lucid dream to notice the difference between the two phenomena. I've now done it.

Until now, my experiences have always taken place close to my physical location—my bedroom. This time I was much farther away in a more subtle reality. I see dreams differently as my experiences evolve. After this new adventure, I tend to agree with the Buddhists, who see dreams as another reality rather than a mere abstraction.

Journal entry, September 29, 2007

I got up at 5:30 a.m. to satisfy a natural need then went back to bed with the aim of doing my usual practice. I was physically relaxed but as always my consciousness was too awake and restless. So, I changed position to create slight physical discomfort. Once in a light trance after performing Robert Monroe's countdown technique, I mentally affirmed: "I demand to leave my body now!" I had no doubt that my wish would be granted. I was between sleep and wakefulness and then fell asleep. I began to dream that I was at work, filling a saucepan in the kitchen sink. It was when I saw the water running out of the tap that I realized I was dreaming, because yesterday I had to turn it off because of a leak. The image became very clear and I found myself "really" in the room, as if I'd been absorbed by the dream image. I took the opportunity to observe the surroundings, which were extremely real and clear. I said to myself, "This is it, I'm out of my body." I walked out of the room into the corridor and then into the main room, noting as I passed that the light in my office was on. I reached up to the ceiling and said, "Take me to Hugues!" Hugues is the co-creator of the Astralsight French forum and also a friend. At the time, we were trying to meet in the astral. Like the last time, I found myself in a grayish environment feeling all the sensations of flight but all I could see was gray. I could feel the very cold wind gliding over my body and I was moving fast. My run came to a halt in a place I couldn't quite perceive, and I wondered if I'd reached my destination. My flight resumed, still in the same conditions. Then I came back into my body; it was 6:30 a.m. For the first time, I noticed very gentle vibrations during the exit; I'm usually quite shaky.

Journal entry, May 31, 2014

Before going to sleep, I programmed myself for a 4 a.m. OBE. I wake up at exactly 4:01 a.m., get up and drink a glass of water to wake me up a bit more. I go back to bed five minutes later, repeating my "Out of body now" affirmation. I decide to target William's house, which I know well from having stayed there. Sometimes I add, "I'm going out now! I'm going to Bill's!"

I have great difficulty falling asleep but after an hour, I finally do. I'm at the edge of a pool and I see a woman waiting for me, sitting and wearing a black headset like the performers have on stage. That's when I spontaneously realize that I'm dreaming, for no reason, and I decide to go to her. Then I start to run involuntarily towards her. I know I'm in the middle of a dream, so I'm having fun. The scenery becomes a blur and I call out, "I'm getting out of my body now!"

I feel as if I'm being transported in the dark; I can't see anything. I feel the fresh air on my face and I find myself in a subdivision of houses; it's night and the buildings seem to be computer-generated images. I walk down the street and affirm again, "I'm getting out of my body now!"

I find myself in a dark environment once again. I can't see anything but I'm flying and once again I feel this astral wind on my face. I say, "I want to meet my spiritual guide." I suddenly feel myself being transported forward and I let myself go; I feel good, confident—to the point of changing my mind for no reason. I ask to experience my higher self. I feel myself moving upwards again. My eyes are closed; I don't dare open them, I let myself be carried along by the movement. My journey stops in the middle of a subway car surrounded by passengers.

I approach each passenger, asking if they are my spirit guide. But I get no answer. Persisting, I concentrate on one young man, questioning him insistently, but he remains silent. Then I lose consciousness and fall back into a dream. I'm in a street, in front of an establishment that looks like a restaurant. I take out a book and decide to read a few pages. By concentrating on the words and deciphering them, I become lucid. I realize that reading the pages of a book could be a good technique for becoming aware that you're dreaming. I manage to identify the words bit by bit, but the meaning seems incoherent; the title sounds like something like "Stretching the Donkey."

Then I wake up in my room, thinking that I've had a restless night, and I have a bit of trouble getting back to sleep. My wife moves, I hear noises, I feel heavy, I have trouble moving. Then I hear a giggle! At first, I'm not sure what's happened, but then I hear it again, more distinctly—an evil laugh. Suddenly I sit up on my bed, furious, shouting, "I'm not afraid of you, I'm not afraid of anything— you can come, I'm waiting for you!" And then, nothing! I went back to bed. A few minutes later I hear mumbling; it's my daughter Tina talking softly to my wife so as not to wake me up. I hear her walk past our bed to leave the room. I try to find out why—if she's ill— while looking for the switch on my bedside lamp. I finally find it but it won't turn on! I then get out of bed to reach the bedroom switch and again, nothing works. I remark to my wife that the meter must have tripped last night. I grope my way out of the room in the dark to turn the power back on. I jostle my daughter a little in the process, which makes me realize that I'm in the middle of a false awakening. The corridor lights up and I see William Buhlman accompanied by an elderly lady. I tell William that I've been looking forward to going to his house. The three of us go out and once outside, I find myself alone with Bill, paying no attention to the senior's disappearance. We understand each other, and to my surprise he speaks French. But I'm having trouble keeping my concentration steady, sometimes losing it. Suddenly I find myself in the back of a dark blue American pickup with William at the wheel and the elderly lady next to him. I've passed into a dream without undergoing a transition while retaining lucidity. It's the first time I've gone from an out-of-body experience to a lucid dream; usually it's the other way around.

I smile because I didn't think I'd be using this means of transportation to get to his house. I find my son Tom sitting next to me and I say to him, "I know I'm dreaming, but I'd like to be more lucid; I'm not lucid enough to direct this dream or get out of my body."

We drove down the road for a while and I let myself go. I lost my lucidity and woke up. It was 6 a.m. A bit shaken from the night, I got up to quickly write down my nocturnal experience.

To conclude

Many people desire multiple out-of-body experiences. And I use the term "desire" for a good reason. We are what we are; whether we're here or elsewhere, we don't fundamentally change. Many people think that being in another reality will bring about a radical change in them. Even if the experience is extraordinary, and you see as a wonderful surprise at first, what happens afterwards is up to you and you alone.

You can have the latest high-performance computer but if you're incompetent with computers, once you're in front of your screen you'll remain the same—just as incompetent.

When you to a different country, you don't become a different person.

Out-of-body experiences are exactly the same way, and if we take it a step further, we can say the same thing about death. Once on the other side, we don't change. We don't turn into angels, we don't become enlightened instantly, and we don't get all the answers about the meaning of life if we don't act in that direction.

That's why it's important to appreciate the present moment, to try to improve ourselves today. And we mustn't expect miracles from mystical or ecstatic experiences, or even from our own death. Nor should we put off our search or our spiritual practice until tomorrow. Death is waiting for us around every corner and can present itself at any moment. We don't have time—it's all here and now.

Journeys into subtle realities—or beyond—are transformative from the moment we use them as a tool for our own spiritual evolution. So it's not important to have multiple experiences; what's important is the quality of those experiences, what they provide us with as material for our evolution. A quality experience is a transformative experience.

58

CHAPTER 2

OUT-OF-BODY EXPERIENCES

Theories and Reflections

Out-of-body experiences confront us directly with the fundamental question of the nature of reality and consciousness. They challenge our usual conceptions of self and world, inviting us to explore the unfathomable depths of our own being.

- Charles Tart

Out-of-body experiences have fascinated humanity since ancient times, touching on both scientific and spiritual aspects of our existence. They represent a phenomenon where a person perceives their "self" or consciousness as being outside their physical body, often observing their own body from the outside. This complex phenomenon has a long history that spans different cultures, eras, and fields of research.

Ancient stories of OBE can be found in various civilizations, each with its own interpretation. For example, in ancient Egypt, the concept of "ka"—a kind of spiritual double of the person—represented the idea of a part of the individual that could travel outside the physical body. The ancient Greeks including philosophers like Plato discussed soul travel, illustrating a precursor understanding of altered states of consciousness.

At the time, accounts of psychic projection were often linked to mystical or religious visions. Christian saints and other spiritual figures reported experiences of being transported to celestial realms or having divine revelations, suggesting out-of-body experiences. In the 1700s, Emanuel Swedenborg extensively documented his spiritual "journeys," claiming to visit heaven and hell and speak with angels.

With the advent of modern science, interest in OBE took a more empirical turn. Figures such as Robert Monroe and William

Buhlman at the end of the 20th century not only shared their personal experiences but also began to explore these phenomena in a methodical way, using astral projection techniques and altered states of consciousness.

In recent decades, neuroscience has shed significant light on this type of phenomenon. Studies have identified specific brain regions such as the temporo-parietal junction, which when stimulated can induce sensations of externalization of consciousness. This suggests that OBEs may have a neurological basis, although their exact nature and function remain the subject of debate.

Near-death experiences (NDEs)—which can be compared to OBE—have broadened the discussion to include aspects of survival of consciousness after death. Researchers such as Raymond Moody and Elisabeth Kübler-Ross have documented cases in which individuals—often in situations of temporary clinical death—report leaving their bodies and observing events they could not otherwise experience.

Today, projections of consciousness are studied from many angles, ranging from individual case studies to neuroscientific analyses to psychological and transpersonal approaches. They are also a popular subject in culture and literature, reflecting humanity's continuing fascination with the mysteries of consciousness.

The history of out-of-body experiences is rich and complex, bringing together reflections from spirituality, philosophy, and science. Although technological and scientific advances have brought new understanding, OBEs continue to pose fundamental questions about the nature of consciousness and human experience.

What is an out-of-body experience?

The nature of out-of-body adventures remains an abstract notion for those who have never experienced them. And the same is sometimes true for experiencers.

My first question was whether these phenomena actually occur outside the physical body. People often talk about out-of-body "exits" and journeys to the astral plane. Certainly, during such experiences, we feel a sense of detachment from our physical body accompanied by a deep sense of freedom. However, similar sensations can also occur in lucid dreaming, i.e., when we take control of our dream environment. Although the sensation of physical exit is not present, the feeling of being detached from one's usual environment remains.

Having experienced various states of altered consciousness, OBE, and lucid dreaming, the primary idea I can express is one of expansion of consciousness. Whatever the type of experience, a link with our physical body is always present. The most appropriate image to illustrate this would be that of communicating vessels. By focusing our mind on a different place, by bringing it to vibrate at different rates, we "pour" 90% or even 95% of our consciousness into a different level. The remaining 5-10% of our consciousness is rooted in the physical plane. And it may even be as small as 1%, or even 0.01%.

In most literature on the subject, it is common to describe the out-of-body experience as an "exit" of the soul from its vehicle of flesh. As a result, many people warn against the risks of these practices, arguing that there is a real danger of getting lost outside this reality or that our physical body could be occupied by another soul—in other words, that it involves a risk of possession. I assure you that there is no inherent danger in OBEs.

I'll come back later to the notion of a continuum of

consciousness, which in my view is important for understanding how the phenomenon works.

The silver cord

Other beliefs are more reassuring, attributing a kind of cable linking the physical body to the spirit, a link more commonly known as "the silver cord." These assertions have been propagated for many years by authors and spiritualists, whether intentionally or not. Its first description is said to be found in Ecclesiastes, a book in the Hebrew Bible, but there may be much older references.

And this has become part of our way of understanding out-of-body experiences. In recent years, however, renowned figures such as Robert Peterson and Jade Shaw—as well as William Buhlman—have questioned the existence of this famous silver cord and, after numerous tests, realized that it was illusory. In his first book, "Out-of-Body Experiences," Robert Peterson did some experiments to see and manipulate it. He even went so far as to try to break it, risking his life in the process according to some theories. But it was not to be. After various attempts, he concluded that this famous cord is a psychological comfort, like a reassuring symbol that calls into question his real existence. Personally, I've never observed it for two reasons. The first is lack of interest and the second is that I've never believed it exists because of my experiences of simultaneous connection between the physical and subtle bodies. I believe that the physical body—like any other energy body—is simply a vehicle for consciousness, and that consciousness is both nowhere and everywhere simultaneously. It simply needs a body to focus its attention and experience a particular dimension.

And if this silver cord really exists, where are the connections linking its subtle part to our physical zones? There must be some kind of "grip" that's both solid and "astral." Some say the connection is at the back of the neck, others at the chakras or the spine. But nothing indicates its true existence. Nevertheless, I respect everyone's beliefs, especially as these are unimportant details and it's difficult to be categorical on such a subject.

Beliefs

If we are to believe the many books that have been written in recent years and certain forums and social networks, more and more people are practicing out-of-body traveling. Some even claim to be experts in the field. And yet, when you read their work you realize that they relate to ancient beliefs. In the end, their writings reveal nothing new and only serve to reinforce mental conditioning regarding this type of experience.

Many of them focus on their journey, the universes, or beings they encountered, without even asking themselves whether their experience was illusory or not. I'm not in any way questioning their stories, I'd simply like to warn the reader not to take anything at face value—and that includes my book. During a journey of consciousness, we travel in universes that are thought-sensitive; in that dimension, our thoughts are capable of creating illusions based on our beliefs.

I've personally made the decision to question everything and I'd advise you to do the same, not to rely on the conclusions or pseudo-truths of others. Even if these experiences are powerful, it's best to avoid giving in to the "charm" of the adventure you've lived. Buddhists warn that these journeys are illusory and distracting, diverting attention from the true spiritual purpose of the experience. More on this later.

Consciousness

Conscience is the voice of the soul; passions are the voice of the body.

- Rousseau

From the Latin *conscientia*: knowledge shared with another person. In ancient times, **consciousness did not exist**: only the "noos"—the knowing mind—had value. It was philosophical modernity that connected consciousness with the human being. Descartes established it as the foundation of knowledge, because consciousness doubts nothing and can therefore serve as the foundation on which all knowledge is built.

From the Latin *cum scientia*: the psychic activity whereby we think about the world and ourselves. By thinking about the world around us, we assert our separateness from it. At the same time, we are *part* of the world.

For Bergson, consciousness is a concrete thing, a reality we experience at every moment. It appears all the more clearly as it is realized in our every relationship with the world, as it accompanies every one of our perceptions and actions.

Consciousness is characterized by memory: a consciousness without memory would be an "unconscious" consciousness; a consciousness without memory could never identify anything and would thus be confronted with a perpetual unknown. Consciousness is the place where events are imprinted. It is defined first and foremost by our perception of the objects that surround us, and this perception implies memory. "To perceive is to remember" (Bergson). To be conscious means to be able to make the link between a present event and a past event, so that the present event can be identified and recognized; therefore I can act in the world and thus live in it.

According to the dictionary, consciousness is defined as the immediate intuitive or reflexive knowledge we have of our own existence and that of the outside world. It's a good idea to start with this definition, as the study in this book concerns various states of altered consciousness.

Several times a day, we pass through varying levels of consciousness, starting with waking up in the morning when we're in a state of half-sleep…then moments of concentration on our work…states of distraction, daydreaming, drowsiness, full presence…then falling asleep, sleeping, dreaming etc. All these represent phases of variation in our perception of ourselves and the outside world during life.

Today, science agrees with the mystics and the religious that consciousness does not reside in the brain.

Consciousness does not move; only the vehicle of consciousness can move.

When we observe our experiences of ordinary and non-ordinary states of consciousness with hindsight and finesse, we realize that we always retain the impression of being behind a camera. Consciousness is not imprisoned in the skull, nor is it subject to the notion of time or space. It can be seen as "installed" at the heart of the Source, and the various vehicles—physical, dream, astral, etc.—can be seen as focal points that lead consciousness to focus on a specific reality.

When we experience Lucid Dreaming, OBE, or meditative states, we don't necessarily reach the Truth, but we do realize that we are an immortal consciousness, part of a whole whose focus brings us into a particular reality. In realities with form, we are subject to the veils of the mind, karma, past lives, beliefs, conditioning, addictions etc.—poisons that distract us from our true nature, from the Source (God?).

Physical reality is the densest, the most difficult, the most "magnetic" reality, but at the same time it is a great environment for evolution. All you have to do is stand back, observe, and use it. Just as we can manipulate/affect the levels of the imaginary, dreams, etc., we can also affect the physical dimension, but it takes longer to manifest because it's denser. However, it's a question of strength of mind because we can dominate the physical with our pure consciousness, which is the strongest power—a divine power.

To work on oneself and one's attachments, to carry out effective spiritual work, one must move one's consciousness away from the physical plane—like a cursor moving along the continuum of consciousness to more subtle levels. The closest and simplest of levels is the imaginary, which is accessed through visualization. But this becomes interesting at levels such as lucid dreaming. We must therefore learn to move our mind away from dense energy so that it can express itself more effectively. Meditations, prayers, etc. are much more effective at these levels.

Consciousness polluted by doubts, beliefs, principles, etc. has very little power. But the pure nature of the mind we encounter in meditation or contemplation has far more potential for action in this physical reality.

In short, the notion of "consciousness" represents who we are—our individuality—at all levels of existence. And our quest is to return to our Spiritual Essence, which we might call "original consciousness." According to certain mystical schools, this corresponds to what is commonly known as the collective unconscious. We can therefore assume that the closer we get to our source (or The Source), the more our consciousness loses its intuitive or reflexive knowledge of its own existence and unites with all other consciousnesses. William Buhlman speaks about the "Higher Self," our highest state of being. In one of these out-of-body adventures, he asks to experience his soul and finds himself in an indescribable environment that he compares to an ocean of pure energy, the source of all knowledge and unconditional love. The best way to understand our true identity is to experiment.

The continuum of consciousness

Consciousness is a continuum extending from physical wakefulness through progressive states of awareness into nonphysical areas of the universe existing far beyond our current scientific vision.

- William Buhlman

The continuum of consciousness is defined by all the "zones" or what I call "different realities" that consciousness can experience. The location we use depends on the balance of concentration in consciousness between this subtle reality and physical reality. More precisely, as we experience the physical dimension, our consciousness is anchored to that reality. The ability to concentrate in a subtle environment—whether we stay within our personal bubble (imaginary, dream) or go beyond it (out-of-body experience)—depends on the relationship of our consciousness to our material body. The more we lose touch with this physical form, the more easily we can move towards more subtle regions.

In order, the continuum starts with physical reality—followed by daydreaming, imagination, dreaming, lucid dreaming, and out-of-body experiences—all of which I personally understand as experiences away from the physical body. Our vehicle of flesh seems to possess a sort of magnetism due to its density, and the further we move away from it the more our experiences occur in regions outside our personal field, i.e., in realities where we are only spectators, not architects. It's true that the notion of continuum can be confusing since it imposes a linear schema, as shown in the image below. At this level, however, there is no question of time and space.

During my various experiences, be they dreams, lucid dreams, or out-of-body experiences, I've always sensed a commonality among them. I didn't know how to explain it for many years, until one day I understood and everything became clear to me. Whenever I had an experience, I always had the impression of being a spectator. As I meditated and experimented, the same thing happened to me in everyday life.

It's a bit like being immersed in a film on television and at some point, the ringing phone takes you out of the picture. You continue to watch the film, but with a certain distance. This was exactly the same thing.

The same goes when we launch into the imagination: we can immerse ourselves completely, indulge in daydreaming, or direct the images. It was then that I grasped the notion of the continuum of consciousness. The various environments/realities are mobile, but consciousness always remains in the same place, i.e., nowhere— because it is everywhere at the same time, unaffected by the notion of time or space. Hence the impression of an observer.

Consciousness should be seen as a beam of light originating at the Source. Each energy body starting with the physical behaves like a magnifying glass, concentrating the light in one spot. And if we move this magnifying glass over the beam, we change the level of concentration.

When we are in our physical body, our consciousness is focused on physical reality. If we shift our point of concentration to another level, we go to the imaginary, then dreams and so on. This is the notion of communicating vessels, which I touched on earlier in the book.

To be a little clearer, consciousness is present at all levels from physical reality to the "astral"—it's just a question of focusing consciousness on a given reality. We each have a "personal field of consciousness"—a zone in which *we* govern the environment; when we move beyond it we access more subtle, consensual levels.

William Buhlman talks about this in "Adventures Beyond the Body," but I didn't grasp its meaning until I experienced it for myself. In the book, he discusses the multidimensionality of humans and the universes. He tells us that at any given moment, however much the notion of time exists, we are simultaneously in a multitude of dimensions ranging from the densest to the most subtle (the Source). We are only aware of the one in which our mind is focused. Some people, like Tom Campbell, a physicist and engineer who was one an early participant of the Monroe Institute, could purportedly switch between the physical and the subtle instantaneously thanks to his experience with altered states of consciousness. He claims he could give a lecture at the physics faculty while riding a motorcycle in another reality. So much so, in fact, that it sometimes led to confusion.

This explains why an out-of-body experience does not result in an exit from the soul but in a shift in focus on the continuum of consciousness.

When we astral travel, there is consciousness in the physical body; nothing has actually left the body, we've just changed our focus of concentration. William relates an inward movement, not an outward one as we might think. The material dimension resides on the surface, with the Source at the core. Astral travel is a journey into oneself. Personally, I haven't felt any inward movement; however, during my experiences, once the sensation of leaving the body has passed, I haven't felt any outward displacement either. On this subject, I remain a walking question mark; I hope to find the answer during future excursions. If so, I'll let the reader know in my next book.

Physical reality is the densest level and acts like a magnet. In the waking state, we can only shift our focus from physical reality to the imaginary. To go beyond this, i.e., in dreams, lucid dreams, and out-of-body experiences, we have to "forget" the physical body by making it fall asleep. In this way, consciousness can easily shift its focus to more subtle realities.

I've given you a linear definition of an out-of-body exit using as an example a beam of light on which a magnifying glass moves, symbolizing the shift to different energy bodies.

The explanation is a little more complex. Consciousness isn't like a beam of light because it doesn't integrate the notion of space and time. It's everywhere simultaneously. It varies somewhat between individuals, but the more we move towards subtler levels, the less the concept of individualization applies. This can be likened to universal consciousness. It's interesting because it translates into the fact that—at the level of our spiritual source—we're all connected. This means that if we do something good or bad to someone else, we experience exactly the same thing because we're all interconnected.

Consciousness can therefore be defined as

a continuum of experiences.

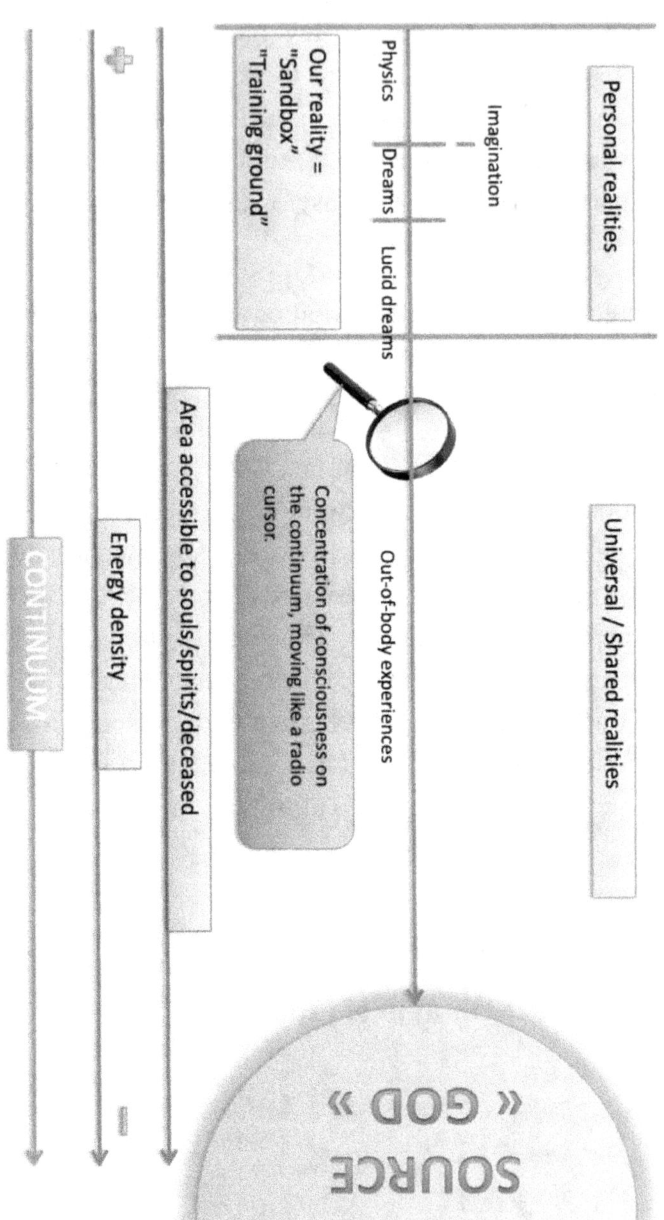

Linear diagram of the consciousness continuum.

Belief systems

To believe without daring to reason about your belief, isn't that already to doubt?

- Eugène Marbeau

A belief is an opinion based on our conditioning.

Our education, our culture, our environment etc., form a whole in which we become accustomed to evolving, and when we leave this context—this comfort zone—we feel uneasy. Confronted with a different opinion, we unconsciously reject it because it doesn't fit into the logic we've built up with the bricks of our environment. Yet it's interesting to stop for a moment our automatic, routine march through life and ask ourselves, "Why is my opinion the way it is? Why do I think the way I do? What would my opinion have been on this or that subject if I'd been born into a different family, in a different country?" Questioning our way of thinking by looking for its roots is a step towards our evolution. It's not by sticking to our convictions that we can move forward; on the contrary, it's by working on them that we can understand our own mental patterns and act on them to become aware of the mechanics of our mind.

A belief system is the creation of a conviction—a "reality" you might say—held by a group of people. It usually starts with a few members, and over time the number increases. Opinions are refined, enriched, and put down on paper to become sacred books. However, the source of inspiration is the same system itself, so it's a self-feeding process responsible for the birth of dogmas. And over the generations, beliefs become so deeply rooted that they become part of a culture.

As a result, the more the years—or even centuries—go by, the less likely it is that anyone will challenge such a belief system. It becomes part of our way of life, part of the "normality" of things, and blends into our lives and our very being. We, in turn, pass it on to our offspring, and if they follow in the same footsteps without ever questioning what they're getting into, they will continue to perpetuate these impersonal convictions. This is just one example.

The same applies to fear. Man has always used this emotion to control his fellow human beings. It's through threat that we control each other. And it's the mortality of our physical body that's at the root of it all. If it weren't for death or suffering, we would no longer be afraid. From a very early age, our upbringing is based on rules laid down by our parents that we must not transgress on pain of correction. It is therefore essential to work on our fears—fear of the unknown, of death and so on—in order to evolve. This is the most important blockage to overcome when practicing altered consciousness or psychic projection experiences.

So why talk about fears and belief systems in a book about spiritual experiences? Simply to make you aware that what we see and think isn't always what we believe. And this is even truer in the field of the paranormal. We must always question our experiences and think critically. The invisible—or the astral as some would say— is a malleable reality that is easily affected by contact with the observer. It's the continent of illusion, and many people have lost their way there, coming up with stories worthy of a Spielberg film.

It's important to understand that as long as we're in a reality where form exists, we can be confronted with our own illusions at any moment. If we wish to explore the continuum of our consciousness in an objective way, we must consider our beliefs and not be afraid to question them.

The holographic universe

The universe itself could be a huge hologram, a three-dimensional projection of a deeper and more complex reality. This revolutionary idea requires us to fundamentally rethink our understanding of the nature of existence and consciousness.

- Michael Talbot

Try to see the dimensions as if they coexisted with each other while vibrating at different frequencies. It's as if they're joined but each has a density all its own. You could compare it to a layer cake, with one layer made of cardboard, another of wax, the next of modeling clay, and so on. Although we perceive matter as solid and unalterable, we are immersed in an environment that is malleable by thought. Each dimension or subtle universe we pass through—whether via the physical body or the various energy bodies—can be infinitely modified. Many experimenters, including me, have been able to verify the reality of our influence on the environment, and the same applies to the experience we have during out-of-body journeys. The God of our heart—as the Rosicrucians would say—has given us an immense power: the power of the mind, and more specifically the power of intention and concentration. It's a power that enables us to travel in different dimensions but it's also a power that locks us in our own jail. Indeed, when we concentrate solely on one reality—such as the physical—we obstruct all the others. A good example of this is dream reality; many people have no recollection of their dream journeys.

Almost all of us have no memory of what we were like before we were born. But in the end, nothing is inaccessible to us—we have no block except those we create. What blocks us is the 99.99% of focus we place in this physical reality, and we judge everything else based on this data. In other words, we use our five senses to observe dense matter and create scientific protocols based on our illusory data. Again, as explained above, from the moment there is form, there is illusion. So, it's important to remember this concept when practicing out-of-body experiences. And as taught in Buddhism and also by altered-states-of-consciousness experts such as William Buhlman, these illusions are there to distract our attention from our true spiritual source. It's a bit like going through a funfair to find the answer to our existential questions on the other side. We'll be distracted by different kinds of attractions and some will be so extraordinary as to make us forget our purpose. And yet we must go through all of these trials and tribulations to reach spiritual awakening.

And that's exactly what out-of-body experiences are all about. Encountering blue or orange beings, little greys, dragons, graphic universes, formless entities, majestic landscapes and so on—these are fantastic out-of-body experiences but they lack self-realization regardless of whether they are consensual or non-consensual realities. Apart from the incredible aspect of the journey—and it's sincerely interesting to experience —what did this bring you in your awakening process?

What we really need to realize is the value of these journeys beyond physical reality as preparation for our own demise. Because, whether in this life or the next, we'll have to get past these formidable distractions if we're to achieve spiritual realization. It's a state where the concept of form no longer exists, where we become one with everything and everyone. The interesting thing to realize at this point is that we are all one and the same. If the whole of humanity had access to this knowledge, the world would be different. When we hurt another person, we're really hurting ourselves because we're all interconnected. This is the essence of Karma, or backlash. Individualism is an illusion; imagine what that means. When you pray, you pray within yourself, with love, fervor, and intention, and all this generates a force that is transmitted to others. When you criticize others, you reassure yourself, but deep down it affects you too. All feelings and emotions are transmitted back into this unity of which we are a part and from which we experience our own states as well as those of others. Everything is in balance; it's the principle of communicating vessels. Knowing this, knowing the true impact of our actions and thoughts on the community, we realize that nothing is trivial and that we must pay attention to what we do.

The concept of reality

Reality is just a point of view.
- Philip K. Dick

On several occasions, I've used the word "reality" instead of "dimension" simply because it seems more accurate and appropriate. So, at this stage of the book and to be as clear as possible for what follows, it would be wise to explore this notion in greater depth.

The dictionary explains that reality corresponds to the character of that which is real—that which really exists (and is not merely an invention or an appearance). From a mystical point of view, reality is either a divine creation, the creation of a group of souls, or the creation of a single individual. This may not make sense to you, but it's true. If you look at our world, the average person will tell you that this is reality—a concrete environment that we can touch, smell, see, hear, and taste. But what about these five senses? Neuroscience describes them as nerve impulses interpreted by the encephalon, i.e., they exist only through the brain. Imagine, then, if we prevented these nerve impulses from circulating. What would happen to our physical reality if we lost the sensations provided by our five senses?

For the duration of our experience on good old planet Earth, our consciousness is rooted in our physical body. The only notions we use are those we experience on a daily basis through our five senses. We are therefore limited—or at least illusorily limited. When we dream we reproduce what we know and feel, and it's the same for other experiences apart from out-of-body travel since the places we visit don't depend on us alone. That's why I call the different dimensions "realities." Each of these places—regardless of its architecture, whether describable or not—exists despite everything. Sometimes we're the designers, sometimes we're not. After all, what is normality—what is reality? We make judgments with the little knowledge we possess. It's worth regularly questioning ourselves and accepting nothing as it is. To take a step back. If you zoom out from the Earth into space, you have to admit that we're like a speck of dust that may seem insignificant in comparison with all this immensity. And yet, we carry the weight of life every day and we attach importance to things that are ultimately trivial. It's all a question of point of view; reality is a point of view. The immensity of the Universe does not represent the Whole; there is also the "other side," the invisible universe.

This infinity can make us feel uncomfortable about the illusory insignificance of our being, I say "illusory" because despite our "smallness" we are not here by chance, our existence has its importance in this Divine organization. Size does not determine value. It is therefore important as a living human being to come down from our pedestal, swallow our pretensions, and accept that we don't know much about life. To doubt is to leave a door open without agreeing. To reject is to cloister oneself in beliefs that have been built up in a restricted environment, and to barricade oneself in order to reassure oneself. Opening your consciousness to the unknown requires courage. Stepping outside your own reality means going beyond your comfort zone to face your fears. Humans tend to rely entirely on science. However interesting, however important, science does not hold all the keys. It remains stunned by many events that it cannot and will never be able to explain. Faced with this concept of reality, we need to adopt a curious humility.

Why this reality?

What could be better than a dense reality as a learning school for the soul?

Life is like living in a playpen; it has bars (our limits) but we're not locked up. We're not prevented from looking beyond, but only under certain conditions and for a given length of time. We're surrounded by "toys"—stuff that distracts us from the fact that the playpen isn't locked, and above all that focuses us on something other than our true spiritual essence. Beyond this universe, deep inside ourselves, we are all interconnected. As a result, the good or bad things we do to ourselves have an impact on all living beings. Hence the need to develop vigilance over our actions, as I wrote in the previous paragraph.

Between the Source and us there are a variety of helpers such as spiritual guides. The love of neighbor that is in each of us naturally makes us want to help those who are struggling in life. This explains the existence of guides, deceased loved ones, and even saints, deities, and others. In our playpen, we find objects that enable us to create our own story. It's the same in the afterlife.

To simplify the diagram, we can imagine that when we jump over our bars, we find ourselves in the first less-dense environment, made of Lego bricks; then when we move on to the next one, we fall into an even less-dense dimension made of modelling clay, and so on. And the "modelers" are both you and other people. That's why experiences are subjective and—whether in or out of the body—can only be unique to each individual. This means that no one holds the Truth as long as it originates in an environment where the concept of form and matter exists. And when this concept no longer exists, our limitations due to being physical beings render our experiences beyond our knowledge and therefore ineffable. Why is this? We mustn't forget that if we are currently focused on this physical reality, it's for a good reason. It's because we need to experience it before moving on. It's only when we leave our little child's form and pass through the bars of our playpen that we'll be able to continue our journey towards other stages, other adventures.

The purpose of out-of-body experiences

As we begin to experience our first out-of-body experiences, we tend to waste time on the separation process…on the environment in which we're traveling…on trying to understand what's happening…on wanting to map our nonphysical places, etc. And this is perfectly normal. It's the natural process of becoming familiar with the unknown. But it's important not to forget that you have in your hands an extraordinary tool for spiritual evolution. To use it solely for futile pleasures would be to overlook the full potential of the experience. Out-of-body experiences allow us to discover the answers to our own existential questions. It's an exercise in spiritual awakening—not mindless leisure. A quality out-of-body experience is not an extraordinary adventure but a transformative confrontation.

The spiritual quest

"We are not human beings living a spiritual life, but spiritual beings who have come to live a human adventure."

- Pierre Teilhard de Chardin

A mystic is someone who is interested in the mysteries of life. If you're reading this book, it's either out of curiosity or because you're one of them. In the latter case, you're probably on a quest for

Truth, looking for answers to your questions. There are many different paths open to you: religious, spiritual, philosophical, etc. You have the choice of trusting just one of them or taking an interest in several, choosing what resonates most with your inner self. Out-of-body experiences and other forms of modified consciousness such as lucid dreaming are extraordinary tools in the quest for awakening. Some see them as a unique path or even an accelerator of spiritual progression. I don't entirely agree with that. I see these experiences as tools, aids, but by no means a path in their own right.

Indeed, the way we look at our physical lives is already filtered through our minds. No two people will perceive the same experience in the same way. These so-called "mental filters" have their origins in life's conditioning, upbringing, personal experience, and so on.

Here's a real-life example. A lady once told me that during Christmas dinner, when the whole family was enjoying being together, her son's wife left the table to go and cry in her room. For the majority, Christmas rhymes with joy, family, and sharing. For this woman's daughter-in-law, this time of year was a reminder of very difficult times spent with her parents. We can see here that every situation in life is experienced according to the angle from which we see it, according to our visual distortions caused by forces that originate in our memory. We find again the meaning of duality advocated by Buddhists, who assert that an object, a person, or a situation cannot exist without an observer. To this notion we must add that those who observe do so through the filters of their mind, not seeing things as they are.

These veils obscure the real scene. They lead us to criticism—good or bad—by referring to the past or the future according to our own experience. And even if we think we're right, it's good to allow ourselves to doubt our judgment. After all, all opinions have a reason to exist, and in the end, anyone can be right or wrong as long as it's reassuring for our ego. And that's what I'm getting at. We look at life through the eyes of the ego. This includes our conditioning—as mentioned above—but also our beliefs and convictions. From the moment we accept a truth—either through our parents or because it suits us—it confirms us and becomes a given. So, at the slightest deviation from this notion, we are extirpated from this mental comfort and we reject it.

So why talk about mental veils, ego, filters, and so on? Quite simply because altered-consciousness experiences take us into regions that are extremely sensitive to thoughts. A belief, a fear, or even a fantasy—whether conscious or unconscious—can very easily affect our experience in dramatic ways. These are called projections of our mind. It's very important not to take our experiences in subtle realities at face value. It's also important not to make judgments based on what you've read or other people stories. Don't let yourself be influenced; venture into these unknown lands with total neutrality.

I also think it's essential to work on *self*-improvement and growth in the physical world. We mustn't lose sight of the fact that we're in this environment for a reason and that we have things to do and learn here on Earth for our own evolution. Meditation—and observing life, our own reactions, and the reactions of others—are important elements of growth. Above all, we need to get to know ourselves to grasp the difficult concept of "reality." Find out more about the nature of our mind and how it works. Then you can step into the invisible worlds with a certain distance, without fear, and with great interest.

We have to wake up here so as not to remain asleep on the other side. And it's on this condition that altered-consciousness experiences will prove to be marvelous tools for personal development. If, on the other hand, you prefer to let yourself be lulled—even fooled—by these experiences, then you'll remain blinded by these illusions, feeding your ego by creating new filters, new convictions.

The spiritual quest is not just a walk in the woods; it involves phases of courage, discipline, questioning, discouragement, motivation, disillusionment, and so on. The path is never a straight line. There are always ups and downs, and it's the effort made at the bottom that takes us to the top. Of course, this is easier said than done. But we tend to picture the other person—the mystic, the meditator, the experiencer—as a gifted person, far removed from what we are. We see the other person as an exceptional being when in fact he's a human being with a conscience, just like us. He encounters favorable periods conducive to practice, and other times he is without conviction, discouraged—sometimes to the point of giving up. But in the end, he can never give up this quest for the soul.

You'll encounter these different phase just as I have and as others—experienced or not—have done. Sometimes, despite our perseverance, we don't get anywhere; sometimes we lack motivation and at other times we are blessed by the gods and our practice spoils us with superb experiences. These negative phases are natural, and all we need to do is be aware of them and use them to our advantage rather than falling victim to them. What's more, the daily practice we put in place bears fruit, and even if the goal isn't there, the journey is just as interesting if not more so.

So don't get discouraged, keep observing yourself and your evolution, watching life through a camera or television as if a film were unfolding before your eyes. Stand on the riverbank and watch the boats go by, avoiding getting caught in one as best you can. The awakening of your consciousness will wipe away the veils of the mind, the blinkers we tend to keep and nurture, and you'll be more Zen, more detached, and much less easily influenced. It's an essential state of mind for approaching metaphysical experiences and, above all, for extracting the very essence of what you'll be experiencing for the benefit of your own self-realization.

Take pleasure in practicing; there's nothing like joy and happiness to help you move forward. Imagine these moments of exercise as bits of vacation that you allow yourself and not as a constraint. Frustration has the opposite effect and if you feel this at any time, let go, take a break, step back…and don't punish yourself, don't react like a victim; see it as a sign of your transformation. The transformation is established with some pain at times, but these are the pains of change—not of destruction.

Our limits

I'd like to stress once again that it's important to understand that when we experience the different states of altered consciousness, we perceive them through the filters of our mind.

We judge and appreciate a situation solely in relation to reference points anchored in our subconscious. These boundaries, as we have already discussed, stem from our upbringing, our culture, our beliefs, our condition as human beings living on earth in the midst of the laws of physics. We are therefore limited in the sense that we access infinite, subtle universes with blinders that restrict our field of perception. And many experiencers report their experiences as Truth, even though they have experienced them through their own "eyes." Our experiences are highly personal. You must therefore be very careful when reading the experiences of others and take a step back from your own experiences.

During an out-of-body journey, for example, we move our consciousness through one or more realities that are not only sensitive to thought but perceived with our reference elements of the physical world. Indeed, we're used to comprehending life through our five senses; and if we refer to Buddhism, a sixth sense is added:

thought. This sixth sense is interesting to consider in our study of different states of consciousness, which is why I name it here.

To return to our example, once we're out of the body we'll continue to unconsciously use these six senses. But these are only valid in our physical reality, you may say. However, just as in a dream or an imagined scene, we have the ability to reproduce these senses. And this is what we do involuntarily during an OBE. We find ourselves in a subtle, infinite universe, but because we're accustomed to using these five senses and know no others, we find ourselves limited and unable to do anything about it. Add to this our beliefs, our education, our culture, etc.—all the conditioning that has forged our critical mind. All these references that we have accumulated over the course of our lives become important limits to our appreciation of altered-consciousness experiences.

This is why certain events experienced during a lucid dream or OBE are difficult to express, as they are almost impossible to describe without sufficient elements of comparison.

These limitations remind us that if we're anchored in the physical world right now, it's for the reason that we need to experience life in this reality. The rest will come later, when our physical body dies.

But that doesn't mean that the doors to the invisible are closed to us. If we have this ability to explore different realities—even when limited—it enables us to carry out very important spiritual work that is especially beneficial to our physical existence.

Attachments

Attachment is the root of suffering.
- Buddha

One of the strongest poisons of the mind is attachment. We are attached to our bodies, to our lives, to our loved ones. And this is at the root of much of our suffering. This doesn't mean it's bad—we simply need to be aware of it to understand our reactions and feelings. Being attached to a child, spouse, or parent is human and normal. But we mustn't forget that each person is an individual with an existence of their own, endowed with a life that belongs exclusively to them and from which they will be separated one day. It's inevitable, and a cause of deep suffering. It seems to me to be one of the most difficult trials to experience in this physical reality. For some, the same applies to material things. Possession—or the desire to possess—is a real problem in our materialistic society. It's a cause of conflict at every level. But even more subtle is our attachment to ourselves…to our body, our identity, our sex, our nationality, and so on.

All these characteristics are part of the panoply of things that will disappear when we die. It's important to remind ourselves from time to time that we're just an entity with no criteria other than those temporarily borrowed for our short stay on Earth. It's illusory to think or believe that we're a man or a woman, that we're American or French, that we're a doctor or a worker, etc. These are only ephemeral qualifiers of no importance at the level of pure consciousness. They only matter here on earth, for a time. We are much more than that. Much more than the criteria of this society whether in terms of beauty or social status. Experiences of altered consciousness teach us to glimpse our true self. In my opinion, it's essential to know this in order to better understand this physical universe and the reason for all the hardships we have to endure. Buddhists report three poisons: attachment, repulsion, and indifference. I've chosen to talk only about the first because—for me—the other two stem from it. Without attachment, there should be no repulsion or indifference. Being "detached" makes us immune to external distractions. As a result, we take an interest in them without focusing or judging.

Life is fragile, and sometimes it's good to stop the mad rush of everyday life and realize this. We all live as if we were eternal. It's a form of non-acceptance of our destiny, a conscious or unconscious refusal of our human condition. The ideal—even if it's not easy—is to submit to it. Rejecting it would only feed our fear of dying. To accept it is to tame death. There are two reasons for rejecting it: fear of the unknown and attachment to our loved ones. That's why it's important to work on these two points through out-of-body experiences and meditation. One Buddhist practice that can complement our training is the practice of meditating on our own death. Bedtime is a good time to do this. I am transcribing here a text by Phra Paisal Visalo translated by Hervé Panchaud on the website http://www.dhammadelaforet.org (thanks for permission to distribute):

Meditating on death at bedtime

The end of the day when it's time to let body and mind rest is a good time to reflect on the inexorable nature of death. Let's meditate on the process of death as if it were happening right now.

Lie down and relax every part of your body, from your head to your toes, especially your facial muscles. Let your breathing come and go freely. Feel the gentle coming and going of the breath at nose level. Put aside all thoughts of the past or future.

As the mind becomes calm, let's think about how we approach death. But we don't know when it will happen. Tonight could be our last. Tomorrow may never come. Think of how our breathing will fade as we approach death. How our heart will stop beating. The body will no longer be able to move and will become cold and rigid, like a useless stump.

Then think of all those possessions, precious to us, that we've amassed and that will cease to be ours. They will become someone else's property. We will no longer be able to enjoy them. All that was so dear to us will no longer be in our care.

What's more, we won't have another opportunity to talk to our children and loved ones. Everything we used to do together will be a thing of the past. We won't be able to visit our parents and we won't be able to do anything for them. We won't even have time to say goodbye to them or to reconcile with those with whom we were at odds.

We'll have to leave behind all our work, even the unfinished stuff. We won't be able to touch it up in the slightest. No matter how important, all activity must be abandoned. The same goes for all the knowledge and experience we've accumulated—they'll disappear with us.

Glory, power, and support will slip through our fingers. No matter how powerful we are, we can't take it with us. Let's not imagine that people will continue to praise us after our death; our very name will eventually be forgotten.

As we meditate in this way, let's look at our feelings. Are we worried, saddened, or attached to all these things? Are we ready to accept all these losses? If not, what is it that still agitates us? Such meditation will help us understand that there are still some things we haven't done (or that remain unfinished) and things to which we are still very attached. This awareness will lead us to prioritize what's really important and what we've been neglecting, and to practice the art of letting go.

Body identity

Body identity brings together all the external elements that characterize our physical body. It's a very important subject to deal with, because out-of-body experiences lead us to detach ourselves from this vehicle of flesh and bones. We must therefore learn to look at ourselves in the mirror while accepting that the reflection we perceive in no way represents what we really are. The image in front of us is merely a temporary vehicle for our consciousness, nothing more. The more we merge with it, the more we remain attached to matter. What is true during our lifetime remains true at our death. Also, it's vital to work on this point, both for our spiritual evolution and to prepare ourselves for our passage.

Our name, our nationality, our age, our social security number, our skin color, etc., all identify our human condition; and as life goes on, the more we see ourselves as such. It's as if as we interact with our car in everyday life, after a while we think of ourselves as the vehicle itself, forgetting what we really are: the driver. Introspection through out-of-body experiences is all about finding our spiritual essence and detaching ourselves from our physical form. This is an arduous task, firstly because we have to admit that we are not this body, and secondly because once we have accepted this, we have to integrate this new concept. This philosophy can be found in Tibetan Buddhism, which employs various meditative practices designed to bring the practitioner to detachment from the impermanent elements of daily life. The physical body is, of course, an integral part of this.

Day and night

To observe life is to find the answers to all our questions.

Think of a day as a 24-hour period divided into two parts: day and night. And why? What is the role of these two periods? Why do we sleep? Why do we dream? We repeat this routine without question. Take a step back and ask yourself what day and night are like—life and death, right? Death is simply a different kind of sleep. Day and night could therefore be an opportunity given to us daily to prepare for our death.

Life is a school, and we're lucky enough to be able to use the daytime to work on our consciousness, our mind, and our heart…and the night to prepare for our passage to that deeper sleep.

Do you appreciate the importance of these days that can seem routine most of the time? Every day is different and every day is an opportunity. Unfortunately, most of the time we waste it. As soon as we wake up, we should express our gratitude for this new opportunity to evolve. All the elements and events that will fill this new day—even if we experience them daily—are different despite everything, and the game is to find in each of them the spark that will bring about an evolution in our consciousness. It could be an encounter…a book…an article…an object…a phrase…a word, etc., that will move us forward in our condition as spiritual beings. Everything is raw material for our quest. And as soon as you consider your days in this way, routine will have no place and every moment of your life will be much more important.

In the evening, the way you fall asleep and your state of consciousness during the day will determine the spiritual quality of your sleep. Dreams are therefore of paramount importance. Dreams represent another reality containing a wealth of information. They are not just images produced by a brain letting off steam. They can even give you an idea of what your death might be like, or at least part of it. It's important to practice being fully present during the day so that you can take control of your nights. It's not easy, but we have every day to practice. Having a clear conscience and no longer being constantly drawn into daydreams will enable us to better manage our passage into the afterlife. And if days and nights come and go—and seasons too—why shouldn't life and death? Which leads us to question the possibility of reincarnation.

Don't forget the essentials

Experiencing different realities can very quickly become addictive, as the experience during these escapades is very intense, even exhilarating. Flying, teleporting, visiting improbable places and meeting exceptional people are all so extraordinary that when we return to our physical reality, with all that this implies, our desire to go back is intense. The trap—just like in the dense dimension of our daily lives—is distraction.

Out-of-body experiences are a precious tool in our evolution. Using them only for pleasure is like having access to a luxury car that you drive only on the street of your neighborhood. It's perfectly normal to explore at first. It's a whole new world opening up to us, an unknown world with infinite possibilities that's so rich you could spend your time doing nothing else. But that would be like a mouse in a wheel. What Buddhists call Samsara. In fact, they practice this type of experience to train for death, to get beyond these various realities and into the clear light. I've known some gifted experiencers who went out very regularly, even quite easily, but who only explored. Knowing that these subtle universes are reactive to our thoughts—whether collective or individual—there are and always will be an infinite number of possibilities. Which makes exploration inexhaustible. The great challenge is to go beyond all that. There's no point in going on thousands of out-of-body experiences if all you get out of them is fleeting pleasure. It's better to have one transformative experience. That's why you shouldn't waste time trying to analyze or understand everything. The most important thing is to experience your soul. All you need to do during an OBE is to ask for it: "Now I experience my soul!"

Experiencing the physical dimension

For a moment, take a step back from the course of your life. Analyze important events—situations that may have been a turning point in your life, dramas, or difficult moments. Then ask yourself, "What has this led to in my evolution, whether physical, family, professional, spiritual, or other?" In the end, something always comes out of it. We can therefore assume that chance doesn't exist. It is an imperceptible logic that leads us to where we need to go in this life.

Sometimes self-reflection is so difficult that we question its efficacy. However, sinking into despair doesn't lead to anything either. Using the situation means turning weakness into strength. And remember that we too are creatures, part of nature and part of this gigantic mechanism, whose author is inconceivable to us. All of this is beyond our understanding, whatever our beliefs.

As chance does not exist, if our destiny was to be born in this physical reality, it is for a well-defined reason. We must therefore bear in mind that if we're here in this dimension, it's because we need to experience it. There's no point in thinking about escaping. Meditation, lucid dreaming, and psychic projections are no escape. We have to face up to the various trials that await us here on earth to enable our soul to grow and evolve. What could be better than a world where the density of illusion makes us believe in its concrete existence? Density also makes us believe that we are separate from each other. We believe that we are unique and distinct from our fellow human beings. Yet before the Big Bang, our entire Universe including us was part of a single, homogeneous element, which then expanded like crazy. All the elements were divided into various forms (planets, humans, etc.) whose imperceptible links still exist today.

Our brief passage through this physical world is therefore an experience we have to live through. Maybe we chose this incarnation before we were born, maybe something else caused it, or maybe neither is true; apart from some people who have "access" to the answer to this question, the majority of us don't know. What we do know, however, is that we are here in this universe and that's our priority. Over time, the succession of our experiences of altered consciousness should reinforce our journey through life and not distract us from our human state in favor of a fantasy world. It's very important to integrate this because it's a guarantee of the quality of our spiritual progress. Getting caught up in an illusory realization—an awakening of paranormal powers or whatever—can quickly lead us to a euphoric stopover from which it can be difficult to escape. To avoid this, keep in mind that we are beings incarnated in this physical reality for a reason; take nothing at face value and always keep a critical eye. Keep this in mind and use it as an anchor. Don't lose sight of what you are, and don't expect to be what you're not.

Matter: support for the spiritual

"Matter is the canvas on which the spirit paints its most profound works."
- Pierre Teilhard de Chardin

At the risk of repeating myself, we are not incarnated by chance. Nature, the physical body, Life, are so well-crafted, so perfect, that there can be no room for coincidence. Faced with this magnificent creation, it's legitimate to wonder why we suffer, why existence is sometimes so hard, even cruel. Good and evil are only human notions. Nothing is negative and nothing is positive; everything is there for our evolution. Physical reality—encompassing both matter and events—is a dense dimension in every sense of the word. Everything is there in a raw and frank way. And this is the cause of our suffering. But it's all a question of perception. What may be difficult for some is not for others. Nature doesn't like imbalance and tends to compensate for every failure in one way or another. Any change in your life—any disturbance whether difficult or ignoble— brings about a change in temperament. The human being has the capacity to adapt to any situation, to strive for a new balance by compensating through the evolution of his soul. In some cases, it's hard to accept this explanation, but it's true.

The place of OBE in life

Some people describe out-of-body experiences as the royal road to enlightenment. From an outside perspective, when we've never experienced this kind of phenomenon, we tend to think that this is where the keys to knowledge and wisdom lie; and that by mastering the exercise we'll experience awakening, answers about life and death, a radical transformation of our being, and even an awakening of our parapsychological faculties.

There's no doubt that this type of experience doesn't leave us indifferent; it can even be said to be life-changing. Our view of reality changes as does our view of death…and of life. Many of our fears dissipate, our apprehension about our mortality disappears, and we realize that we are much more than we think. However, accessing altered states of consciousness doesn't make us any wiser without real work on ourselves. I've known people who emanated unconditional love, who were full of compassion, and who devoted a large part of their lives to helping others; some had achieved a state of wisdom without having had a single out-of-body experience in their lives, at least consciously. On the other hand, we come across renowned (or not) experiencers with hundreds—even thousands—of out-of-body experiences under their belts, who are no more awake than you and me.

I think it's important to look at the place of OBE in our lives and how this extraordinary practice can help us in our evolution.

Various spiritual paths, religions, and tools have been available to us for millennia. None of them is better than another, and taken at face value they remain mere belief systems or just food for the ego. The most important thing is to put them into practice. In the West, we tend to think we know something because we've read about it, rather than putting it into practice. Nobody can do the work for you.

Out-of-body experiences are a great tool as long as you use them properly. But it's not the most important element in life. Remember, we're in this physical reality for a purpose. Spiritual alchemy, the transformation of defects into qualities, the quest to become better—these are what's most important. And it's not by simply wandering into other dimensions that these virtues will magically appear. However, it will help you greatly and accelerate your progress.

The out-of-body experience is therefore a tool of understanding and evolution of great transformative power. Some people compare them to a mystical experience, but how we react and use that power determines whether we achieve transformation or an illusory trap. It is therefore important also to study the knowledge of "ancient" experiencers and to include disciplines such as prayer or meditation in our daily spiritual practice, and not make OBE the focal point of one's life.

I've long thought the opposite, and I know that many authors have made this their main avenue of evolution. My heartfelt advice is that—even if you have to devote time and substantial energy to your practice to get results—you must never close yourself off from life or other people by taking this path. I want to emphasize this important point. You want to start practicing OBE; you're highly motivated and that's great. I encourage you to do so, but do it with a sense of perspective: don't reject differing opinions, don't feel different or superior, don't turn away from other people. In short, beware of ego traps. The more we discover the wonders of nature, of life, the greater our humility becomes. It's much easier to get out of your body than to become an enlightened being—a great sage. So, approach all this with passion, wisdom, humility, and respect. And if your wish is just to go for a walk on the Moon, visit the neighbor or aliens, you're free to make that choice, but you'd be wasting the benefits of the experience and you risk being faced with your own illusory projections.

As far as I'm concerned, out-of-body experiences are the best way to get closer to the true nature of your soul.

CHAPTER 3

THE INTERFACE BETWEEN OBE AND NEUROSCIENCES

Exploring the Frontiers of Consciousness

Neuroscience is both a window on the mind and a door to the unknown.
- David Eagleman

This part of the book explores how recent discoveries in neuroscience align with or challenge existing theories of the out-of-body experience. We'll take a brief look at the brain mechanisms potentially involved in OBE, and see how these phenomena might be better understood through the prism of modern science. Personally, I doubt that purely biological research is sufficient to fully elucidate the mechanisms of experiences that transcend physical reality. However, I find such research highly relevant and worthy of interest. It could eventually open the way to the development of faster, more effective induction techniques.

1- <u>Introduction to neuroscience and out-of-body experiences</u>

Neuroscience is a multidisciplinary branch of science that studies the nervous system, including the brain, spinal cord, and neural networks. It seeks to understand the structure and function of the nervous system at different levels, from individual molecules to complex neural circuits and human cognition.

This discipline encompasses a wide range of fields, including neuroanatomy (study of the structure of the nervous system), neurophysiology (study of the functions and processes of the nervous system), neuropharmacology (study of the interactions between drugs and the nervous system), neuroimaging (use of imaging techniques to visualize the brain and its activity), neurology (study of neurological disorders), and cognitive psychology (study of mental processes such as perception, attention, memory, language, etc., in relation to brain functions).

Neuroscience has applications in many fields, including medicine (for the diagnosis and treatment of neurological and psychiatric diseases), psychology, robotics, artificial intelligence, education, and other areas related to human behavior and cognition. But what interests us here is its involvement in the field of altered states of consciousness.

The study of out-of-body experiences by neuroscientists is a fascinating and complex field. Out-of-body experiences occur when someone has the sensation of detaching from their own body and perceiving the outside world from a position distinct from their physical body. These experiences can occur spontaneously or be induced by conditions such as trauma, illness, meditation techniques, or hallucinogens. Neuroscientists are interested in understanding the brain mechanisms underlying these experiences.

Some research has suggested that out-of-body experiences may be linked to alterations in brain regions responsible for multisensory integration, where information from different senses is combined to form a coherent representation of the bodily environment. Brain imaging studies such as functional magnetic resonance imaging (fMRI) have shown specific brain activations during out-of-body experiences, notably in regions involved in the processing of spatial orientation and proprioception (awareness of the body's position in space).

However, it should be noted that out-of-body experiences are still poorly understood, and current neuroscientific explanations are only theories. Moreover, out-of-body experiences are often subjective phenomena and difficult to study objectively in the laboratory. Ultimately, the study of out-of-body experiences by neuroscience represents an evolving field of research that seeks to demystify these fascinating phenomena while offering new insights into the nature of consciousness and human experience.

2- Brain mapping and out-of-body experiences

Neuroimaging techniques such as fMRI and EEG (electroencephalography) are used to study out-of-body experiences and other phenomena related to consciousness and perception.

fMRI (functional magnetic resonance imaging):

- fMRI measures changes in cerebral blood flow, which correlates with neuronal activity in different brain regions.

- During an out-of-body experiment, researchers can use fMRI to identify brain regions that show abnormal or different activity compared to baseline, which may provide clues to the neural mechanisms underlying OBEs.

- fMRI can also be used to map the functional connections between different brain regions during a consciousness projection, helping to understand how the brain integrates sensory information and constructs a coherent representation of body space.

EEG (electroencephalogram):

- EEG records the brain's electrical activity using electrodes placed on the scalp, providing a direct measure of neuronal activity.

- During an out-of-body experience, the EEG can detect changes in the brain's electrical activity patterns, such as specific oscillations or evoked potentials, which could be associated with alterations in perception and consciousness.

- EEG can also be used to study the synchronization and desynchronization of brain activity between different brain regions during OBE, which may help identify the neural networks involved in this phenomenon.

By combining these neuroimaging techniques with other experimental approaches, researchers can gain a deeper understanding of the brain mechanisms underlying out-of-body experiences, helping to illuminate our understanding of human consciousness and perception.

3- <u>The neurochemistry of out-of-body experiences</u>

The role of neurotransmitters and brain chemicals in out-of-body experiences is not fully understood, but some theories and research suggest some possible mechanisms.

Central nervous system and neurotransmitters:

Neurotransmitters are chemical substances that transmit

signals between nerve cells (neurons) in the brain. Neurotransmitters such as serotonin, dopamine, norepinephrine, and glutamate are involved in the regulation of mood, sensory perception, and consciousness. Fluctuations in these neurotransmitters can potentially influence perception and subjective experience, potentially contributing to OBE.

Neurological triggers:

Some researchers suggest that out-of-body experiences may be triggered by abnormalities or imbalances in normal brain function. For example, conditions such as epilepsy, migraines, or other neurological disorders can sometimes induce experiences of dissociation or depersonalization that could be perceived as astral travel experiences.

Vestibular system:

The vestibular system, which is responsible for balance and the perception of spatial position, may also play a role in out-of-body experiences. Research suggests that abnormalities in this system—or disturbances in its signals—may contribute to the floating or out-of-body sensations associated with OBE. The latter involves sensations, but not visual experience.

Altered states of consciousness:

Dissociation experiences can occur during states of altered consciousness such as deep meditation, hypnosis, and near-death experiences. These states can be associated with changes in brain activity and neurotransmitters, contributing to the subjective experiences experienced during these moments.

Endorphins and feelings of well-being:

Some out-of-body experiences can be associated with the release of endorphins, neurotransmitters that act as natural analgesics and can induce sensations of well-being and physical detachment.

DMT

DMT molecule

Dimethyltryptamine, or DMT, is a powerful psychedelic substance that exists both in nature and in the human body. It is produced naturally in the brain, notably in the pineal gland, although its exact role in normal brain function remains largely unknown. The potential link between DMT and out-of-body experiences is often discussed in psychedelic research circles and in communities interested in altered consciousness. Some have put forward the hypothesis that DMT could play a role in modulating out-of-body experiences, particularly when released in large quantities, for example during altered states of consciousness such as dreams, near-death experiences, and deep meditation.

However, it is important to note that our understanding of the relationship between DMT and out-of-body experiences is still very limited and subject to debate. Further research is needed to elucidate DMT's precise role in these phenomena as well as its mechanisms of action in the brain. Some people have reported having out-of-body experiences under the influence of DMT, but individual testimonials do not constitute conclusive scientific evidence. It's also important to consider the psychological, cultural, and environmental factors that can influence these experiences.

It's interesting to note DMT's relationship to the pineal gland. This gland, also known as the epiphysis or cerebral epiphysis, is a small, pinecone-shaped endocrine gland located in the center of the brain, between the two hemispheres near the midbrain. In esoteric tradition, it represents what is known as the third eye. It's an area that can be stimulated by visualization or by intoning a specific mantra such as "OM" or "AUM." I've mentioned it before in this book, particularly as a way of remembering dreams more easily. However, I have also been known to induce an out-of-body experience by visualizing a white energy light in the pineal gland.

Journal entry, February 2, 2024

After waking up at night, I concentrated on my pineal gland. In a state of relaxation close to sleep, I visualized a strong white light in the center of my head. I imagined that this light had the power to purify and stimulate my pineal gland. The sensations were intense, and I could feel a powerful energy flowing through my skull. Then I lost consciousness for what seemed like a few seconds and was propelled out of my body like a rocket. I was flying through an environment shrouded in thick fog, while the atmosphere seemed charged with electricity. Everything was tinged with an orange glow. Then my flight came to a sudden end and I saw myself drop like a stone to the ground. The sensation was dizzying, and I suddenly returned to my physical body, overwhelmed by intense vibrations.

4- Stimulation-induced out-of-body experiences

Transcranial magnetic stimulation (TMS) has been explored in certain contexts to induce sensations similar to out-of-body experiences. TMS is a non-invasive technique that uses magnetic fields to stimulate certain regions of the brain. When applied to specific areas of the cerebral cortex, it can influence neurological processes and produce a variety of perceptual and cognitive effects. Some studies have used TMS to stimulate regions of the cortex involved in the perception of body and space, such as the parietal cortex or temporal cortex. Experiments have shown that stimulation of these areas can induce sensations of disembodiment, distorted sense of self, and sometimes even OBE-like experiences. However, it should be noted that TMS-induced sensations are not necessarily identical to spontaneous out-of-body experiences. OBE are complex, multifactorial phenomena that can involve neurological, psychological, and sometimes even spiritual or cultural processes. TMS can provide interesting insights into how the brain generates bodily and spatial perceptions, but it cannot fully recreate the richness and variety of subjective out-of-body experiences.

5- Challenges and controversies

By their very nature, altered-consciousness experiences are beyond our understanding. Researchers who study them encounter various obstacles in their studies. Firstly, out-of-body experiences are subjective phenomena, meaning that they are experienced differently by each individual. This makes it difficult to standardize study protocols and compare results across different studies. What's more, because of their subjective nature it's not easy to measure these experiences objectively. Researchers often have to rely on participants' reports, which may transcribe an experience biased by faulty memory or interpretation. It can also be complicated to reproduce these experiments in the laboratory, validate results, and generalize conclusions.

Also, there is no clear consensus on the definition and classification of altered-consciousness experiences. Some scientists may include similar experiences under different terms, making it complex to compare results between studies.

An important aspect to bear in mind is that certain study methods—such as artificially inducing an experiment in participants—can pose ethical challenges. Scientists must ensure that their practices respect ethical principles and do not put participants at risk.

Our understanding of the mechanisms underlying out-of-body experiences is still limited. It can be complicated to design relevant experiments and research hypotheses without a clear understanding of the neurological and psychological processes involved.

It should also be borne in mind that—because of their association with paranormal or spiritual experiences—out-of-body experiences can be stigmatized in certain academic circles. This can make it difficult for researchers to obtain funding or recognition for their work.

6- <u>Bridges between Science and Subjective Experience</u>

Discoveries in neuroscience could enrich our understanding of accounts of out-of-body experiences in many ways. And by establishing a relationship between the scientific and the spiritual—

the material and the immaterial—can lead to an interesting balance. You could compare it to balancing + and - or Yin and Yang polarities. The confrontation of extremes always produces an enriching result.

Neural correlates:

Neuroscience can help identify brain regions and neural processes associated with out-of-body experiences. For example, brain imaging studies could be used to map brain activity during experiences, providing clues to underlying neurological mechanisms.

Neuropharmacology:

Studies into the effects of certain drugs on perception and cognition could shed light on the biological mechanisms of OBE. For example, psychoactive substances such as hallucinogens could be used to induce experiences like OBEs, enabling specialists to study their effects on the brain.

Neurology of similar experiences:

Neuroscientists could study other related phenomena, such as near-death experiences and lucid dreaming, which share similarities with OBE. By better understanding the neurology of these related experiences, researchers could also shed light on our understanding of out-of-body travel.

Conversely, accounts of out-of-body experiences could also contribute to neuroscience research in several ways:

Identification of neural mechanisms:

Detailed descriptions of OBEs could help neuroscientists

identify the brain regions and neural processes involved. These accounts could provide clues to the brain structures and neural networks associated with mind-body dissociation.

Research hypotheses:

OBE stories could inspire new research hypotheses in the neurosciences. For example, if several people report similar experiences during out-of-body experiences, this could prompt researchers to explore further to determine the specific brain regions or neural pathways that might have been involved in the coincidental experiences.

Validation of results:

Stories of out-of-body experiences could also be used to validate the results of neuroscience studies. For example, if a brain imaging study identifies a particular activation in a brain region during an OBE, the stories of people who have experienced an OBE could be used to confirm that this region is indeed involved in these experiences.

By combining the insights of out-of-body experience stories with the tools and methods of neuroscience, we can deepen our understanding of the mechanisms underlying these fascinating phenomena.

7- <u>Implications for the future of consciousness research</u>

The integration of neuroscience and out-of-body experiences could open up new perspectives and greatly enrich research into consciousness. OBEs offer a unique opportunity to study altered consciousness, in which the subjective experience of awareness is dissociated from normal sensory inputs. By integrating experiential accounts with neuroscience findings, researchers could better understand the neural mechanisms underlying altered states of consciousness.

Out-of-body experiences challenge our traditional understanding of consciousness and personal identity by enabling individuals to perceive their consciousness independently of their physical bodies. By integrating insights from this phenomenon with advances in neuroscience, researchers could explore the limits of human consciousness and the nature of personal identity. OBE narratives could also serve as empirical data to develop and refine theoretical models of consciousness. By combining these stories with neuroscience findings, more accurate and comprehensive models of how consciousness emerges in the brain and interacts with the outside world could be developed.

Our conceptions of subjective reality change with experiences that seem to defy the laws of physics and space-time. By integrating accounts of out-of-body experiences with advances in neuroscience, scientists could explore the nature of subjective reality and the relationship between individual consciousness and the external world. Together, the integration of neuroscience and out-of-body experiences could open up exciting new avenues of research in the study of human consciousness, helping us to better understand its underlying mechanisms, its limits, and its relationship with subjective reality.

Future opportunities for collaboration between scientists, OBE experiencers, and 'insiders'—individuals who have undergone other altered-consciousness experiences—could be very enriching and open new perspectives in research into human consciousness. Researchers could collaborate with insiders and experiencers to share their respective knowledge and experiences. Experiencers could offer insights and traditional methods for inducing similar experiences, while individuals who have experienced other consciousness projections could provide detailed accounts of their experiences, helping to better understand these phenomena. It would be possible to develop rigorous study protocols while taking into account the subjective and spiritual aspects of these experiences. And by combining empirical data with spiritual perspectives and accounts of experience, it would be possible to explore the different dimensions of consciousness—including its subjective, cultural, and spiritual aspects—in a more holistic way.

In short, collaboration between specialists and experiencers could open up new avenues of research in the study of human consciousness, integrating diverse perspectives and recognizing the complexity and richness of human experience.

PART TWO

PRACTICE

To know, to will, to dare, to be silent

Knowing, willing, daring, and remaining silent sum up the path of the initiate, and as an explorer of the subtle dimensions, we can rely on these four fundamental pillars. Each of these key words represents a virtue or principle that experiencers are encouraged to cultivate in their spiritual and personal quest.

Knowledge - This involves the quest for knowledge and understanding. It's about understanding the profound laws of nature and the universe as well as developing an inner understanding of oneself and the mysteries of existence.

Willingness - This means having the strength of will to pursue one's spiritual goals despite obstacles and challenges. It's the motivation and commitment to a chosen path, the ability to persevere and dedicate oneself fully to one's quest.

Dare - This represents the courage and audacity to cross conventional boundaries and confront the unknown. It means exploring uncharted territories of consciousness, engaging in practices that defy established norms, or simply having the courage to question and transcend one's own limits.

Keeping Quiet - Those around us are not always able to hear the story of our experiences, even if enthusiasm arouses the desire to share. This can also indicate the value of listening, reflection, and silent meditation as means of deep understanding.

CHAPTER 1

PREPARATORY STAGES

Prerequisites for out-of-body exit techniques

Preparation is the key to success. In every business, the preparatory work is as important as the final effort.

- Alexander Graham Bell

Being an experimenter - persisting despite oneself

Those who have had a near-death experience are commonly referred to as "experiencers." But this title also applies to practitioners of out-of-body experiences.

Non-experiencers ask a lot of questions about why we do what we do. And that's perfectly understandable. What's more, death-related subjects are often avoided in the West. The general tendency is to ignore them and get on with our daily routines, hoping to postpone the moment of having to face it as long as possible. And yet death is part of our lives. And nothing can change that. Some people—including me—choose to look it in the face and try to understand it and discover whether our fear is justified or not. Like all fears, the fear of death is rooted in ignorance. Human beings are always apprehensive about what they don't know. But in every field, there are a handful of people who feel compelled—despite themselves—to go ahead, to brave their emotions, to find out more.

It's a force within, something indefinable, that drives them on. Some would say it comes from a past life or a spiritual force. Practicing out-of-body experiences requires courage, perseverance, and a great deal of patience. It's a lifetime's work. Without this enthusiasm of unknown origin that burns deep inside, it's impossible to stay on this path. Once you've had this kind of experience—even once in your life—you can't forget it. And that's one of the most common reasons why people devote so much time to it.

To outsiders, we can easily come across as enlightened or

dreamy. But when we dare to broach the subject, one of two things happens. Either we come across someone who has had a similar experience but didn't want to talk about it for fear of being misjudged…or by telling our story with humility and honesty, we convey our experience with sincere enthusiasm. This will arouse the curiosity of your interlocutor and—even if he's doubtful—won't leave him indifferent.

Welcome to the "practical" part of this book. You've decided to join the underground community of experimenters, and that's a great decision. Here you'll find everything you need to know about experimenting on your own. First there's a preparatory stage, then the techniques themselves, and finally solutions to the most common problems. I've also added a section on the three major keys to successful experimentation, which I recommend you read carefully.

Keeping a journal

A personal journal is an essential tool for every experimenter. It allows you to record any type of experience in order to appreciate your evolution, to become aware of your mistakes, and to understand the way you function. It's a personal thing, and it's up to you to write down everything you want to record: your dreams, your techniques, your experiences, your spiritual theories and reflections, your discouragements, the solutions to your problems, your energetic feelings, or whatever—just like a travel companion.

It's important to note the date and it's practical to change journals every year. And even if we're on digital time, it's much more beneficial to the subconscious to write in pen in a notebook. Taking the step of forming words or creating drawings on a paper medium sends a powerful message to our subconscious, speeding up our results. Writing on a sheet of paper imprints our mind. Don't hesitate to write down your affirmations. It's advisable to write several of them a day for greater impact.

The journal also allows you to write down your goals. For example, to go and visit a specific place or contact a specific person. This not only feeds your motivation, but also helps you prepare for the experience so that you don't get disoriented, not knowing what to do once out of body and panicking. Choose a goal for your next experiment, mark it down, and come back to it regularly to keep it on track and support your determination. You can also draw up a work plan to structure your days. For example, practice meditation in the morning, repeat affirmations several times a day, and perform out-of-body or lucid dreaming exercises in the evening and at night. When we're structured, we impose a discipline on ourselves that enables us to practice effectively and—above all—to maintain our training over time. Because once a habit is created, it takes over on days when you're not motivated. Write down your daily practice strategy and don't hesitate to correct and improve it as the days go by. Personally, I gauge the effectiveness of my practice according to my dreams. I take notice of whether they are clearer, if I dream of dead people, if my dream adventure was especially realistic, if I felt like flying in my dream, if I felt like slight vibrations or other energetic phenomena during my dream or just after, the time when I woke up, etc. All this informs me of the progress of my practice. It tells me the degree of impact of my exercises.

Ideally, then, we should be on the lookout for all these kinds of clues, for it is only through them that we can know whether our practice is efficient, whether we're on the right track…and it's also food for our determination. If after a few days we have seen no clues in our dreams, we need to readjust certain points. First of all, we need to be self-critical of the seriousness of our involvement, and then we need to make a few small modifications such as adding visualization, modifying our affirmations, changing our position in bed, etc.

Some of my journals

For example, this is how I structure the pages of my journal:

Journal entry, March 21, 2020

Technique used: *affirmations*

Other practices of the day: *20 minutes silent meditation, 15 minutes energy practice*

General condition: *a little tired, some worries at work*

Bedtime: *relaxation countdown + affirmations*

Night-time awakening: *around 3 a.m., I tried not to move, affirmations again*

Dream:

I dreamt that a friend was giving me a surprise. I was to follow him to a field behind his house. When we got there, a huge hot-air balloon was waiting for us, attached to the ground by ropes. We climbed aboard, I cut the four ropes with a large scissor and we took off. I could feel the fresh air on my face, and I felt happy.

Note:

Average practice, I had trouble maintaining my concentration on reciting my affirmations. However, I persisted, and repeated myself two or three times.

On the other hand, I'm happy with the dream because the notion of flight is present, which tells me that the subconscious has heard my request after all. So, I don't change a thing, I continue in this direction.

I've gotten into the habit of writing next to the date in parentheses, "LD" for "Lucid Dream" and "OBE" for "Out-of-Body Experience." Also, I can see at a glance when I've had an experience and what it was. This is just one example. It's up to you to organize your journal as you see fit. But gathering as much information as possible will help you later. Don't hesitate to make a note of the "white days" as I call them; that is, periods without results, without recollection of dreams or anything else, and sometimes even without practice. White days can be due to temporary fatigue, worries of the moment, etc. It's common and human. Make a note of it though, even if it's only the date and the fact that you didn't do anything, feel anything, or achieve anything. This doesn't mean you've wasted time or gone back to zero: even in periods of pause, we are evolving in one way or another. Putting it down on paper is a sign of your interest in the practice, of your concern that you've missed an opportunity or a session, and all of this reflects that deep inside yourself the work continues to be done. Take a step back from this type of event—there's nothing negative about it, just use it to improve your strategy.

Tip: Use one journal per year. Even if your journal isn't finished and you still have blank pages on December 31, it's better to organize your writings on a yearly basis. It'll be much easier the day you want to go back to them.

Optimizing the Environment for Out-of-Body Experiences

Preparing the space where your practice will take place is crucial. Ideally, you should have an area dedicated to out-of-body experiences, such as a sofa in your office or an extra bed in a room. Having an area dedicated to astral exploration is already conditioning our subconscious to the significance of your quest. The more you practice in this area, the more likely it is that as soon as you go to lie down on your sofa or bed, the process will begin even though you haven't started practicing. It's even possible that after a while, you won't even need to use any method at all.

If setting up an exclusive space is impossible for you, don't worry. The key is to find a quiet, welcoming space—like your bedroom—where you can practice in peace.

Silence must reign, and if ambient noise is unavoidable, sound-reducing plugs can offer an effective solution. You need to relax deeply, free your mind of distractions, and focus on a specific technique. Without absolute calm, it is very difficult to implement the various steps.

It's also advisable to wear loose, comfortable clothing to avoid any physical strain and to be warm. When you enter a deep trance, your body slows down and cools down. Use a blanket to keep warm.

One last practical but essential tip: make sure you empty

your bladder before you lie down. It may seem trivial, but an urge to empty your bladder can interrupt your session and bring the experience to a premature end.

Tip: There are some very comfortable night masks with built-in headphones. This allows you not only to be unaffected by brightness—which is preferable for a good quality of relaxation or sleep—but also to listen to hemi-sync music.

Goal

Clearly defining your intention is a very important step in preparing for a projection of consciousness. Ask yourself: why do you want to have an out-of-body experience? It could be as simple as visiting your surroundings or a friend. But it could also be to see a departed loved one, explore distant planets or different countries, investigate the existence of other life forms, venture into the heart of the Earth, or fly over Mount Everest.

Your imagination will be the only limit to your aspirations. Let your wildest dreams guide your desire to explore beyond physical reality. The important thing is that this goal provides a powerful motivation, because a goal is a subtle anchor that will ease the transition into your energy body.

Start by writing down your main goal in your journal—the one you want to achieve first. At the end of your notebook, you can also draw up a list of future adventures to explore over time. However, keep your focus on your primary intention and engage in the practice of out-of-body experiences with determination until you reach that first goal before turning to the next ones.

Autosuggestion

The effectiveness of affirmations is well established these days. Ever since the work of Émile Coué, whose research aimed to "mechanically" induce a suggestion in the unconscious by repeating a positive phrase, the immeasurable benefits of this exercise have been undeniably proven. The principle is quite simple: a persistent thought that invades our mind eventually becomes reality. To do this, you need to repeat a positive, motivating phrase.

The unconscious doesn't take negation into account. For example, if I say to you, "don't think of an apple," the image of an apple will unconsciously appear in your mind. That's why it's important to use a positive sentence.

Autosuggestion can be a very important ally in maintaining a quality of practice and determination that lasts over time. It can also multiply your chances of success and speed up the triggering of an experience.

Here is an example of a sentence I repeat several times a day:

"I'm more and more motivated to have out-of-body experiences!"

"I practice more and more and better and better, and I have more and more conscious out-of-body experiences!"

Autosuggestion is also an effective way to work on those fears that prevent us from successfully completing an outing. Fear of the unknown—apprehension about this type of experience—is the number one cause of failure. In such cases, we can effectively use the Coué method with an affirmation such as:

"I am a soul like any other who experiments outside her physical body, serenely and safely!"

Or:

"I get out of my body easily, safely, protected by my divine nature!"

Feel free to create your own phrase; the simpler it is, the more impact it will have. It's a good idea to repeat it aloud several times a day. You can also write it down; the very act of putting it down on paper somehow imprints it on your subconscious. The important thing is to do it every day. It's a very simple technique, and extremely effective if applied properly. All you need is patience and perseverance, and the benefits can come quickly depending on the individual, the quality of the practice, and the number of repetitions. The key is to believe in it, to feel that the request is effective on the spot.

A trick derived from this exercise is to print your suggestion on colored paper and place it in a place you often walk past. This could be the bathroom, your bedroom, the office, etc. When I was at the Monroe Institute in Virginia, William gave us an A4 sheet of yellow paper with the words, "NOW I HAVE A CONSCIOUS OBE!" written on it. We were to stick this little poster to the ceiling of our Chek Unit (our practice cabin). Don't hesitate to do the same. The more tricks you use to saturate your mind, the better the results.

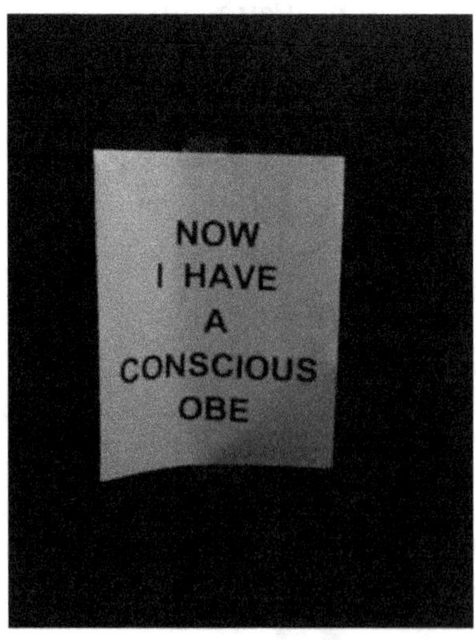

The advice I personally give and apply is to take your time and build your suggestion. Choose the words that speak to you—that appeal to you. Once you've done that, sit down comfortably, close your eyes, and start reciting your affirmation. Observe its impact on you, how it makes you feel as you repeat it, any images it conjures up in your mind, how it soothes or stresses you. All this will tell you whether it's right for you or not. And if you feel it's not working, you can replace a word or change the wording to suit you. In short, modify your sentence to make it perfect for you.

Tip: In the section of this book entitled "Natural Aids," you'll find a hypnotic induction method called "The Sensory Spiral." Don't hesitate to use it to reinforce the effectiveness of your affirmations.

The Vision Board

The vision board is a powerful motivational tool that helps you visually materialize your goals and dreams. To create one, assemble images, photos, quotes, and affirmations that embody your aspirations and stick them on a board or a piece of cardboard. Then put the board in a place you frequent regularly so that every time you see it, it reminds you of your ambitions. This concept can be applied to wishes of any kind, but also to conditioning ourselves for out-of-body experiences.

Energy Work

Our bodies—both physical and subtle—need energy to function. So does consciousness. Energy work is not essential for out-of-body experiences but it is of considerable benefit. It helps to develop concentration, improve vitality, and enhance health. The vibratory state—which is the first sign of an outing—is easier to reach by those who practice energy work, as it has a direct relationship with the energy system. The practice will also have an impact on consciousness—which will be re-energized and therefore clearer— and also on dreams and their recollection. By working on certain energy centers such as the Ajna (or third eye), you can even *induce* lucid dreams and out-of-body experiences.

Among reputed authors, you'll find two categories of approach in terms of techniques. There are those who place chakra or kundalini work at the forefront, like Akhena and Robert Bruce, who consider that without this work it is difficult to have access to quality experiences. And then there are others for whom it represents an interesting but nonessential alternative. As you'll have gathered, I fall into the latter category, and the reason is simple: most of my experiences have taken place without prior energy work. On the other hand, I have tested techniques related to the psychic centers or the spinal column that have enabled me to trigger separation or lucid dreams that I have transformed into OBEs. All this is valid and interesting, not only in the field of altered states of consciousness but also in others such as health. It depends on the individual but also on our life phase.

To illustrate my point, there have been times in my life when I couldn't get the slightest result, the slightest dreamlike sign, even though my practice was daily and—in my opinion—of fairly good quality. It was against this backdrop that I introduced the energy exercises and they have borne fruit.

I'm going to present here a summary of the main energy systems, bearing in mind that there are already a large number of books on the subject (see bibliography), and I'll share some simple but effective techniques for creating an OBE through energy work.

Energy Centers

In Hindu culture, the so-called first energetic body—which some call the "etheric"—is said to be located as close as possible to our physical body and containing the energy centers known as chakras. This term translates as "wheels." These centers are seen as luminous wheels that rotate, drawing energy from the surrounding environment into their center and redistributing it throughout the body via a complex network known as the nadis. These channels are similar to the concepts of meridians found in Chinese medicine.

Ancient texts list no less than 88,000 chakras, but here we'll concentrate on the seven main ones. As body and mind are one, each chakra has a very specific role to play in maintaining balance in certain parts of the body as well as in certain psychological aspects of the human being. It's not essential to know all this by heart in order to carry out energy work, but energy follows intention and even with a minimum of knowledge, the impact of the exercises will be more precise and effective. Here, then, is a list of the main energy centers, located on a central axis between the genitals and the top of the skull.

The seven main chakras

1-   Muladhara chakra or root chakra

The Muladhara chakra—more commonly known as the root chakra—is located in the perineum, between the anus and the genitals. This is where transcendent energy awaits awakening. Physically, it is associated with the nose and sense of smell. The color associated with it is red. A balanced root chakra provides stability, "grounding," and is an important element to consider when practicing out-of-body experiences.

2-   Svâdhistâna chakra or sacral chakra

The sacral chakra is located about two inches below the

navel. It is usually perceived as an orange disc. Its significance is that Kundalini originally resided here before descending to the root chakra. This is where the karma of our past lives and the link to the collective unconscious reside. It is therefore a very important energy center for our spiritual evolution.

3-   Manipûra chakra or solar plexus chakra

The Manipûra chakra is traditionally positioned behind the navel, but its location may differ from book to book. It is often placed between the umbilicus (the belly button) and the xiphoid process (the tip of the sternum) because it is made up of a main energy center and secondary centers whose functions are similar to those of Manipûra. It is therefore considered a single chakra. It radiates a yellow color. This chakra, linked to the element fire, symbol of purification, represents our sun, the starting point of our spiritual development.

4-   Anâhata chakra or heart chakra

The Anâhata chakra is located at heart level and its associated color is green. It links the three lower centers with the three higher ones. It is the center of unconditional love. It is said that the awakening of this chakra results in the birth of a number of paranormal faculties, including that of healing through the laying on of hands. Home to our feelings of love, it's also considered the gateway to the soul, maintaining a close relationship with the Ajna or sixth chakra.

5-   Vishuddhi (or Vishuddha) chakra or throat chakra

This energy center is located in the throat very close to the thyroid gland. It's considered the chakra of purification and is represented by a blue disk (actually, blue-green). It's also the communication center responsible for expressing our feelings…such as laughter, anger, tears, and so on. As far as the practice of altered-consciousness experiences is concerned, it is of particular interest as it is responsible for fulfilling our desires and transmitting our intentions.

6-   Ajnâ chakra or frontal chakra

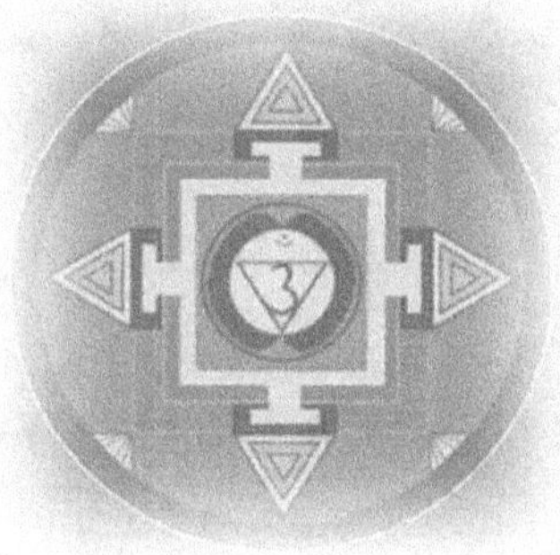

Located about a finger above the root of the nose in the middle of the forehead, it's a chakra you can feel when you concentrate on it. Just reading the description of its location can induce a sensation of light pressure in the area mentioned. It is known as the "third eye" and its Sanskrit etymology means "to command," hence its function as a "command center." This chakra is closely linked to the pineal gland, an important part of the nervous system, and considered a "spiritual antenna."

Activating the forehead chakra puts us in touch with higher consciousness and gives us access to clairvoyance. It generally radiates an indigo blue light, but can sometimes turn violet. This explains why—depending on the book—it is sometimes one color or the other. In this book, however, we shall retain the traditional color of indigo blue.

7-   Sahasrâra chakra or coronal chakra

Represented by the color white or violet, it floats above the head. Sahasrâra's role is to connect us to the Divine Essence and to act as a channel for the transmission of cosmic energy to all the other chakras. Anecdotally, some experiencers report exiting through this center during an out-of-body experience.

Chakra Stimulation

Here are a few simple but effective techniques for stimulating the chakras. If you wish to go further, there are methods such as Reiki or New Energy Ways, which are proving highly effective in this field. The Monroe Institute has also published a set of CDs created by energy-center-development specialist Patty Avalon. The product is called "Healing Journeys Support with Hemi-Sync."

Exercise 1 - opening your chakras

As a first exercise, here's a particularly effective technique recommended by William Buhlman during his workshops.

Simply concentrate on a chakra, starting with the root, and

imagine it opening like a door or window. As with all the exercises suggested here, the important thing is to feel beyond imagining. Feel the center opening up like a flower blooming. You can also visualize a double door opening gently. Feel the energy center expand and open. You may feel slight pressure, warmth, tingling, or rotation. In the root chakra you can easily feel as much as a slight burning.

Do this for each chakra, starting with the root and working up to the coronal. You may concentrate on a chakra for a period of a few seconds to a few minutes. As soon as you feel the zone is active, move on to the next one. On the other hand, if you don't feel much—which is common when you're new to energy work—try to maintain your concentration for thirty seconds to a minute.

Exercise 2 - using colors

Here's an exercise similar to the first with the difference that instead of using the notion of opening the chakras, you'll imagine the corresponding color of each chakra shining brighter and brighter. Always start with the root and work towards the coronal. As in the previous exercise, it's essential to get a good feel for the area you're working on. As soon as you feel the energy center shining brightly, move on to the next one.

As a reminder, here are the corresponding colors:

- Root chakra : red
- Sacral chakra : orange
- Solar chakra : yellow
- Heart chakra : green
- Throat chakra : blue-green
- Frontal chakra : blue-indigo
- Coronal chakra : violet

Exercise 3 - tactile imagination

For this exercise, we're going to use an interesting faculty called tactile imagination. This involves imagining touching an area mentally until you actually feel it. For example, focus your attention on the palm of your left hand and imagine the fingertips of your right hand touching the area in a rotating motion.

If this exercise seems a little complicated, if you can't feel this "imaginary rubbing," then start by doing it for real. Close your eyes and focus on the sensation of touch, feeling your fingertips rubbing the skin in a circle around the palm of your hand. Then, keeping your eyes closed, stop the rotating movement and continue the exercise in an imaginary way, trying to retain the sensation you had during the previous practice.

You can do this on any part of the body, the important thing being to really feel the action of the imagination on the area.

The same applies to chakra development. You simply need to focus your attention on the desired energy center and apply a rotational movement through intention. You can use the direction that suits you or the recommended one. In fact, some books recommend alternating the direction of rotation—one to the right, one to the left—starting with the root chakra, which is rotated to the left for men and to the right for women. The rotational directions of the other energy centers will thus alternate according to the first chakra.

However, don't feel obliged to follow this rule, as stimulating a chakra in any way will automatically activate it.

Kundalini or Fire Energy

Some authors, such as Akhena and Robert Bruce, recommend working with Kundalini—which belongs to the Indian philosophy and is also known as fire energy—to promote out-of-body experiences. This simulation can also be useful for dreams, lucid dreaming, and even certain types of meditation, such as Yogani's spinal breathing pranayama. The idea is to activate this energy and then store it in the first chakra, or in the area below the navel known as the Hara.

This has a positive impact on both physical and spiritual health, clarifying consciousness and purifying the nervous system. It can then be used to induce awareness in any state of consciousness. On a personal note, I have used Kundalini practice on several occasions in my research into out-of-body experiences, and have indeed been able to verify its benefits. My first observation concerned the impact of this exercise on dreams. I happened to spontaneously induce lucid dreams following the activation of this energy.

Each person will benefit from it according to their needs. But it's worth testing and observing the results because it's a virtuous practice. I'm not proposing in-depth, intense work on Kundalini. Indeed, it's something that needs to be handled with care and practiced in the company of qualified people. As I'm not a specialist, I'd like to share with you a method that you can use in complete safety. In Akhena's words, it's a simple practice of stimulating the energy stored in the first chakra and there's no risk of awakening the Kundalini by using this exercise.

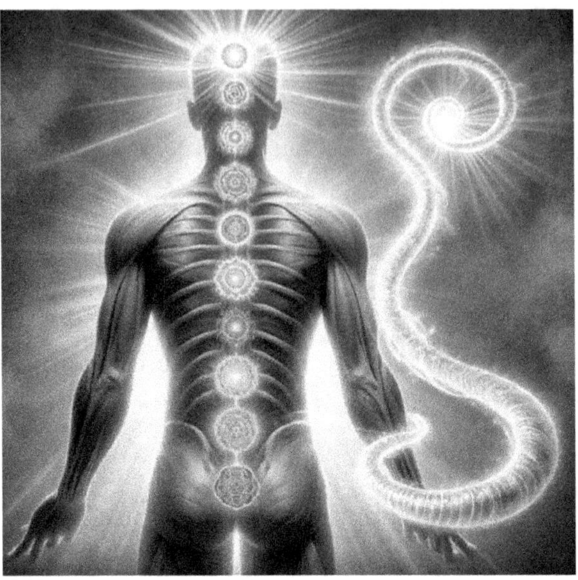

Kundalini

Put into practice:

Phase 1:

We're going to use our tactile imagination again, but this time in association with breathing. First, focus your attention on the first energy center—the root chakra—located between the anus and the genitals, and imagine feeling a rotating movement there. Feel this well, as it's very common to feel heat in this area, which in some people can become quite intense to the point of a burning sensation. A little trick is to use the breath to fan this "fire" by imagining blowing on this energy center like a bellows with each exhalation. It's extremely effective. Concentrate on this exercise for about five minutes.

Phase 2:

Now that the energy present in this first psychic center is awakened, feel it gradually rise up your back, along your spine. If you're comfortable with this kind of tactile imaging, add a rotational movement to the rising energy. It's as if—like a snake—it is wrapped around your spine rising to the top of your head. This trick amplifies the action; it's not rare to feel a sensation of heat and fire in your back. You may also sometimes lose this perception in the middle of the back, as if it were difficult to feel the energy all along your spinal axis.

There may turn out to be a "blockage"—an imbalance—in this pathway, which is known as the Governor Vessel or Du Mai in acupuncture. If this is the case, concentrate for a few moments on the location of the blockage, focusing a little more on it. You can try to visualize a blowtorch or a laser to encourage stronger action. Or try to imagine a very intense white light with the ability to dissolve blockages. Don't hesitate to use your infinite power of visualization and feeling to restore good circulation in the spine.

Phase 3:

You can feel the energy, the heat, rising to the top of your head. At this point, there are two possible outcomes:

As Akhena advised, you bring the fire down into the first chakra, followed by back and forth along your spine. And after a while (5-15 minutes) you finish by bringing the energy down to the root center and leaving it there. In this way, you store energy that will be used automatically later when you seek to trigger an out-of-body experience or lucid dream.

Or, you move the fire energy to the front of the body, i.e., over the top of the skull to the central axis of the face, then the thorax, and finally the abdomen, following the central channel (Ren Mai or Conception Vessel) to the Hara (or lower Dan Tien), i.e., in the area below the navel.

Illustration of Dan Tien by a Tai Chi practitioner

The hara is another energy storage site that can be used in future experiments.

This Kundalini work is very simple and easy to set up. The most important thing is to *feel*. Perceiving sensations and shifts of consciousness in the body are far more effective than visualization alone. Combining imagination and perception is the most efficient way to achieve fast, convincing results.

With a little practice, you can do the exercise in front of the TV, while walking, or while at work (depending on your job, of course). As the days go by, you'll be able to appreciate the evolution of your practice through your feelings, your sensitivity, your dreams, your clarity of mind, your renewed energy and so on.

By way of an anecdote, there was a period in my life when I practiced the New Energy Ways method revisited by Robert Bruce, the source of which is said to be a "bone-breathing" technique considered by yogis to be a secret way of influencing prana. In addition to exercises on the minor and major chakras, Robert proposes a Kundalini exercise similar to the one I've given you. At the time, I used to do them whenever I could during the day, the evening, in front of the TV, before going to sleep, and sometimes even after waking up at night.

After a few days of intense practice, I woke up one night with a feeling of intense fire that started at the root chakra and went up the spine to the lumbar region. It was so intense that I was afraid I was burning from the inside out. Then the sensation slowly faded. This is an example of what can sometimes happen.

It's worth pointing out that if you've never used an energy technique before, it's common to feel tired for the first week or two. This is perfectly normal, a bit like returning to a sport after a long break. You just have to persevere, even if it's inconvenient to do exercises in the evening or at night as sleep may come more quickly and concentration may be more difficult to maintain. Remember that this is a positive reaction; it means that something is happening that you will reap the benefits of later.

Tip: If you're interested in this approach to developing Kundalini energy to induce out-of-body experiences, then Akhena's techniques (see Bibliography) are for you.

Neon Body Technique: Energetic Activation

I'd like to introduce you to a method of energy stimulation I've devised to energize the body, the chakras, and the Kundalini. This approach—which I imagined and tested in my quest for an exercise encompassing all areas of the body—is particularly powerful. It's ideal to start the visualization in a state of deep relaxation to maximize effectiveness and enhance the sensations experienced, but it's possible to practice it in a state of normal consciousness. The key is to focus on the sensations to reinforce the visualization. The protocol begins with stimulation of the various parts of the body, followed by the chakras, and ending with the Kundalini.

<u>Energy stimulation method</u> :

1- Body stimulation :

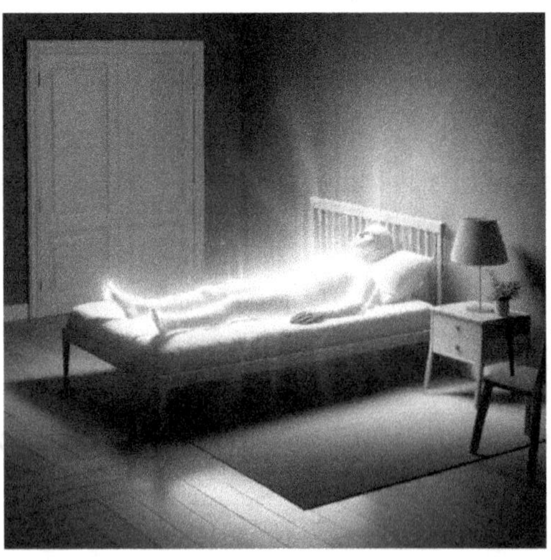

- Imagine every part of your body lighting up like a neon light. At first, it may flicker before emitting a powerful, warm, and vibrant white light. Feel the light's tiny vibrations of sound and touch.

- Starting with the right leg, visualize the foot and ankle, then the calf, and finally the thigh lighting up intensely in white. Feel the warmth and vibrations.

- Repeat the process for the left leg, passing through the foot, ankle, calf, and thigh. These light up one after the other, like a neon light. Feel all the sensations described and visualize the white light gradually illuminating the room.

- Then visualize your pelvis, abdomen, and chest lighting up, warming your upper body and intensifying the vibrations.

- Continue with the arms, starting with the right one: hand and wrist, forearm, then arm and shoulder. Take your time to see the white light and feel its effects.

- Do the same with your left arm. Progress gently, feeling the heat and vibrations.

- Finish with the head. Imagine it lighting up like a streetlamp, radiating a dazzling white light.

- At this stage, every part of your body is stimulated by this powerful white energy. You feel warmth and well-being enveloping you, and the vibrations are more intense. Enjoy this moment for a few seconds, then move on to the next step.

2- Chakra stimulation :

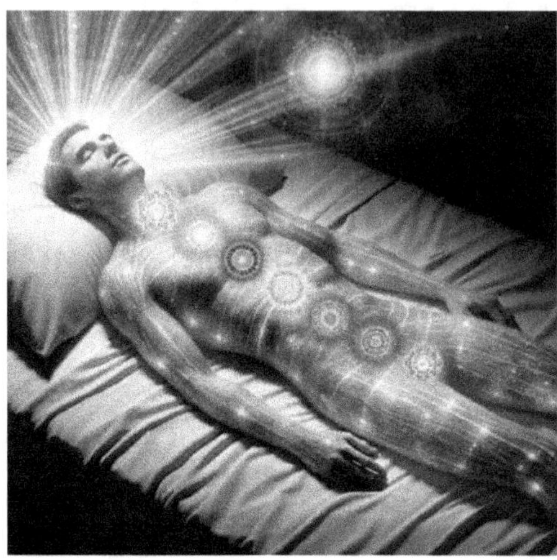

- Now imagine a ball of red light gradually intensifying between the coccyx and the perineum—the root chakra. It gets brighter and brighter, and more sensitive people may feel a warmth or even a burning sensation. Once the visualization and sensation are well established, move on to the next chakra.

- Below the navel this time, an orange ball begins to appear. Its light gradually intensifies, radiating both in front and behind the back. This orange glow running through the body corresponds to the sacral chakra. Here again, once you've got the feeling and visualization right, move on to the next step.

- Direct your intention above your navel. A ball of yellow light illuminates, gradually increasing in intensity. This activates the solar plexus chakra. The luminosity is penetrating, radiating not only to the front of the body but also to the back. When visualization and sensation are sufficiently clear, activate the next chakra.

- Now you are at heart level; the ball of light is green. It becomes brighter and brighter, warming the area more and more intensely. As soon as you feel the stimulation, move on to the next chakra.

- The throat chakra is activated by blue light. A ball of blue light emits an increasingly luminous, penetrating beam. You feel sensations in your throat. When these are clear and unmistakable, move on to the next step.

- Now stimulate the Ajna chakra, i.e., the third eye, located slightly above the area between the eyebrows. A ball of blue-indigo light shines brighter and brighter on either side of the head. Feel all this before moving on to the last energy center.

- The coronal, the last of the chakras, sits like a crown on top of your head. Visualize it as a fairly large ball, violet or white in color, with an intense radiance that extends all the way to the sky.

- Enjoy this moment when all seven chakras are stimulated, and appreciate the vision of them shining intensely on your body, radiating pure white light. The spectacle must be magnificent and the sensations powerful. Feel purified by the action of all these energies.

3- Kundalini stimulation

Once the body and chakras are powerfully glowing, imagine red hot lava entering the root chakra and running up the spine to the coronal chakra. Feel this gradually, don't rush. It's as if the heat were extreme in the spine. If you've practiced well up to this point, you should feel a very warm energy moving up your back to the top of your head.

- Move this energy up and down several times. Continue for a few seconds or minutes if you wish, and finish by moving it back down into the root chakra.

- If you have trouble feeling the energy in any part of your spine, imagine a ball of white light coming to "unblock" the area concerned. Blockages can sometimes occur. For example, you may feel the energy rise to the middle of your back and then stop. In this case, you need to persist or else use the white light beam.

4- End of process :

-   Once you've completed the exercise, gently regain awareness of your physical body, take three deep breaths, and start wiggling your fingers. When you feel ready, open your eyes, stretch, and drink a large glass of water.

Tip: If you practice Reiki, use it for your energy preparation. I also recommend Robert Bruce's New Energy Ways (see Bibliography), especially the "Full-Body Circuit."

Mudras

I'm sharing with you some Taoist knowledge on the use of small, finger-only gestures known as "Mudras." They're a precious help in my practice of out-of-body experiences, especially when I'm having trouble relaxing. That's why I wanted to integrate this notion into this book. What's more, they have an energetic action, which interests us on several levels in our practice.

The word Mudra comes from Sanskrit and means "seal." If we look at the syllables of this word, we find:

- "**Mud,**" meaning "joy"

- "**Ra,**" meaning "trigger".

Mudra is a seal that brings joy.

Mudras are gestures involving the fingers or hands that promote the circulation of energy in the human body. They have always been used in Eastern civilizations as a therapeutic aid.

It's interesting to note that hands often instinctively form a Mudra at just the right moment. It's as if the body possesses an inherent wisdom that always seeks and finds a way to express itself.

There are a multitude of gestures, and if you're interested in the subject I refer you to Gertrud Hirschi's excellent book "Mudras for Body, Mind and Spirit." Below, I'll explain Mudras in terms of Taoist philosophy.

- <u>The five elements:</u>

To understand the use of Mudras, we need to start by studying the five elements because they form the basis for the use of these gestures.

To understand the workings of the Universe, Easterners divided the components of this world into two parts, each containing a set of similar aspects. One part contains aspects such as day, masculine, hot, etc., and the other, night, feminine, cold, etc. They named these two groups Yang and Yin. Then, in order to go into even greater detail and understanding, they divided these two groups into five subsets: the famous five elements.

This formed—and still form today—the basis of Asian medicine. Physical disorders are caused by an alteration in the balance among the five elements. And there are techniques for acting on them, such as acupuncture and the use of Mudras.

Here's a list of the five elements and their psychological influence:

Metal: a lack of this energetic quality will translate into sadness, anxiety, and stress, while an excess will express itself in over-excitement or over-confidence.

Water: a lack of Water will give rise to fear, apprehension, and indecision, while an excess will engender extravagance and authoritarianism.

Wood: a lack of the Wood element makes us sensitive to anger, while a plethora of it makes us hot-tempered and even sectarian.

Fire: a lack of Fire translates into crying and anguish, while an overabundance of Fire translates into laughter (joy).

Earth: a deficiency of Earth leads to depression, mental fatigue; an excess leads to obsessions.

Each of these elements controls one of the others, and this is where Mudras come into play:

Fire controls **Metal**

Earth controls **Water**

Metal controls **Wood**

Water controls **Fire**

Wood controls **Earth**

So, for example, if you're feeling anxious, it's because you're lacking Metal. Thanks to a Mudra, we can "recharge" Metal. If we're angry, we have an excess of Wood. Two solutions then present themselves: either we remove Wood or we get Metal, because Metal controls (or "crushes") Wood.

Mudras can help you control your emotions.

These gestures are also useful for physical problems. I can't go into detail here, as the use of the five elements requires a fairly lengthy training course and you won't be able to understand everything with just a brief explanation. Nevertheless, I will give you a few tips.

Most of the problems we encounter are due to the elements Wood or Fire. All inflammation is due to Fire (coughs, cystitis etc.), so either remove this element or bring in Water, as the latter controls Fire. For all problems related to Wood (such as asthma, stress), either remove Wood or bring back Metal.

- <u>In practice</u>

Here's what each finger on the hand represents.

Note that the thumb represents the intermediary between the elements and their origin.

The first phalanx (bone) of the thumb corresponds to the Sky (Heaven), and by placing your fingers in contact with it you'll either seek out the element you need or send back the unwanted one.

The second phalanx corresponds to the Earth, and its function is the same as for Sky/Heaven; therefore, we have a choice between two sources—Earth and Sky—for drawing or returning energy.

So how do you choose? Most of the time, we use Heaven because cosmic energy is quickly available. But it's a question of feeling. If you feel that your gestures work better with Earth, then do them that way.

To fetch the element you need, you bring the pad of the corresponding finger into contact with the part of the thumb you've chosen. For example, if I'm having an asthma attack or I'm anxious, I'll go for Metal in Heaven (or Earth if you prefer) by connecting the pad of the ring finger with the first phalanx of the thumb. To remove the unwanted element, contact the base of the finger with the chosen part of the thumb.

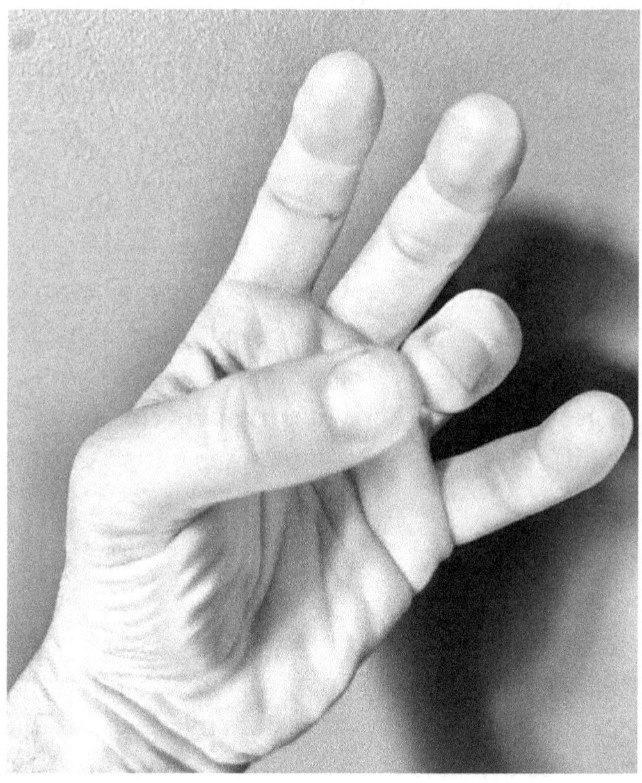

Metal Mudra (to Heaven)

Returning to my example, I can also remove the Wood that bothers me by "sending" the Wood back to Heaven (or Earth) by bringing the base of the index finger into contact with the first phalanx of the thumb.

Mudras are performed with both hands at the same time, and are maintained until a result is achieved.

In the context of out-of-body experiences, we'll be using the one pictured above. In fact, if you're having trouble relaxing for whatever reason, or if you're having trouble breathing when you're on your back, make this gesture and you'll feel the effects in a matter of seconds. If you're having trouble maintaining the correct finger position, you can place your hands against the mattress to hold your Mudra in place while relaxing your body.

The two fingertips should simply be in contact, there's no need to press hard.

- <u>To conclude</u>

Mudras are small, discreet gestures that can be performed in a pocket or behind the back, for example, and which can make a big difference in many situations. If a symptom worsens while performing a gesture, do the opposite of mudra (return the energy if you've fetched it) or stop immediately by separating the pulps.

Relaxation

Whatever techniques are used to bring about a change in the state of consciousness, relaxation remains the most important preparatory practice. The effectiveness of any lucid dreaming or out-of-body experience depends on it. Most reported failures are due to poor relaxation. Do not neglect this phase. Its importance is paramount and deserves appropriate time. Nowadays, there are several aids available to simplify and speed up the process, from breathing exercises and sophrology to more complex procedures such as the Monroe Institute's Hemi-Sync sound creations. The aim is to achieve a state of deep trance in which the body sleeps and the consciousness remains alert.

Start by trying out each of the suggested methods—don't hesitate to glean others from the Internet or books—then stick with one and apply it on a daily basis. With a little practice, you should be able to relax deeply in no time. Depending on when you do your exercises, the hardest part will be keeping your consciousness awake. It's important to find the right balance because we're often either too agitated or too sluggish.

Techniques

There are many ways to relax your body and I'd like to share with you the ones I find most effective and easiest to use. I advise you to try them all at least once to find the one that suits you best. Of course, if you know of a technique that's not on the list and that works better for you, use it.

1-   <u>Basic technique</u>

The basic relaxation technique is very simple to perform but highly effective.

It simply consists of lying down in the same position you usually use to fall asleep. Relaxation is a natural ability we all have, and we use it every day at bedtime. All we have to do is rely on what our body knows how to do naturally. The only difference is that we must keep our consciousness awake.

Breathe slowly and regularly, and never move. Try to keep your eyes fixed, but without tension. Relax a little more with each exhalation, "expelling" physical and mental tensions. To keep your consciousness awake, focus on one point: your breathing, your heartbeat, or the darkness behind your eyelids.

2-   <u>Self-hypnosis technique</u>

Self-hypnosis is very simple to use. It's an exercise that many practitioners enjoy before repeating affirmations or using a visualization method, whether during the day or after waking up at night.

Once you are lying down in a comfortable position, count slowly from 10 to 1 and suggest to yourself by repeating:

10... "I'm relaxing!"

9.... "I'm relaxing!"

8.... "I'm relaxing!"

Continuing the count until…

1... "I'm totally relaxed, my body asleep while my mind stays awake!"

Here again, expel your internal tensions—physical or mental—on each exhale.

Before starting the countdown, you can suggest to yourself, for example:

"I'm going to count from 10 to 1, and with each number my relaxation will be deeper and deeper, and once I reach one, my body will then be asleep and my consciousness awake."

3-   Progressive relaxation

This technique requires a little more concentration, but is nonetheless fairly simple to perform. It appeals to the unlimited power of your imagination, particularly in terms of sensations.

Lie down, as usual, in a position conducive to relaxation. The method requires you to review each part of your body for tense muscles, starting with your feet, calves, thighs, one leg then the other, then continue with your pelvis, abdomen, and thorax. Then review your arms in the same way as your legs, starting with your hands, forearms, arms, shoulders, and ending with the head, jaw, eyes, scalp, ears, and neck.

For each of these areas of the body, you will imagine that it relaxes by becoming heavier and heavier. Then this heaviness will begin to give way to a lighter and lighter feeling until the limb disappear as if it had been amputated. Once this is done, "forget" this part and move on to the next.

At the end of the exercise, once your whole body has relaxed, you should feel "expanded." Again, imagine that your physical body has completely disappeared and you're nothing more than a floating consciousness in the space of your room.

4-   Variant of progressive relaxation

There is a well-known variant of progressive relaxation; the approach is exactly the same except that instead of imagining each body part disappearing, you are asked to tightly contract the area to be relaxed for a few seconds. Once the muscle is released, the area relaxes on its own. Apply this method to the whole body. Once the exercise is complete, contract all the muscles simultaneously, hold for a few seconds, then release. Then let yourself relax; enjoy the sensation of relaxation and encourage it by deepening the relaxation on each exhale.

5- The Tibetan technique

The dead man's position.

Tibetan relaxation is a very pleasant method taught in Buddhist monasteries. The starting position is that of the "dead man" (see image above). Lie down on a mat on the floor or on your bed, arms and legs slightly apart, as if you'd been shot and slumped on your back. Think back to your childhood, when you played cops and robbers or cowboys and Indians and had to fake your death.

Once in position, remain still. Like the progressive relaxations, you'll need to go through every part of your body. The variation here will be to use the characteristics of the five Tibetan elements to progressively relax you until you no longer feel your body.

The chronology of the zones to be visualized is as follows:

The 1st, 2nd, 3rd, 4th, and 5th toe of a foot.

Then the calf, knee, and thigh.

Do the same with the other leg.

Pelvis, buttocks, abdomen, thorax, back.

The 1st, 2nd, 3rd, 4th, and 5th finger of one hand.

Forearm, elbow, arm, shoulder.

Do the same with the other arm.

Jaw, cheeks, eyes, ears, scalp, back of head, nape of neck.

You need to go through all these parts at the same speed as you speak the text. That is, neither too fast nor too slow. You can mentally repeat the relevant areas as you go along.

The method consists of feeling an element in each part of the body being used, starting with the **EARTH** element. Feel the heaviness of the Earth in each zone, following the chronology presented above. Your body should feel heavy at the end of the exercise. Feel the sensations.

Then switch to the **WATER** element in the same way. Feel as if something is flowing through each area of your body, repeating the circuit from your toes to your head. Once you've done the exercise, feel your whole organism "move" like a pleasant, fluid circulation throughout your body.

It's time to go back to the toes and imagine the **FIRE** element this time. Feel the warmth of this element gradually develop throughout your body until it invades it completely.

At the end of the circuit, your body should feel warmed up or on fire.

Resume the chronology of relaxation with the **AIR** element. Each area addressed in sequence becomes lighter and lighter, and once all the parts have been reviewed your whole body becomes light as a bird's feather. You should feel yourself floating or levitating above the ground.

And finally, starting again from the beginning, we use the **SPACE** element. Every part you focus on will disappear. As the exercise progresses your physical body will be consumed in space, leaving you as a mere point of consciousness. You lose the sensation of your physical body—it no longer exists. If you've done the exercise properly and without falling asleep, you should be in the ideal state of consciousness to induce an experience.

This method may seem a little tedious to read, but it's actually very easy to implement. And above all, it's a pleasure to use. Don't hesitate to try it out.

Tip: if you find it hard to relax, envision imaginary hands massaging your head. Feel with awareness the movements on your skull and temples and this should relax you completely more easily and quickly. You can add an affirmation such as, "I'm relaxing more and more, I'm calm and safe!"

ISC or Ideal State of Consciousness

What I call the Ideal State of Consciousness (ISC) is the optimal condition for inducing an altered-consciousness experience such as lucid dreaming, remote viewing, and out-of-body experience. You could call it a "launch pad." This is the most important element to know and know how to induce. Once you know what it is, what it "looks" like, it's much easier to appreciate when to use an induction technique and also to access the state more quickly. Just by remembering this particular state, we can reach it very easily.

This is often the most difficult part of consciousness-expansion techniques but it's not as complex as it sounds. Unfortunately, this is a stage that is often underdeveloped in books.

All out-of-body experiences and lucid dreaming exercises—whether visualization or affirmations for example—will only be effective if you practice them in this ISC. I'm stressing this point because it'll save you time. It's by starting there that you'll be able to reproduce this state with ease and thus modify your state of consciousness very often—even on demand for the most gifted and those who practice with perseverance.

There are different approaches, which I'll share with you here:

The hypnopompic state

One of the simplest techniques is to wake up without moving a single part of your body, keeping the body asleep while consciousness focuses on having an OBE. It may seem difficult at first, but rest assured it's very easy to learn. This state of consciousness is called the "hypnopompic state" and it's an ideal state for leaving the body.

The method simply consists in programming yourself before you fall asleep, whether in the evening or following a nocturnal awakening or a nap. As soon as you start to fall asleep, repeat an affirmation like, "I wake up at 4 a.m. without moving" or, "When I wake up, I don't move!" You'll usually see results very quickly, even on the first attempt. It's better to repeat the phrase few times—with conviction and without doubts—and to emphasize that you're going to succeed instantaneously.

If you can sleep in, you can repeat the hypnopompic state several times to increase your chances of success. To do this, program yourself to remain motionless each time you wake up during the night or in the morning. For example, if you wake up around 4 a.m., mentally repeat an affirmation like, "I'll wake up in half an hour without moving" or, "I'll wake up at 5 a.m. without moving." And if you missed it when you woke up, do the same thing again, changing the time. It's very effective, but it can be tiring. That's why it's best not to use it on a daily basis.

The hypnagogic or deep-trance state

Another method, which requires a little more practice, is to put your body to sleep while staying awake. This is Robert Monroe's famous "mind awake, body asleep" (MABA) state. To achieve this, you need to approach sleep without being drawn into it. There are a number of tricks you can use to achieve this.

Choose a semi-comfortable position. If you usually fall asleep on your side, lie on your back or somewhere in between. Simply changing position will slow down the process of falling asleep.

1- <u>Relaxation</u>

If you're wide awake, then start a relaxation exercise. For example, you can use a countdown from 10 to 1 and combine it with a statement like, "My body falls asleep while my mind stays awake." Having worked with the Monroe Institute's "Wave 1" CD from the Gateway program, which enables you to go into Focus 10 (Mind Awake, Body Asleep) by counting from 1 to 10, I use this technique because it enables me to reach this state of consciousness in a very short time.

Tip: After doing my relaxation exercise, when I see that sometimes I start to drift off to sleep, I change the axis of my eyes behind my closed eyelids. I've noticed that when I fall asleep, unlike most people my eyes tend to move downwards. Becoming aware of this and raising them as if I were looking straight ahead, or even slightly higher, woke me up from the lethargy.

2- <u>Calming the mind</u>

Once the body has relaxed, it's important to calm the mind. Concentrating on the breath remains the most widely used and effective method. However, focusing attention on a single point remains a difficult approach for some people, especially if they haven't practiced it before. One trick is to practice an energy technique. This makes it easier to concentrate and because it stimulates inner energy, it facilitates the out-of-body experience. The exercise I like to do is to bring the energy up from the spine to the top of the head while inhaling and back down on the exhale. We're working here on what's more commonly known as the Kundalini (please refer to the section on the subject). You should feel a gradual warmth, which may even intensify in the spine. It's quite possible for vibratory phenomena to appear at this time.

At this point, we can apply one of the induction techniques for consciousness projection, which I'll detail in the next section.

However, it is crucial to emphasize what I consider to be the most important aspect of the practice. Indeed, you could master all the out-of-body techniques, but unless you reach the appropriate trance state your efforts will be in vain. Achieving the trance state is therefore essential for successful consciousness projection.

Concentration

Concentration is the key to mastery. When we can focus our minds on a single task, we are capable of accomplishing miracles.
- Swami Sivananda

If you're having trouble centering yourself in one spot, then you're going to need some practice. You have the choice between practicing out-of-body exercises until you improve concentration, or speeding up the process by practicing a centering method every day.

Go gradually, starting with five minutes once or twice a day, then increasing by five minutes each day until you reach 20 minutes. Ideally, you should use something that doesn't require you to have your eyes open, as the aim is to help you use this ability to induce an astral projection. You can focus your attention on breathing, on a sound such as tinnitus, on your heartbeat, or on a mental affirmation. I recommend using a timer to free your mind from thinking about time.

Concentrating on the breath is a widely used method of calming the mind prior to the vibratory phase. Its advantage lies in the possibility of adding complementary elements to reinforce our attention, thus facilitating the process. For example, we can combine focusing on breathing with energy exercises. Visualize energy rising up the spine with each inhalation and descending towards the base with each exhalation, as described above.

Or you can add an affirmation like "Now" on the inhale and "I'm out of my body!" on the exhale. Or simply count "One, I breathe in, Two, I breathe out, Three, I breathe in, Four, I breathe out, etc."

Completing your breathing by imagining movement is an out-of-body technique in itself. With each inhalation and exhalation, feel yourself floating higher and higher above your body, then above your room, above your house, in the sky, in space, and so on. You can feel the temperature of the air. The air feels cool in your nostrils as you inhale and warm as you exhale. Observing this sensation helps you to concentrate more effectively.

There are many other methods, but this is not the subject of the book. Sometimes we find it difficult to concentrate for various reasons, and knowing these little tricks will enable us to carry out a meditation exercise during the day while developing an ability that will be of great use in our preparation for the out-of-body experience.

Consciousness moves from one body to another according to the law of communicating vessels. When we imagine a scene, we project part of our consciousness into the image. And when we dream, we are almost totally immersed in this dream world. The same applies to out-of-body experiences. The idea is to transfer our consciousness into a subtle vehicle.

But why can't we do this when we're awake? The reason is the existence of the five senses. I include thought as a sixth, a perspective shared by Buddhists. These are considered the six anchors of consciousness to physical reality. When they are awake, they hold us in this vehicle of flesh. This is why—during practice—the aim is to induce a state of bodily sleep, thereby turning off the senses to facilitate the relaxation of consciousness. In theory, it is possible to go out of one's body in the waking state; but this requires the ability to block out all of one's senses in any given situation—which in turn requires unwavering focus and a high degree of concentration on an object or place far from one's physical body until consciousness is moved completely out of the awake body.

Some renowned authors report experiences of bilocation, where a person is simultaneously in two different places, whether in physical reality or in a parallel dimension. As I am neither an expert nor have had such experiences, I will refrain from sharing an opinion on the subject. What you need to remember is that when you're doing your exercises, it's important to focus on your object of concentration, bearing in mind your goal of transferring your consciousness elsewhere—away from your material body. Understand that mental emptiness and concentration are two extremely important elements in the success of your experiment.

Tip: Don't hesitate to use affirmations to calm the mind. For example, say to yourself, "My mind calms down with every exhalation!" Use the incredible power of the mind.

Sleep interruption

The sleep interruption technique involves setting one or more alarms to wake you up in the middle of the night so you can practice after at least two sleep cycles, i.e., around three hours after going to bed. The mind is often clearer and more ready to practice at this time, while the body is partially rested but still crying out for rest. It is generally advisable to get up for a few minutes and drink a glass of water or go to the toilet to fully awaken before going back to bed and starting the practice.

This is known as the Wake Back To Bed (**WBTB)** technique. It's already a method in itself because just by having the intention, you can quite easily induce a lucid dream or out-of-body experience. However, I advise you to use your usual OBE technique for a better chance of success.

I carried out several tests of the technique including setting three nighttime alarm clocks, one at 3 a.m., another at 4 a.m., and the last at 5 a.m. I did this for a week, wearing my sports watch on my wrist so that it could measure my sleep quality. Each time I woke up, I positioned myself on my back and held myself for a period ranging from 15 to 45 minutes in the hypnagogic state, where the body is asleep but consciousness remains awake. Despite these sleep interruptions and this practice, my watch always indicated that the quality of my sleep was good.

Tip: When I can't do a WBTB, I do what I call a "Wake Back to Back," i.e., I position myself on my back. In this posture, I personally find it very difficult to fall asleep. This allows me to prepare for practice by waking up a little more without having to get out of bed.

What follows is a series of non-essential elements for your practice. For some it may even seem rather amusing but it's interesting nonetheless. It's conceivable that some aspects will resonate with you and help to enrich your practice. I've put them together here as a bonus.

Adapting practice to different times of day

The idea of adapting OBE/astral projection practices according to the time of day is based on an understanding of circadian rhythms and states of consciousness that fluctuate throughout the day. Here's how you can program your practices according to the time of day and natural variations in energy and concentration:

When you wake up in the morning

- <u>Ideal time for</u>: Gentle conscious-awakening techniques. This is the moment when the boundary between sleep and wakefulness is at its thinnest, potentially stimulating OBEs with less effort.

- <u>Approach</u>: Remain still when you wake up, then use movement techniques such as hand rubbing or rocking to try to project yourself out of your body.

Mid-morning

- <u>Ideal time for</u>: Meditation and mental preparation. After the morning energy peak, it's a good time for meditative practices that prepare the mind for a potential experience later in the day.

- <u>Approach</u>: Meditate while focusing on mental calm and clarity of intention, visualizing the desired experience.

Afternoon

- <u>Ideal time for</u>: Short nap or relaxation. The afternoon—especially after lunch—can be a time of fatigue, which can facilitate altered states of consciousness. Try not to nap too close to mealtime and avoid alcohol.

- <u>Approach</u>: Practice deep relaxation or conscious nap techniques, where you stay mentally alert while letting your body relax deeply.

Evening

- <u>Ideal time for</u>: Intensive practice. We often have more time and fewer distractions in the evening, allowing for longer, more concentrated sessions.

- <u>Approach</u>: Employ detailed visualization techniques, deeper meditation practices, or listen to OBE-specific audio guides.

Before going to bed

- <u>Ideal time for:</u> Preparing for nocturnal out-of-body excursions. Use this time to prepare your intention and schedule an hour of experimentation about three hours after bedtime.

- <u>Approach:</u> Use targeted visualizations and/or affirmations, or listen to binaural frequencies designed to encourage states of consciousness conducive to OBE.

In the middle of the night

- <u>Ideal time for:</u> WBTB techniques. Waking up voluntarily to practice after two sleep cycles significantly increases the chances of a successful out-of-body experience.

- <u>Approach:</u> Wake up after three to five hours of sleep, stay awake briefly, then return to bed with the intention of leaving the body.

Each moment of the day offers unique opportunities to explore OBE practices according to your natural cycle of energy and awareness. Personal experimentation is the key to determining which techniques work best for you at different times. It's important to consider your personal schedule, rhythm of life, and daily responsibilities to integrate these practices harmoniously and effectively.

Adapting your technique to your sleep pattern

Out-of-body techniques can vary according to individual preference, circumstances, and sleep pattern. They may be more effective or more appropriate depending on whether you practice them before sleep, during light sleep phases, or upon awakening. Here's a general overview of different techniques and how they can be integrated with sleep cycles:

1. Visualization technique before going to sleep

- <u>Description:</u> This technique involves relaxing deeply in bed and visualizing a specific place or object, then imagining stepping out of your body to get there.

- <u>Suitable for:</u> This is good for people who have trouble falling asleep or who want to practice before going to sleep. The deep relaxation required can help you fall asleep.

2. Vibratory state technique

- <u>Description</u>: This technique involves manifesting the sensation of energetic vibrations in the body, often used as a prelude to an out-of-body experience. This state is achieved through relaxation, visualization, and sometimes sound.

- <u>Suitable for:</u> Practice upon awakening or after a sleep cycle. The vibratory state is often more accessible when you're still close to sleep.

3. WBTB technique

- <u>Description</u>: This method involves waking up after 3-5 hours of sleep, staying awake for a short period (5-30 minutes), then returning to bed and attempting a projection technique.

- <u>Suitable for:</u> This technique takes advantage of REM sleep cycles, which are longer and more frequent in the second half of the night. Ideal for those who can fall back to sleep easily.

4. Waking up with mental imagery

- <u>Description</u>: This method involves waking without moving then closing your eyes and imagining a specific scene or activity. The idea is to slip from a waking state of consciousness directly into a conscious dream state or OBE.

- <u>Suitable for:</u> This method works well for people who are able to wake up naturally without an alarm, allowing a smooth transition between states of consciousness.

5. Meditation and deep relaxation

- <u>Description</u>: This is the use of meditation techniques to achieve a state of deep relaxation and expanded awareness. It can be practiced at any time, but is often recommended before bedtime. The use of a mantra such as "OM" or "AUM" is interesting on several levels.

- <u>Suitable for:</u> This is good for all types of sleepers, especially those who prefer a more spiritual or contemplative approach.

Adapting your technique to your astrological sign

This is information I found a few years ago and which I'm sharing more for the knowledge than the efficiency of this data. But it remains an interesting approach nonetheless. The association of out-of-body experience techniques with astrological signs is more in keeping with a symbolic and spiritual approach. Although there is no real foundation establishing a direct link between zodiac signs and astral projection techniques, certain astrological beliefs may suggest methods or approaches that could resonate differently depending on the personality traits associated with each sign.

Here are a few playful and symbolic suggestions for each sign:

Aries (March 21 - April 19)

- <u>Character traits</u>: Adventurous, energetic.

- <u>Suggested technique</u>: Dynamic techniques such as active visualization or awareness movement (balancing, flying, etc.).

Taurus (April 20 - May 20)

- <u>Character traits:</u> Sensual, seeks comfort.

- <u>Suggested technique</u>: Meditation in a comfortable environment with sensory aids such as soothing scents or Hemi-Sync music.

Gemini (May 21 - June 20)

- <u>Character traits:</u> Curious, adaptable.

- <u>Suggested technique</u>: Visualization techniques involving dialogues or encounters with other beings.

Cancer (June 21 - July 22)

- <u>Character traits:</u> Intuitive, emotional.

- <u>Suggested technique</u>: Guided meditations on water or other environments that encourage emotional introspection.

Leo (July 23 - August 22)

- <u>Character traits</u>: Dramatic, confident.

- <u>Suggested technique</u>: Visualize yourself as an epic hero or daring astral explorer.

Virgo (August 23 - September 22)

- <u>Character traits</u>: Methodical, practical.

- <u>Suggested technique</u>: Structured, detailed approaches such as specific visualization or relaxation sequences.

Libra (September 23 - October 22)

- <u>Character traits</u>: Balanced, seeks harmony.

- <u>Suggested technique</u>: Deep relaxation and meditation techniques focusing on balance and harmony.

Scorpio (October 23 - November 21)

- <u>Character traits</u>: Deep, mystical.

- <u>Suggested technique</u>: Exploration of mystical or transcendent themes, perhaps incorporating powerful symbols or archetypes.

Sagittarius (November 22 - December 21)

- <u>Character traits</u>: Philosophical, loves adventure.

- <u>Suggested technique</u>: Astral travel with a goal or quest for knowledge.

Capricorn (December 22 - January 19)

- <u>Character traits</u>: Disciplined, patient.

- <u>Suggested technique</u>: Regular, methodical practice with an emphasis on patience and progressive skill-building.

Aquarius (January 20 - February 18)

- <u>Character traits</u>: Innovative, independent.

- <u>Suggested technique</u>: Experiment with unconventional techniques or create your own.

Pisces (February 19 - March 20)

- <u>Character traits</u>: Sensitive, intuitive.

- <u>Suggested technique</u>: Guided meditations that explore deep inner or spiritual worlds.

These suggestions are based on the characteristics traditionally attributed to each zodiac sign and should be taken lightly. The important thing is to experiment and find what resonates best with you, regardless of your zodiac sign.

Adapt your technique to your psychological profile

Adapting an out-of-body experience technique to your psychological profile can be highly relevant, as certain methods may suit you better depending on your personality, preferences, and mental state.

For Analytical and Logical Profiles

- <u>Character Traits</u>: Rationality, appreciation for structure and order.

- <u>Suggested technique</u>: Methodical approaches such as progressive relaxation techniques, the use of specific mantras, or structured visualizations that follow a logical sequence.

For Intuitive and Creative Profiles

- <u>Character Traits</u>: Vivid imagination, tendency to think outside of traditional frameworks.

- <u>Suggested technique</u>: Free-visualization techniques, creating detailed imaginary landscapes or scenarios where you can explore freely.

For Emotional and Empathic Profiles

- <u>Character Traits</u>: Sensitivity to your own and others' emotions, strong empathy.

- <u>Suggested technique</u>: Emotion-focused guided meditations or the use of music and sound to induce altered states of consciousness conducive to OBE.

For Pragmatic and Down-to-Earth Profiles

- <u>Character Traits</u>: Preference for concrete, tangible approaches, skepticism towards the vague or overly abstract.

- <u>Suggested technique</u>: Techniques based on physical sensations such as concentrating on breathing, the sensation of floating, or the use of light pressure techniques on the body.

For Adventurer and Experiencer Profiles

- <u>Character Traits</u>: A taste for novelty, adventure, and exploring the unknown.

- <u>Suggested technique</u>: Experimenting with various methods including vibratory states, direct departures during awakening, and exploring various realities during projections.

For Introverted and Reflective Profiles

- <u>Character Traits</u>: Prefer quiet environments and inner reflection, tendency to introspection.

- <u>Suggested technique</u>: Deep meditation practices, exploration of states of consciousness through introspection and guided visualization.

For Anxious or Stressed Profiles

- <u>Character Traits</u>: Prone to anxiety or stress, may have difficulty relaxing.

- <u>Suggested technique</u>: Stress-reduction techniques such as deep breathing, progressive muscle relaxation, and soothing visualizations to calm the mind.

For Determined and Focused Profiles

- <u>Character Traits</u>: Strong willpower, ability to focus intensely on goals.

- <u>Suggested technique</u>: Practices requiring sustained concentration such as focusing on a specific visualization object or using long, complex mantras.

It is important to note that these suggestions are generalizations, and that individual experience may vary considerably. Personal experimentation and adaptation of techniques to meet your specific needs are important. OBE practice is highly individual and may require time to find the method that works best for you based on your personality and personal preferences.

Adapt your technique to the different days of the week

Adapting out-of-body experience techniques to the days of the week may seem unusual, but this approach could fit into a personal routine and exploit the variations in energy and mood that many feel throughout the week. This is a fun approach assigning different OBE practices to different days of the week, considering general activity and energy patterns:

Monday - Day of New Beginnings

- <u>Approach</u>: Intention-focused meditation for the week ahead. Use this "new beginning" energy to set clear intentions for your astral explorations.

Tuesday - Day of Action

- <u>Approach</u>: Dynamic techniques, perhaps using visualizations that involve movement or adventure.

Wednesday - Day of Reflection

- <u>Approach</u>: Introspective practices. The middle of the week is a good time to reflect on past experiences and plan for the future. The use of a journal in this work is recommended.

Thursday - Expansion Day

- <u>Approach</u>: Exploration of new techniques or areas in astral travel. Thursday carries the energy of growth and expansion, which can inspire more daring explorations.

Friday - Liberation Day

- <u>Approach</u>: Freer, more spontaneous approaches. With the weekend approaching, it's time to experiment with less structure and more freedom in your practice.

Saturday - Relaxation Day

- <u>Approach</u>: Relaxing techniques. After a busy week, opt for practices that promote winding down and deep relaxation.

Sunday - Day of Reflection and Preparation

- <u>Approach</u>: Guided visualizations or preparatory meditations for the week ahead. Use this day to integrate your experiences and prepare yourself mentally and spiritually for the challenges ahead.

These suggestions are designed to integrate OBE practice into the rhythm of daily life, considering the variations in energy and availability you may feel throughout the week. Of course, the best approach is the one that resonates with you personally and adapts to your schedule, energies, and aspirations.

176

CHAPTER 2

Techniques for inducing an out-of-body experience

Techniques for inducing an out-of-body experience

"Realization lies in practice."
- Buddha

Today, numerous books and digital media of all kinds have given us access to a multitude of astral projection techniques, each with its own variations. Nevertheless, it would be unthinkable to exclude this theme from a book dedicated to altered-consciousness experiences. That's why I'm going to share with you the most widely practiced and recognized methods. However, rather than simply listing them, I'll include tips and practical advice designed to make them more effective and easier to understand. Another key to exploring beyond physical reality is letting go. In all the approaches you're about to tackle, let go, relax, enjoy, and trust.

1- Awakening technique

You must have read or heard on several occasions that you naturally leave your body every night. I can confirm this, as I've seen it in some of the personal experiences I've recounted in this book. The question then arises: why are most people unaware of this? Why, too, are we unaware when we dream? What's the common factor in all this?

It's simply a question of consciousness. We experience our adventures, dreamlike or otherwise, in the same way as we do our daily lives. Habit and routine mean that we function mechanically 99% of the time. We're hardly aware of what we're doing every day in this dense reality, so why should we be aware anywhere else?

This notion was taught to me in Tibetan Buddhism during retreats in a monastery. If we appreciate and pay more attention to every moment and every mundane object, we achieve a higher consciousness in everyday life as well as in the most subtle experiences. This is first and foremost a method of awakening, but it is also an exercise conducive to experiences of altered consciousness without practicing any particular technique.

Let's be honest, it's not easy to integrate mindfulness into your life; it's generally said that the subconscious takes 21 days to transform an action into a habit. Challenge yourself to be more and more present every day without feeling any tension.

During the day, take the time to stop and observe your surroundings. Whether you're performing a task or contemplating nature, works of art or the people around you, pay special attention to your hands, objects, and everything else around you. After a while, you'll naturally become aware that you're dreaming or that you're outside your material body.

2- Affirmations

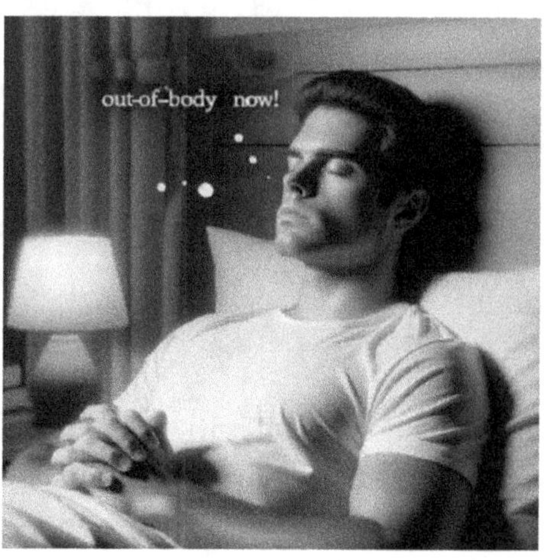

This method is both simple and highly effective. The difficulty lies in practicing it properly. Intention is the most important aspect of this technique. So much so, in fact, that you should almost be able to practice it without words. When constructing your affirmation, try to *feel* the intention, using it first on its own and then supporting it with your phrase. Words should be no more than a support for your determination, a means of planting it in your subconscious.

Combining it with visualization can be even more effective. Isn't it said that a picture is worth a thousand words? Intention is often accompanied by voluntary or involuntary visualization. When we have a strong desire to achieve something, most of the time we imagine the scene spontaneously.

To illustrate this, let's take the example of someone who irritates you to the point of wanting to slap him. You are seething and you really want to slap him, but you're not going to say, "I'll slap you right now!" Nor are you really going to slap him. But in the context of an out-of-body experience, it's this intensity of emotion you want to capture in your intention.

There are three crucial elements in the success of this technique, beyond persistence of course:

1- A strong intention

2- Knowing that it's going to happen immediately

3- Having no doubts

Repeating, "I'm out of my body!" 50 times mechanically while thinking about something else is doomed to failure. You need to feel deep down and without a doubt that you're going to dissociate from your body immediately, regardless of your technique. The mind then focuses on the goal of the journey as if we were already out. We think of our affirmation in such a way that each repetition takes us out of our physical body. We feel the force of the words, expecting the experience to unfold immediately.

Another small difficulty—but one that can be managed very quickly with experience—is that you create a kind of internal tension while at the same time maintaining deep relaxation. It's essential to let go, to trust, and to maintain a sleeping physical form.

Personally, I find it more effective to use a combination of two affirmations. I've experimented several times with reciting a simple phrase like, "Now I'm out of body!" with conclusive results. However, every time I've combined two affirmations, I've seen effectiveness right from the first use. My combination is: "I remain conscious while my body falls asleep!" and, "Now I'm out of body!" The word "conscious"—recommended during an intensive course at the Monroe Institute in Virginia with William Buhlman—exerts a phenomenal power on the subconscious. As soon as I incorporate this word into my practice, I immediately notice several extremely clear dreams in a single night, lucid dreams, and even waking up one or two hours later in a vibratory state. I've observed that the simple fact of telling ourselves that we remain conscious as our body falls asleep allows us to gain a few precious extra seconds of rehearsal before drifting off to sleep, compared to a session without this affirmation. Don't overlook this point, and above all, test it to see if this little trick changes the effectiveness of your practice.

I also sometimes use with success this affirmation alone: "I am aware of being outside my body!"

Singing the affirmation is a fun and effective approach. Choose an "Earworm"-type composition, i.e., a song that tends to get stuck in your brain.

It took me a long time to discover the method that suited me and, above all, that enabled me to transcend my physical body. Reading books and trying out various techniques (Monroe, Bruce, Buhlman, Hemi-Sync etc.) was very enriching, as it enabled me to get to know myself better.

To find your method, you first need to consider the time you can devote to it each day, as well as external factors such as family and professional life, etc. But the most important thing of all is to feel no constraints when practicing. To avoid frustration, you need to enjoy doing it without worrying about the result.

Patience and perseverance are equally important. Without them, you won't get any results. The key to success lies in rigorous daily practice. It's true that the vagaries of life don't always allow for regularity in the quality of exercises.

William Buhlman points out that the results obtained are directly proportional to the commitment and regularity of the practice. I've found this to be true on several occasions.
Periods of fatigue and low motivation yielded little or no experience. On the other hand, when I had a strong desire to succeed, I was sure to get results.

The technique that has proved to be the best suited to my life and my personality is affirmations. I think the combination of its simplicity and extreme effectiveness is what attracted me to it in the first place. It's this method that has given me most of my experiences. Once again, it took me a few months to realize that I had to persevere in this direction without worrying that other techniques were better.

As this exercise was not covered in sufficient detail in most of the books I had read, I turned to works in the fields of the subconscious, hypnosis, and autosuggestion.

<u>Technique:</u>

- Make yourself comfortable on your bed.
- Take a few deep breaths and relax on the exhale.
- Mentally motivate yourself by thinking of a goal (e.g. meeting a deceased loved one, or taking on a simple goal as mentioned in the previous chapter).
 - As soon as you begin to doze off, start mentally reciting the affirmation.

- Repeat it slowly and continuously until you reach the vibration stage or until you fall asleep.
- Leave your body.

<u>Remarks:</u>

1- Use this method every day before going to sleep (during a nap, when going to bed, following a nocturnal awakening).

2- Relax, stop moving, and focus all your attention on your phrase.

3- Repeat continuously, so as to leave no room for extraneous thoughts. Repeating your affirmation over and over again in a state of deep relaxation is akin to hammering a nail into the unconscious. Each repetition drives the suggestion deeper and deeper into the mind, ensuring proportionately greater effectiveness.

4- The affirmation should be short and positive: "Now I'm out of body!" or, "I'm leaving my body now!"

5- Absolutely expect the method to work immediately; don't doubt it.

In discussions on forums, some people claim that recitation should be performed out loud so that it passes through the ear and registers more easily in the subconscious. From personal experience and the testimony of other acquaintances, I can confirm that mental recitation alone is totally effective. You can start out loud and finish mentally, but the latter is more than sufficient. The most important thing is to focus totally on your affirmation.

Others claim that repetition is not necessary. In some cases, stating your affirmation two or three times before going to bed may suffice but this depends on several factors, and above all on the practitioner. By repeating it, you leave no room for parasitic thoughts, thus maintaining your concentration on the out-of-body exit until you fall asleep. In this way, you achieve better results in a shorter time.

Examples of affirmations for out-of-body experiences:

- "Now I'm out of body!"
- "I'm free of my physical body, now!"
- "I'm leaving my body now!"
- "I'm completely relaxed and ready to explore beyond my physical body!"
- "I'm safe and protected, free to travel outside my body!"
- "I separate from my physical body easily and safely!"
- "My mind is open to the experience of astral projection!"
- "I am conscious and lucid, floating freely out of my body!"
- "With each exhale, I feel lighter and ready to leave my physical body!"
- "My mind is powerful and able to travel beyond physical constraints!"
- "Instantly, I free myself from my physical body in complete freedom!"
- "I'm now ready to safely leave my body!"
- "My mind easily detaches from my physical body now!"
- "I project myself out of my body instantly!"

The method in detail

- Definition of autosuggestion

According to the dictionary, suggestion is the act of proposing something, the art of bringing an idea or feeling to life without openly expressing it. It is therefore an incitement, an act committing a person to admit or perform something. "Auto" is a prefix meaning "of itself" and thus the desired phenomenon occurs within a closed system without influence from external factors.

Autosuggestion is therefore a tool—conscious or unconscious—we use to encourage ourselves to manifest a desired outcome.

- The subconscious

" You know a lot more things than you know than you know!"
-- Milton Erickson

The subconscious mind is an important ally not only in the practice of astral projection but also in everyday life. Knowing its role and how to use it will be a major tool in preparing for out of body experiences and managing our lives. Far removed from Freudian considerations, for Milton Erikson the subconscious is wise, protective, and the holder of all our resources and knowledge.

"The unconscious: it's everything that is not yet conscious."

The subconscious regulates and coordinates biological functions such as body temperature, blood circulation, heart rate, breathing, etc. It acts as a reservoir of knowledge. It stores all the memories, learning, resources, and know-how we've experienced consciously or unconsciously. This is where information enters and exits after passing through our ego's filters. It protects us by removing traumatic events and information that is obsolete and useless or has become so in the conscious mind.

The subconscious is distinct from the conscious and has its own modes of operation. It perceives, feels, thinks, and reacts autonomously. It is under no obligation to the conscious mind. It protects it and helps it to operate with patience and indulgence. It has its strengths and weaknesses and it can be happy or unhappy, just like you. The subconscious is a facet of yourself that you are simply unaware of.

It is capable of processing far more information than the conscious mind; it automatically takes charge of many complex and varied tasks, it manages our memory and can store forgotten experiences, it is hyper-creative and abhors a vacuum, and it has a simple yet complex mode of operation.

The subconscious is separated from the conscious by the

barrier of thoughts and inattention. Repetitive gestures or thoughts, imagination, and autosuggestion break through this barrier with the help of one element: habit.

The subconscious mind controls gestures and physiological functions, enabling us to work, walk, breathe, and drive—for example—while thinking about other things. Thanks to the subconscious mind, all of our physical mechanisms work without conscious volition.

Those who use autosuggestion, the repetition of a gesture, or their imagination during their daily activities will be trying to inculcate notions in their subconscious in the midst of all these unconscious functions. It's a bit like talking to a friend in the middle of a crowd singing at the top of their lungs. With patience and perseverance, you will succeed.

Let's take the example of driving a car: at first, you have to learn gestures such as shifting gears, braking, etc. You apply yourself to performing them with great attention so as not to make a mistake and after a while—through repetition—you're able to drive while thinking about something else since the driving technique has become unconscious.

However, if we don't move or think and if we reduce organic functions, we can access a much more available subconscious. The crowd is no longer singing, your friend can hear you. It's a bit like taking him aside and talking to him eye-to-eye so that he doesn't miss a single word of what you're about to tell him.

It's important to know that the subconscious doesn't differentiate between reality and imagination, so whatever you imagine will be considered. On the other hand, mental images are the means of expression of the subconscious, so we'll need to observe our dreams during our practice session to see if the subconscious really understands our wishes.

Here are a few examples of dreams that indicate that our subconscious has heard our desire for an out-of-body experience. This list is based on the book "Adventures Beyond the Body" by William Buhlman and my own personal experience:

- Feeling or seeing yourself in or near any vehicle.
- Recognizing a change in your everyday environment.
- Feeling numbness or paralysis, waves of energy, or unusual sounds.
- Recognizing any unusual event, situation, or ability (such as flying).
- Feeling yourself falling or sinking; feeling sensations of upward or downward movement (elevator, stairs).
- Being in a rapidly changing environment.
- Being in an environment you can easily manipulate or control.
- Recognizing a problem or conflict.
- Recognizing a bridge, tunnel, or any kind of passageway.
- Being instructed or guided.
- Finding yourself in a small group of people in a classroom or conference atmosphere.
- Encountering multiple levels or floors of any kind.
- Reading a book or computer program containing unusual or advanced information.

The subconscious can put us to the test. Here's a concrete example from my personal journal:

Journal entry, September 26, 2006:

Since the beginning of September, I've resumed my practice with a warrior's soul. I'm fed up with doing little experiments here and there, I want to take it to the next level and transcend my body on a regular basis. Not that I don't have patience, but I draw my motivation from my frustration and turn it into a personal challenge.

I observe my dreams to see how my subconscious reacts to my request. In the last two days, I've had dreams that reveal, for me, a subconscious understanding of my desire to leave my body.

In the first dream, my father confirmed that I would indeed succeed in traveling both physically and astrally, but that I was too tired and needed to take a course of trace elements. Is this a message from my subconscious telling me that I don't have enough energy to make a projection? It's true that I'm tired because of work, but my determination allows me to put that behind me.

In last night's dream, I had to take an elevator and when I got in, one of the ropes which supported it gave way and the cabin became wobbly and therefore unusable. I then took the stairs to a large pool overlooked by a high diving board. I climbed to the top of it with the fear of jumping in my stomach, but once I got to the top a horde of children came and stood in front of me to stop me. I therefore feel that my subconscious is hindering my practice.

- The ISC

Autosuggestion is a technique for programming the subconscious mind and—as we saw earlier—the ideal time to act is when the conscious and subconscious minds work closely together, in other words when we're in the ideal state of conscious, or the ISC.

In the waking state, the conscious mind takes precedence, while in the sleeping state the subconscious mind takes the lead. Remember, the ideal state of consciousness for making suggestions lies at the boundary between wakefulness and sleep, i.e., in the hypnagogic state. This boundary is also known as the hypnotic or deep-trance state. In practical terms, this level of consciousness is reached when the body is asleep and the mind is awake, as we studied before. However, a light trance may be enough to persuade the subconscious.

This is why in most astral projection techniques the first step is to relax—to achieve a light trance. There are two schools of thought regarding the next step: either we continue our exercises until we reach a state of deep trance, or we use our natural ability to fall asleep. Indeed, practicing autosuggestion just before falling asleep is a highly effective method.

Tip: One hypnosis tip is to modify your mental voice to have more impact. For example, if you're a woman, repeat your affirmation in a man's voice. You can also vary the speed at which you speak. All these variations surprise the subconscious, which then pays more attention to the words.

3- Visualization

A picture is worth a thousand words.
- Confucius

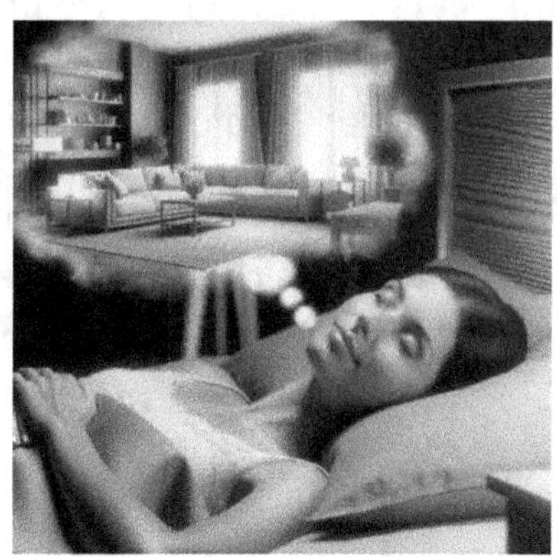

Imagining what you want has a greater impact than repeating an affirmation, but it also depends on each person's profile. The visualization method is well known and has been used in many books. In a nutshell, it involves imagining yourself in a familiar environment—such as your living room—and focusing your attention on various objects such as a trinket, a lamp, a photo, a plant, etc. The aim is to concentrate on a place far away from your physical body until you fall asleep. This is what William Buhlman calls the target technique. Walk through your living room during waking hours; choose between three and five objects and analyze them in physical terms to better involve the senses—such as touch—in your visualization.

Then during practice, imagine yourself walking down the hallway and opening the door to the living room. Perhaps you can detect a particular smell—like a wood fire, or a sound—like a bird in the garden. Live the scene to the fullest as if you had already left your body. Feel the joy of success. At this point, move on to the objects you studied in the physical. Start with the first one; touch it, visualize it in as much detail as possible. Once done, move on to the next while enjoying the journey from the first to the second element. Do this for each one until you fall asleep. A little trick to increase the sense of immersion in the image by imagining what's behind you while visualizing what's in front of you. This has the effect of encompassing us fully in the imagined environment. If you're still not asleep by this time, you can imagine going outside and taking a walk, reciting affirmations like, "I'm conscious out of my body!"

Another variation is to relax and then fall asleep imagining yourself sitting on the edge of the bed. Pretend you're already out of your body, feeling the joy of success. Keep concentrating until you fall asleep.

You can also visualize an imaginary place, a kind of personal paradise. This requires more concentration, since you have to create a complete image. Using a real place that you know well will require less mental effort.

The idea here is to persuade yourself that you're already far from your physical form while letting your body fall asleep. Falling asleep during visualization is the best approach to a successful out-of-body experience. The hardest part is staying focused, and that's something you have to work at. With practice, the exercise becomes easier and easier, and the visualization clearer and clearer.

Based on this principle, you can create your own visualization method.

Tip: To increase immersion, don't hesitate to play with the image. Zoom in, change the climate, the brightness.

4- Motion-based techniques

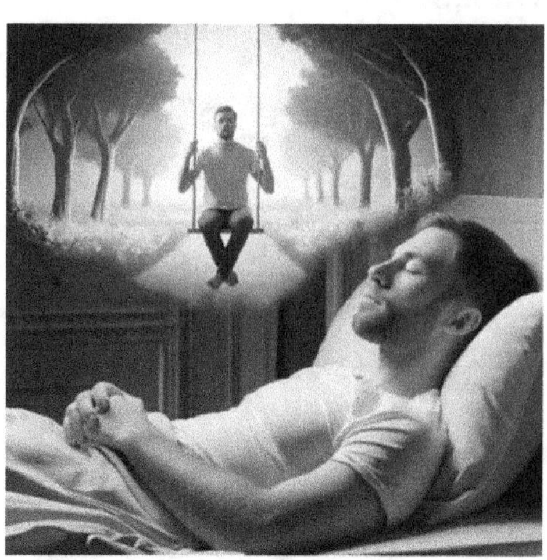

Motion-based techniques offer a fun way to induce an OBE by imagining a movement and trying to feel it. You do not need to visualize; it won't hinder the exercise in any way. You simply need to really feel the movement without actually moving. This is a very effective technique because it can induce dissociation.

Here is a non-exhaustive list of different motions-based techniques:

- Rocking forward and backward, imagining yourself on a swing or rocking chair.
- Driving at full speed, visualizing yourself in a car or on a motorcycle.
- Flying, feeling like you're really moving above the mountains, the sea, or the clouds.
- Clapping your astral hands.
- Sitting on the edge of the bed.
- Rolling over yourself like you're rolling down a sand dune.
- Spinning around as if trying to induce vertigo.
- Running or cycling.

Any type of movement is worthwhile as long as you enjoy doing it, and especially that you feel the sensations as if you were actually doing it.

5- Tactile techniques

Here again, you are asked to feel, not visualize. The advantage of this method—like the motion-based techniques—is that it offers a solution for people who find it difficult to visualize as well as for the visually impaired or people with aphantasia.

The best-known is the rope method described by Robert Bruce in his book "Astral Dynamics." It involves imagining a rope falling from the ceiling into your hands, feeling the texture of the strands, the hardness of the rope, etc., and pulling on it as you feel yourself being pulled out of your body. As you grasp the rope and move your hands forward, one above the other, feel the weightlessness and lightness as you move upwards. During workshops with William Buhlman, he would give us a piece of rope so that—with our eyes closed—we could record our tactile perceptions of it. He taught us a variation in which we visualized a ladder instead. The principle is the same: it's all about sensation.

We practiced this method when I was at the Monroe Institute, and it was the only time I ever managed a brief out-of-body exit with this exercise. The difference was that I felt like I was being pulled by the rope as if it were attached to a winch, and instead of making the effort to climb, I let myself rise towards the ceiling.

In the same vein, you can try moving around your bedroom or any other room as if you were visually impaired, feeling your way around furniture, objects etc., imagining tactile sensations as you go along.

6- Combined techniques

There are other methods that despite a few differences are essentially identical. Only the form changes while the principle remains the same. To increase the effectiveness of a technique, you can combine these different approaches. For example, you can mix visualization and affirmation. As you imagine yourself moving around a room in your house, say, "I'm out of my body now!" This will support your intention.

Set your imagination in motion. Visualize a swing in your garden then sit on it. Start swinging gently then gradually increase the speed as you admire the details of your surroundings. Use your imagination and, above all, have fun.

7- Other unclassified techniques

Out-of-body experiences have captivated human imagination and curiosity for millennia, giving rise to a wide variety of techniques across different cultures and eras. Some of these techniques are well documented and widely practiced, while others remain less well known or are specific to certain traditions.

Here are some of the lesser-known OBE techniques:

The mental rotation technique

This technique involves imagining oneself turning or pivoting on a horizontal or vertical axis. The idea is to disorientate the physical consciousness to facilitate separation.

Visualizing the breadcrumb trail

Inspired by Greek mythology, this method involves visualizing a thread or rope that connects you to your physical body, allowing you to venture into the astral while maintaining a secure link to return.

Journey in the tunnel

A technique in which a tunnel or passageway is imagined, often with a light at its end. The practitioner visualizes himself going through this tunnel, thus facilitating the exit from the body. We can add the sensation of vibrations that increase as we move through the tunnel.

The anchor object technique

In this method, you select a physical object as an "anchor" for consciousness. By concentrating intensely on this object before falling asleep, the practitioner can attempt to "find" himself outside the body.

The mirror technique

For this technique, you use a mirror to facilitate projection. The practitioner visualizes entering or exiting the mirror, using the mirror as a portal to out-of-body experience.

The practice of dual consciousness

This is an advanced technique for simultaneously maintaining awareness of the physical body and the astral experience. This can enable a smoother, more conscious transition out of the body.

Converting a lucid dream into an out-of-body experience

Lucid dreaming gives us the opportunity to navigate the depths of our consciousness and discover unsuspected worlds.

- Stephen LaBerge

The easiest OBE method is to convert a lucid dream into an out-of-body experience. A lucid dream is one in which we regain our waking lucidity. In other words, we become aware that we are living a dream experience. It's a bit like waking up in an imaginary place as real as everyday reality. There are several very simple techniques to achieve this. But the first skill to work on is remembering your dreams, if you don't do that naturally.

Techniques for remembering dreams or having clear dreams.

1. <u>Contemplation:</u>

Contemplation is a meditative technique that invites you to appreciate the present moment. Cultivating mindfulness for even 15 minutes a day will have an impact on the nature of your dreams and their recollection. Ideally, it should be practiced during the day and also just before going to sleep. A meditation done in this way is a kind to a purification of the mind. Just as daily bodily hygiene is important, so too is spiritual hygiene.

For daytime practice, sit with your back straight, in complete relaxation, hands resting on your thighs or one on top of the other. Having a straight back shouldn't cause any particular tension, but you should feel as if the vertebrae are resting on each other, forming a straight, welded, solid column on which you can let go and relax without breaking the straightness. It's as if you were "suspended" by a stick that replaces your spinal column. If I insist on good posture, it's because it plays an important role in the quality of meditation.

Regarding the eyes, there are two schools of thought: either keep them open or leave them closed. If you decide to practice with your eyes open, looking straight ahead, adopt a panoramic gaze so you're not staring at anything; your eyes should simply bathe in the ambient light, seeing without looking. The axis of the gaze should be turned downwards at around 45°. Understand well the notion of non-fixation: nothing should catch your eye. This is the ideal choice because meditating in this way brings the benefits of this practice into everyday life since we live with our eyes open. Meditation is a training of the mind that should have an impact on our daily lives. The same is true at night during our dreams, as we use our dream eyes.

If you find it difficult to perform the exercise due to mental agitation, you can close your eyelids to focus. On the other hand, if you're a little tired or prone to lethargy, keep your eyes open but look straight ahead or slightly higher, always with a panoramic field of observation so as not to stare at anything. Altering your field of perception helps you to stay awake.

A lama from a Tibetan Buddhist monastery in France told us

during a retreat that meditation is a bit like sleeping with eyes open. We're relaxed both physically and mentally, and in this stability of mind we appreciate the present moment, its quietude and inner peace. Another lama from the same community likened meditation to time off, regarding sitting on the cushion as a short vacation taken during the day.

For those familiar with Buddhist meditation, you likely recognized the practice called Vipassana in the previous paragraph. However, if you prefer to sit with your eyes closed, this is perfectly valid.

Once you've done this, turn your attention to the parts of your body that come into contact with the chair, meditation cushion, or floor. Pay attention to temperature differences in different areas and hear external sounds without actually listening to them. Don't fix your attention on a specific point. Then shift your awareness to the tip of your nose. Feel the air enter your nostrils; appreciate its freshness and purifying benefits and then feel it emerge, warm and laden with the negative aspects of your being and your muscular and mental tensions. Appreciate the relaxation you experience as you release these internal stresses.

Little by little, your mind will become calmer, just as the rough sea calms down in the evening. Clarity, purity, and stability will appear—if only for a moment—but you will experience them, just as troubled water becomes translucent when it calms. Appreciate the true nature of your soul and if the storm starts up again, if thoughts return, observe them, don't chase them away; simply turn your attention back to your breathing. It's a wonderful refocusing tool we can also use in everyday life, always at our disposal and terribly effective. Keep your attention on your breath in the background as you watch the mind stabilize. In moments of anguish and anxiety, focus on the ebb and flow of the air to establish yourself in the present moment.

As I advised at the start of this chapter, you should repeat this exercise in the evening or at night, lying on your bed with eyes closed just before falling asleep. By "purifying" your mind before going to sleep, you'll find it easier to remember your dreams and they will become clearer and longer.

This will influence the nature of your dream adventures, as you'll avoid taking the worries of everyday life with you. Your dreams will take on a personal and sometimes symbolic dimension rather than simply serving as an outlet, an evacuation of daily worries, or an extension of current concerns that are weighing you down. This method alone can trigger awareness in a dream. As well as strengthening your dream memory, this practice can also increase your capacity for conscious awakening, both in your dreams and in your everyday life.

2.   <u>The third eye</u>:

Stimulation of the sixth chakra—the Ajna, more commonly known in the West as the third eye—promotes the production of exceptionally clear dreams, the memory of which persists after awakening. As this has already been covered earlier in the book, those wishing to deepen their knowledge on this subject may refer to Dr. Hiroshi Motoyama's reference work "Theories of the Chakras: Bridge to Higher Consciousness."

This energy center is located between the two eyebrows, about 0.4 inches above the root of the nose. To stimulate this area, simply imagine it opening like a window—for example—or a flower. You can also imagine an imaginary finger massaging this spot or a luminous white ball radiating from it. The very fact of focusing your attention on this chakra stimulates it.

Practice this just before going to sleep in the evening or after waking up at night. It's not necessary to stimulate for a long time; sometimes five to 10 minutes is enough.

3. <u>Autosuggestion</u> :

Autosuggestion is a technique that recurs frequently in this book, as it takes advantage of a natural human capacity that is both simple and effective. It can be used for a variety of purposes, and in this case, to improve dream memory.

The principle is always the same: the conscious mind must approach the subconscious in order to speak in its ear. To do this, you need to enter a hypnotic trance, i.e., deep relaxation. The more relaxed you are, the better the message will be perceived. Ideally, your body should be asleep and your consciousness awake. But let's keep things simple in practice: simply repeat the affirmation just before falling asleep. Choose a short, positive, affirmative phrase such as, "When I wake up, I remember my dreams!" or if you haven't been dreaming for a while now but were before (following a bereavement or any other disruptive event) try, "I'm now able to dream again!" It couldn't be simpler, and it works pretty quickly.

4. <u>Journal</u>:

As with all spiritual practices, it's essential to keep a journal to record your exercises, feelings, and experiences. Writing down your dreams just after waking up not only ensures that you don't forget them afterwards but also shows your subconscious mind that you're interested in studying them. Paying attention to your dreams develops your dream memory.

The next step is to use a method that allows the dreamer to take control of his or her nocturnal escapades by training the consciousness to awaken in the middle of a dream scenario. There are several effective and proven approaches to this. As this book focuses on out-of-body experiences, I'm sharing with you the best-known exercises. If you are interested in lucid dreaming, I invite you to read the references cited in the bibliography section at the end of this book, particularly those by Stephen LaBerge, Robert Waggoner, and Charlie Morley.

Affirmations

As with out-of-body experiences, we can use the power of words to induce lucid dreaming. The rules remain the same: start by relaxing deeply, then focus on a positive affirmation. Repeat it mentally with intention just before falling asleep. It's important to charge the phrase emotionally, not to repeat it automatically.

Example of affirmations for lucid dreaming:

- "I realize that I am dreaming!"
- "Tonight, I realize that I am dreaming and I control my dreams!"
- "I remember my dreams vividly and I am conscious during my dreams!"
- "I direct my dreams with clarity and intention!"
- "I recognize my dream signs and become lucid immediately!"
- "Every time I dream, I become lucid and take control of my experience!"

Reality checks

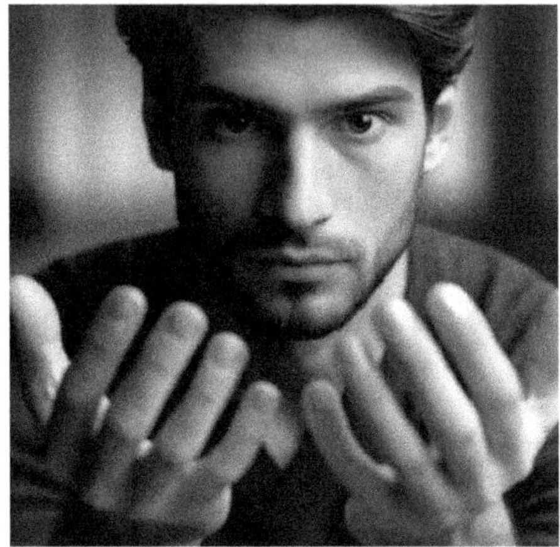

A reality check is an exercise that leads us to question the reality in which we find ourselves at a given moment. With daily practice, this exercise becomes a habit that accompanies us even in our dreams. The major difference is that—when practiced in a dream context—this questioning causes an awareness that we are dreaming. This enables us to become lucid and actively participate in the direction of our dreams.

This technique was discovered by a pioneer in dream research, the German psychologist Paul Tholey. He sought a way to direct dreams in order to study them. And by developing a critical mind in real life, he was able to do the same in his nocturnal adventures. It's possible that he was inspired by Tibetan Buddhism, one of whose age-old practices is dream yoga, i.e., the control of one's dreams to pursue the quest for awakening during sleep.

The principle is simple: several times a day, interrupt what you're doing and ask yourself what reality you're in. Is it possible that you're dreaming at this very moment? Even if you're convinced you're awake, what clues are there that you're not really asleep? This regular questioning can lead to a heightened awareness of your state, whether in a dream or in reality.

Observe carefully: in your usual dreams, you don't question the dreamlike nature of your surroundings; you accept the circumstances without questioning them, passively experiencing the dream without ever doubting that you're asleep. To change this, regularly question your state of consciousness throughout the day until it becomes routine. This exercise can awaken deeper reflection on your perception of reality.

To do this, use tips such as:

- Look at your hands and see if they're really yours and whether they change shape.

- Plug your nose and see if you can still breathe, because in a dream your nostrils don't get blocked.

- Try jumping into the air: if you float for a moment, or if your descent to the ground is abnormally slow, you're probably dreaming.

- Read text on a poster, a door, an advertisement, a book etc. Turn your head then come back to the text to read it again; do this two or three times and if the text or the photo changes, you're not in everyday reality.

- Try to walk through a wall.

When you do these tests, say to yourself: "I don't think I'm dreaming, but I need to confirm this by doing my tests. Then I'll decide." You'll discover that in your first lucid dream, the dream environment seems as tangible as everyday reality. This experience shows that it's indeed relevant to question the environments in which we exist at every moment.

We tend to go through life lost in our own thoughts, without asking ourselves where we are. Day or night, we're like sleepwalkers whose stress, worries and daily tasks numb our awareness. Working with reality tests can be likened to "mindfulness." It's an awakening exercise, and that's why it's so interesting to practice.

Dreams reflect the clarity of our consciousness. The proof is that when we practice meditation on a daily basis, dream memory improves considerably and dream clarity becomes increasingly intense. I therefore invite you, from now on, to question your reality several times during the day and look for proof to eliminate any doubt by using the tricks I've listed above.

Tip: *A useful strategy is to create an anchor, i.e., to identify a recurring element in your dreams such as your hands, a specific object, or a character. Then, every time you encounter this element in real life, ask yourself if you're dreaming. This practice sows doubt and can help you become aware during your dream adventures.*

Vigilance

I touched on this subject in the section on contemplation. With a view to triggering lucid dreaming, I'd like to emphasize the notion of vigilance. It's a term that's becoming increasingly popular, particularly under the heading of "mindfulness"—a concept that's been gaining in popularity for some time now. It's no longer a question of practicing a well-defined technique at specific times but rather of adopting a lifestyle model. Applying this concept to our daily lives leads to changes in the mind (and brain) that are felt even in our dreams at night.

Most of the time, whatever we do, our mind is rarely focused on what we're doing but wanders in the stream of thought. It does as it pleases, so to speak. Vigilance therefore implies a commitment to regaining control of it, to anchor yourself in the present moment, and to use your thoughts wisely most of the time.

Vigilance is what Buddhists call the right concentration. It's simply "Being."

When you drive…drive!

When you eat…eat!

When you walk…walk!

Don't get caught up in internal monologues or daydreams that obscure the only important moment in your life: the present moment. As you try to be more vigilant, you'll begin to appreciate existence and you'll start to notice things that you'd previously overlooked.

But it's not just about the environment, it's also about you and your behavior. You'll learn to know yourself, to analyze your reactions. Little by little, you'll become an observer of life and—by extension—an observer of dream realities. Your dreams will begin to become clearer and clearer until one day your consciousness achieves lucidity. Once you've taken control of your life, you'll take control of your dreams.

Of course, the practice of mindfulness is first and foremost an element of a personal spiritual quest, the primary aim not being to use it as a trigger for lucid dreaming. It's essential to always consider this type of experience as a gift, the fruit of in-depth personal work rather than as a main objective to be achieved.

Journal of my lucid dreams

To illustrate my point, I'd like to share some of my lucid dreaming experiences with you. Lucid dreams are extremely interesting experiences that should not be denigrated; however, I'm not a specialist in the field in the sense that I haven't sought to go into the subject in depth. Most of the time, I've used this method to induce an out-of-body experience but had a lucid dream instead.

Journal entry, July 14, 2012

Last night, after reading a book on lucid dreaming and its possibilities, I fell asleep using a technique I'm very fond of: affirmations. I woke up at around 6 a.m. and, as I drifted back to sleep, I kept the idea in mind of achieving lucidity in my next dream. I found myself in a dream environment that I spontaneously took control of. I thought, "I'm conscious, I'm having a lucid dream!" and lifted off the ground to start flying. I was flying in a fog that surrounded me and that I couldn't get out of. Then I found myself in another dream, in the middle of a hairdressing salon. I was aware of the dream environment but not aware enough to direct the dream. I asked a man present what year it was and he replied 3010. I laughed, noticing that barbershops hadn't evolved at all.

Journal entry, November 12, 2012

I repeated my usual affirmation to myself several times as soon as I went to bed around midnight: "I realize I'm dreaming!." A restless start to the night, awakened every hour or so, I finally got up at around 3:30 a.m. to get a glass of water. Back in bed, I resumed my technique until I fell asleep.

I dreamed I was staying with friends. Their home was different from what it really was. It was smaller. They had built a plaster partition to create a small room for their two children. Then my wife and I went to bed in the guest room. Moments later, I woke up in my dream, thinking that I'd forgotten a friend who was waiting for me in the next room for an acupuncture treatment. Tired, I went there anyway. He was indeed there, lying patiently on the bed. I stimulated him at a few Chinese medicine points. At the same time, my friend—the owner of the premises—appeared and invited me to follow him into the basement, where workmen were at work. It was at that precise moment that I realized it was all a dream, and I became lucid. I made my way to a glass skylight in the ceiling and flew through it, ghost-like, without breaking it. I decided simply to fly, trying to keep lucid as best I could. Sometimes I could see the landscape on the ground clearly, sometimes it was hard to perceive. I had to adjust my view constantly. Then I landed near an old Western motel and lost my lucidity.

Journal entry, November 20, 2012

I went to bed around 10 p.m., but around 11:30 I was woken by my daughter, who was feeling ill. Then I managed to get back to sleep, but only until 1:30 a.m., when she woke up again for the same reason. Not knowing how the night was going to go, I decided to try my hand at lucid dreaming. I went back to bed and—agitated by the situation—relaxed as best I could by reciting my "I'm aware I'm dreaming!" affirmation.

I found myself walking along a path with an ancient building in front of me with a sort of old gate like you might find at the entrance to a city. This place reminded me of Rome, only smaller— an ancient city with remains everywhere.

That's when I did a reality check, asking myself whether I was in the middle of a dream or not. It's a question I ask myself several times a day now to get into the habit of doing the same in the middle of a dream adventure. And that's what happened, but I didn't react immediately.

Convinced I was lucid but wishing to remove any doubt, I decided to test my reality by attempting to fly. To my surprise, I rose slightly above the ground. At the same time, a small black dragon appeared from behind a ruined stone door. I realized I was in the middle of a dream.

As I began to explore this enchanting place, I felt a presence beside me. It was my daughter, Tina, who seemed to be sharing this magical adventure with me. I stopped, put my hands on her shoulders and said, "Look at me Tina, you're in my dream; look at me carefully and remember you're in my dream—you have to remember it when you wake up!" Hopefully, she would remember the experience the next morning. I then wanted to see my guide. There were some people there including a bearded man who seemed to be the leader of the group. I asked him to give me a moment to chat. I wanted to ask him about my spiritual evolution, to tell him that I was fully aware of this dreamlike place.

He asked me to wait a moment, as he had a task to complete before he could continue. While I waited, I gradually lost my lucidity. To pass the time, I joined the other characters who were having fun jumping on small trampolines. I was then pulled out of my dream by our cat, who started meowing. It was about 3:20.

The night was restless; I had other dreams and made other attempts but remained unsuccessful. The next morning, I asked my daughter if she remembered seeing me in a dream, but she did not. It would seem, then, that I had simply interacted with a creation of my dream mind.

Journal entry, February 7, 2013

Awakened several times by our dog and my wife, I went back to sleep around 5:30. I had one clear dream—maybe several—then found myself running with a "friend" down a road when I realized I was dreaming spontaneously. I said, "Wait, stop running! Am I dreaming?" And I became lucid on the spot. The dream figure accompanying me stopped moving; I watched him for two seconds and then my vision became blurred, so I asked for clarity. The environment became clearer.

I immediately thought of provoking an out-of-body experience. I said, "Now I'm getting out of my body!" I began to fly; I felt as if someone was holding me from behind to transport me. Losing consciousness, I asked for clarity again.

Stuck in this dream world despite my request, for some reason I suddenly thought of visiting William Buhlman. I asked aloud to go to his house. The "thing" that was holding me changed direction and within seconds I found myself at William's house. He was there, eating with his wife Susan, who couldn't see me. I said to him, "William, can we talk in another room?" He motioned for me to follow him, and I woke up in the corridor.

Journal entry, March 29, 2013

Awakened around 3 a.m., I went back to bed while repeating my affirmation: "I'm aware I'm dreaming! I am aware that I am dreaming!" This practice preceded a series of dreams, heralding a rather restless night.

In one dream I passed a mirror and observed myself. It wasn't my face. I was a young, clean-shaven man, but when I touched my cheeks, I could feel my beard. Then I found myself in the hall of a building similar to a small reception hall.

We were received by an actor who was giving a private performance. Once in the room, I was given a shell and a five-euro coin. The coin had been modified, and was larger with a Buddha engraved on the reverse side.

It was as I left this place that I became lucid. The landscape in front of me became clearer, and I realized I was in the middle of the city in a sort of suburb with American-style houses. Finding myself in the parking lot of a fast-food restaurant, I tried to fly away. After an initial failure, I finally managed to get a few inches off the ground but only for a short time.

As usual when I become aware that I'm dreaming, my first thought is to take advantage of the situation to trigger an out-of-body experience. This I did without success. I resorted to trying to communicate with my guide. But here again I came up empty-handed.

Letting go in disappointment, I flew skyward, completely out of control. I gained more and more speed and height, perceiving less and less of the dreamlike environment until the experience suddenly came to an end.

<u>*Journal entry, November 24, 2013*</u>

I go to bed with the intention of waking up at 4 a.m. without moving. To do this, I use an affirmation to program my subconscious. Finally, I get up around 4:30 a.m. to use the bathroom, then go back to bed to begin my lucid dreaming method again.

My sleep is disturbed; I wake up several times and have a series of very clear dreams.
Then, I fall asleep and find myself with my wife in a village square. There's music in two places, and it's something I can't stand. Confidently, I try to stop the cacophony with a simple wave of my hand, as if I knew deep down that I could control the situation. One of the two pieces of music came to a screeching halt but not the

other.

Suddenly, I realize I'm dreaming. It's as if I'm absorbed by the dream, by the scene. I see a man dressed all in white with a scarf over his head trying to escape. He quickly runs behind the Plane trees in the square.

As with the music, I try to stop it with a gesture, but to no avail. I feel as if something is pulling me backwards and preventing me from moving forward. I consider that my consciousness—perhaps due to insufficient concentration—is acting as if it were trying to hold me back. Then I look at my hands: they're clearly visible, the image is clear. Then I wake up, putting an end to the adventure.

Journal entry, April 30, 2014

I got up at 3:30 then went back to bed, reciting my affirmation to induce lucid dreaming: "Now I'm aware that I'm dreaming!" I continued until drowsiness began to overtake me.

The atmosphere was strange. I approached a door behind which I could hear wailing and strange noises. It reminded me of spirits trying to frighten me. I grabbed the handle and opened the door only to find that the room was pitch-black. I could still hear the moaning. Then dancing figures appeared. Working up courage, I rushed in as if entering an arena, ready to face whatever awaited me. Feeling fearless, I immediately became lucid. It was as if I were absorbed by the dream image, a sensation that was both surprising and very pleasant.

I asked for total consciousness several times. The images were not always very sharp they kept changing and there was little color. Overall, it was rather gray and the atmosphere was "heavy." I couldn't get out of this environment that was weighing me down, engulfing me.

I came to my senses and drew on my resources to soar Superman-style. My lucidity was stable: I was flying through the dream landscape; it was the only thing I could do. It was impossible to direct or change anything. I asked for consciousness again several times, and as usual, tried to get out of my body but nothing worked. The experience lasted a long time and I finally gave in to the dream, losing my lucidity.

Journal entry, August 11, 2014

I'm currently getting back into the practice of lucid dreaming. I find the idea of using dreams as a tool for personal development— with the aim of facilitating deeper and more enriching out-of-body experiences—fascinating.

Last night I woke up several times, and each time I made sure to repeat my affirmation as soon as I regained consciousness. Overall, my dreams were very clear.

I got up to satisfy a natural need. I was urinating and looking at myself in the mirror above the toilet when I said to myself, "If I were in a dream, I'd be flooding the whole bed!" And that's when I saw a third arm come up to comb my hair, as if a new limb had sprouted on my right side. Then I thought, "Gosh, I'm in a dream!" and again, my new hand came back to do my hair.

I thought I'd give lucid dream meditation a try. I just stood there, doing nothing but contemplating the moment.

I could see myself very well, even if the reflection didn't really match my real physique. My eyes were blue, which is not the case in reality. Suddenly, the image began to shake; I struggled to maintain my concentration and slowly woke up.

It was a wonderful experience of lucid dreaming. Buddhists use lucid dreaming to practice meditation during sleep—to extend their practice—but also because the benefits are increased tenfold in this altered state of consciousness. This is what they call dream yoga. As a practitioner of Samatha Vipassana on an almost daily basis, I've seen first-hand what these people are talking about.

Journal entry, February 2, 2016

After a busy day at work, I was exhausted. I fell asleep like a baby around 11 p.m. I was sleeping soundly and dreaming profusely.

I was in a beautiful 1930s-style elevator, the kind you find in some palaces. Staring at the control panel, I spontaneously became lucid. I was admiring the gilded interior and the buttons at eye level to the right of the door. There were gold designs. I just stood there for a moment looking at them. I didn't feel like doing anything. Then I lost my lucidity and fell back into my dream. Tiredness meant I could only remember a few snatches. This lack of energy was felt in my dream, which explains why I didn't do anything.

However, I notice that—as is often the case—when I start staring at an object in a dream for a few seconds I become spontaneously lucid.

Journal entry, June 5, 2016

I woke up at around 2:45 a.m. and took the opportunity to do a WBTB (see techniques section). Once back in bed, I mentally repeated my phrase: "I realize I'm dreaming!"

I fell asleep only to regain consciousness a few moments later, lying in bed but in a different place. I was in a room similar to the one I had as a child. Sleeping on my right side with my head turned towards the door, I couldn't move. I could hear my wife talking to me, then my son Tom came in. Both thought I was sound asleep, but it was as if I were pretending. I was aware of my surroundings. I was in the middle of a false awakening. Then I found myself in a large apartment in Paris where a party was taking place. It seemed to be at a friend's place. It was crowded. I went into the bathroom and spontaneously realized I was dreaming.

I looked at myself in the mirror, then saw that I wasn't one-hundred-percent lucid, that I could get caught up in the dream at any moment, so I concentrated on my hands and they began to melt and then change shape—sometimes missing fingers, sometimes stabilizing. A young man appeared in the room, and knowing I was dreaming, I asked him to introduce himself and tell me why he was there. He didn't answer; his silence made him seem like a robot. I then realized that he was simply a dream character and didn't insist. Then I began to lose my lucidity and rushed to the apartment door to get out. I found myself in a huge hall with a staircase running along the wall. The walls were painted with magnificent, ancient frescoes. My consciousness became stable and clear again. I took the opportunity to take off flying towards the roof of the building. It was fun going up and down. Then I flew up to the dome of the building, trying to cross it to get outside, but I got stuck. I insisted a little and lost control of the dream.

Journal entry, June 22, 2016

Awakened at around 4 a.m., I got up to drink a glass of water and then—once back in bed—resumed trying to become lucid in my dream. I found myself walking along the city sidewalk crossed by a road and a median strip with young trees and grass. Something in the sky calls out to me and I see a triangular shape—light in color, blending in with the clouds—flying majestically across the sky. The craft gradually moves away, then slowly turns and comes back towards me. I realize I'm dreaming. What follows is a wave of UFOs appearing out of nowhere above my head. Feeling my consciousness failing, I turn my attention to one of the shrubs. My vision quickly regains its clarity. I perceive in detail the gray bark, the veins, and the texture of the trunk, but when I touch it, it turns out to be as soft and hollow as a rubber hose.

Surprised by this unexpected sensation, I suddenly lose my lucidity and am swept away by the dream. I wake up lying in bed and start a discussion with my wife about the possibilities of lucid dreaming. Then I regain full consciousness, realizing that I had just experienced a false awakening.

<u>Journal entry, September 23, 2018</u>

I woke up around 5 a.m. Having trouble getting back to sleep, I meditated using a Rosicrucian method. I had trouble concentrating, but I did it in several stages. All the while, I repeated my usual affirmation: "Now I'm out of body!"

Eventually I fell asleep and the dream world opened up to me. This time my son Tom accompanied me. We were back from a trip and had just landed. Suitcases in hand, we entered a souvenir store. Our luggage was bulky, and it didn't take long for the shop assistant to point this out to us. She was in the middle of yelling at me when I saw that one of the two wheels on the suitcase was dislocated. The lady told me I was "antepane" (which means "nothing"). I put her back in her place and my son and I took the exit in anger. I then went to look at the time and realized that my watch wasn't on my wrist. I remarked to myself that I must have had it since I was planning to participate in some sport later. That's when I realized I was dreaming. We walked out of the store onto a quay, mooring cleats, and the sea stretching out in front of us. The light was beautiful, the view magnificent. I said to Tom, "We're in a dream, wake up, look!" and began floating through the air to demonstrate to him that we were in a dream environment. He didn't seem to understand. So I took to the skies. As I soared towards the firmament, I thought of my mother—who had died two months earlier—and shouted, "Mommy!"

But nothing happened. I woke up in tears, thinking that I must have woken my wife by screaming. The bedroom light came on and I kept my eyes closed. I felt her watching me to see if everything was all right. Then I realized I wasn't in my bed but in another dream, a false awaking. And then I woke up for real.

<u>*Journal entry, December 2, 2023*</u>

I was walking in the countryside; it was daylight and I had planned to go to the beach behind the hill. When I reached a farm, I was on the usual path except that there was a huge pile of logs in the way. Then night fell. I wanted to try another path but ended up on the roof of the shed. I looked down; it was very high and I felt dizzy. I wanted to get back down but I didn't know how. A white canvas protected the flat roof and I thought I could use it to reach the ground. Finally, looking to the right I saw that the wall ran along a ridge to reach the gate and that it was much lower. I took this exit and went on my way. I arrived in a brightly lit area that looked like a funfair, with stores selling sweets, sweetened electronic cigarettes, etc. I bought myself a candy-flavored electronic cigarette. Then I found myself in front of a small airport and I went inside. There were lots of Chinese and Japanese people. The signs were in Japanese. On a screen was a clip from 1979 with Dalida (French singer) and Delon (French actor). I came out of the building and noticed that it was very bright daylight. That's when I doubted I was dreaming. I looked at my hands and became lucid. My hands were hyper-detailed, and I observed the surroundings, the sidewalk and so on. There was a man to my right whom I watched for a while. Then for some reason, seeing groups of people coming out of the airport I decided to sing to see their reactions. Some ladies laughed, but nobody took offense. An elderly couple came up to me and I lost my lucidity. I followed them as if they were my grandparents, but somehow they also seemed like strangers. We passed by the funfair and they bought some food. They offered me something and I refused. I preferred to smoke a gum cigarette.

Converting a lucid dream into an out-of-body experience

If your aim is to use a lucid dream to induce an out-of-body experience once you're aware that you're in the middle of a dream adventure, don't waste any time. Lucid dreaming is an exciting experience, and finding yourself in a lucid dream environment with incredible possibilities such as flying can quickly cause you to lose sight of your goal. It's important to keep your goal in mind so that once you've become aware of it, you remember to induce the exit directly. There are various ways of doing this. Some people let themselves fall backwards. William Buhlman asks for full awareness until the scenery gradually dissolves. Personally, I've gotten into the habit of flying towards the sky or a ceiling while repeating the affirmation, "I'm getting out of my body now!" Most of the time I pick up speed, start to feel the cool wind on my face and pass through greyish layers, feeling stronger and stronger vibrations until I find myself standing in my room or directly in a subtle environment.

I've written about some of my experiences in my journal in the out-of-body experience section.

Create your own out-of-body exit technique

Creating your own technique is like sculpting your own path to excellence.

- Tony Robbins

Creating your own out-of-body technique can be a rewarding process, allowing you to adapt practices to personal needs, preferences, and characteristics, including sleep cycle and psychological profile. Here's a step-by-step guide to developing your own method:

1. <u>Personal Assessment</u>

- Understanding your Sleep Cycle:

Note your sleep patterns—including when you fall asleep and wake up naturally, the phases of light and deep sleep, and how your energy fluctuates through the night and when you wake up.

- Analyzing your Psychological Profile:

Think about your personality traits, what motivates you, what relaxes you, and what activities capture your attention and imagination.

2. <u>Timing</u>

- Based on the Sleep Cycle:

Identify the times when you're most likely to be in a state of light sleep or on the borderline between wakefulness and sleep, often early in the morning or during a nap.

- Based on your Psychological Profile:

Choose a time when you feel naturally more open, relaxed, or intuitive, depending on your personal characteristics.

3. Basic Techniques

- Deep relaxation :

Develop a relaxation routine that works well for you, perhaps incorporating elements of meditation, deep breathing, or visualization.

- Clear intention:

Clearly formulate your intention to experience an OBE before you begin your practice, and don't hesitate to write it down so that it permeates the subconscious.

4. Experimentation and Customization

- Visualization techniques :

Create visualization scenarios that resonate with you personally, whether by imagining a specific place you'd like to go or visualizing a process that symbolizes leaving your body (like climbing a rope or floating upwards).

- Sense integration:

Depending on what stimulates your mind most (sight, sound, touch), incorporate sensory elements into your practice, such as listening to specific sounds or imagining the feel of various textures.

- Energy practices:

If this resonates with you, integrate practices that manipulate or perceive energy, such as visualizing light or energy flowing through your body.

5. Logging and Adjustment

- Document your experiences :

Keep a journal of your attempts, including when you made the attempt, what technique you used, how you felt before, during, and after, and any successes or obstacles you encountered.

- Adjust according to results:

Use your journal to identify what seems to be working and what isn't, and adjust your practice accordingly.

6. Patience and Perseverance

Recognize that developing an effective OBE technique can take time and requires patience and perseverance. Don't be discouraged if results aren't immediate, and keep experimenting and refining your approach.

The important thing is to listen to your body and your intuition, and to remain open to adjustments and discoveries along the way. In the end, the method that works best for you will be the one that considers your unique characteristics and fits harmoniously into your life and routines.

Controlling the out-of-body experience

Once out of the body, we need to learn how to master the experience. To do this, two key methods emerge: the use of affirmations and the practice of visualization. These techniques, although widely discussed by many authors, have been particularly developed and refined by William Buhlman in his exploration of the subtle planes.

The use of affirmations may seem simple on the surface: reciting a concise, positive phrase is not in itself complex. However, the real challenge lies in the need to accompany these words with a powerful intention, without which they will have no more effectiveness than a car without fuel.

It's essential to issue your commands with conviction, saying them out loud as if their realization were inevitable. If the desired effect is not achieved on the first attempt, persevere by repeating your affirmations insistently until the desired result manifests.

This method will initially enable you to improve your visual perception. It's not uncommon for vision to become blurred immediately after separation from the physical body. In this context, use the mantra, "Clarity now" or, "More consciousness now."

Affirmations can also facilitate travel to specific destinations; whether you want to explore the Moon or change dimensions, commands such as, "I demand to go to the Moon!" or, "I'm changing dimensions now!" will guide your journey.

As for visualization, it can be used to reconnect with a departed loved one by imagining their face and saying their name. It can also be used for healing, by visualizing energy emanating from your hands and moving towards a person whose face you can visualize.

There is no single method that guarantees success; the key is personal experimentation with what resonates with you. For a deeper understanding of these concepts and other examples of affirmations, I highly recommend reading "Adventure Beyond the Body" by William Buhlman.

Memorizing experience

Some people find it difficult to remember the details of their out-of-body experience once they've returned to their normal state of consciousness, sometimes forgetting small details or even a large part of their adventure. However, there are a few tricks you can use to improve your subtle memory:

Immediate recollection :

Immediately after your return, try to recall every detail of the experience. This helps to fix memories before they fade. Then write down everything you can remember in a journal dedicated to your experiences. This simple method has proved effective for many experimenters.

Positive affirmation:

Before fully reintegrating your physical body, take a moment to affirm aloud, "I will remember every detail of this experience!" This statement can help anchor the memories in your mind.

Autosuggestion:

During the day, practice autosuggestion by repeating positive phrases such as: "After each out-of-body experience, I can easily remember all the details of the adventure." This mental-reinforcement technique can significantly improve your ability to retain information from your experiences.

Although these experiences are generally memorable, and our consciousness and memory are fully awake during an OBE, some people may nevertheless find it difficult to remember their experience. That's why I've included the following tip on the subject to help you maximize your retention of memories of these extraordinary moments.

Tip: If you're worried about forgetting important details of your experience in the absence of your journal, an effective method is to use associations to organize your memories into clear categories. Let's take the example where you leave your body, meet an entity, travel to a place like the planet Mars, then propel yourself through space to an ocean of light. You can divide this adventure into three striking sub-sections: the entity, Mars, and the ocean of light. To easily remember these elements, you can either create an acronym, or group them into thematic categories. For the acronym, use the initials of each key element to form an easy-to-remember word. In our example, this would be "EMO" (Entity, Mars, Ocean). Alternatively, you can classify them by category, such as "encounter" for the entity, "planet" for Mars, and "divinity" or "elevation" for the ocean of light. These methods will help you not only to memorize significant experiences but also to retrieve them more easily for later reflection or sharing.

CHAPTER 3

BLOCKS, ERRORS, AND SOLUTIONS

Failures are the means by which we discover our limits. They force us to explore new paths to success.

- Josh Waitzkin

Preliminary out-of-body experience phenomena

As an explorer of consciousness, you will have to face new phenomena due to the change in frequency of your consciousness. You should know right now that none of them are dangerous. They can be quite surprising, but the fact that we've informed you in advance will lessen the surprise, enabling you to better manage the situation.

Here is a non-exhaustive list of the preliminary phenomena of an altered-consciousness experience:

- Strong vibrations as if you were in the heart of a jet engine.
- The feeling of being touched by someone.
- Feeling like a fresh breeze is blowing on your face.
- Hearing voices, even a scream.
- Hearing a sound like a gunshot close to your ear.
- Feeling like you're swelling or expanding.
- Feeling a sensation like an electric shock throughout your body.
- Feeling yourself rise gently; feeling as light as a feather.
- Seeing through closed eyelids.
- Feeling small vibrations in the back of the neck or head.
- Feeling like you're in two bodies at once.
- Feeling that your physical body is paralyzed.
- Hearing footsteps, bells, or music.

These manifestations are always surprising, especially the first time. But with time, we come to realize that all of this is illusory and harmless. They are the natural phenomena of a vibratory shift in consciousness. When you're faced with one of these, first tell yourself that you're almost out of your physical body and that's a very good thing. Secondly—and this is very important—you must remain calm and concentrate on an affirmation or visualization to induce the exit, so as to move quickly as far away from your physical form as possible. If you feel vibrations, encourage them to become stronger and spread throughout your body. To do this, let go and allow yourself to be carried away by these sensations.

It's important to note that not everyone perceives these warning signs, nor are they a prerequisite for a successful out-of-body experience. Over time, these vibratory sensations tend to diminish for many individuals.

Fears and how to overcome them

Fear is the emotion most often used to control humans. It provides security for the preservation of the species, but above all remains the number-one barrier to our progress. It is a tool that has been used to prevent the layman from gaining access to knowledge that could challenge well-established systems.

Fear has also been used to deter laymen from attempting to experiment with altered-consciousness experiences. People have experienced separation from the body since the dawn of time; yet the concept has only recently been made public, thanks to certain contemporary authors who have experienced it spontaneously and devoted their lives to research in the field.

Even today, there are books extolling the dangers of out-of-body experiences, revealing authors who are undoubtedly inexperienced but simply reporting facts they have read here and there.

Is there any danger in deliberately inducing out-of-body experiences? If that were the case, I don't think I'd be here writing this—and even less so the seasoned explorers of the invisible such as Robert Monroe, Robert Peterson, and William Buhlman, to name but a few.

However, the risk cannot be considered to be zero because as with all practices there may be contraindications. But these are not always where we think they are.

The discorporation of consciousness is a natural capacity of living beings. Several authors have reported that every night, we emerge a few inches above our physical form to regenerate energetically. I can't confirm this based on personal experience. On the other hand, I *can* confirm that our energetic body does indeed detach itself from our physical body during sleep.

Note: if the following journal entry looks familiar, it's because I used the same dream as an illustration of Continuum Experiences earlier in the book. I think you will agree that it is a good illustration of both subjects.

Journal entry, February 22, 2006

Following a nocturnal awakening, I was concentrating on my usual affirmations as I drifted off to sleep when suddenly I had the impression of being in two bodies at once. It was as if I had separated from my body and was floating a few inches above my physical form and facing it. I could feel my ribcage breathing, but in a different way. In other words, I was aware of my breathing but at the same time watching my body breathe as an outside observer. It was as if there was another person's rib cage facing me, the two chests in contact. The only difference was that I could clearly perceive inhalation and exhalation, as if my physical and nonphysical lungs were overlapping without getting in each other's way. It's hard to describe; the experience was certainly strange but not at all unpleasant. It could be that I became aware of the situation just as my subtle body began to exude slightly. According to many authors and experiencers, this is a process of energetic revitalization common to everyone that occurs every night.

There is therefore no danger associated with the outing itself. We are an immortal spiritual essence that takes as its vehicle a body—whether physical or energetic—to experience the corresponding environment.

As I discussed earlier in this book, a link called the "silver cord" anchors our consciousness to our flesh form during our life on earth. Whether it's real or symbolic, I can't say at present. However, during my out-of-body exits I've noticed the existence of a magnetic field that extends about 16 feet outward from my body, the property of which is to pull you back to the physical body. The magnetic pull of the physical body diminishes when I move beyond this boundary; I have also observed that my vision improves beyond this field.

It's difficult to know what's really going on, so it's best to rely on your own experience. Some people are quite adamant that entities can cut this cord and take over our physical vehicle, while others believe that our body can be possessed by a wandering, malicious soul while we're traveling outside of it. This is absolutely false. The "link" between our consciousness and our vehicle of flesh is strong and constant during an experience; we are securely connected to it whatever happens. The impression I personally get is that of a line of communication.

If I think of my physical body, my consciousness will feel it; if I stay focused on the experience, I feel myself entirely in the environment with a tenth of my consciousness remaining in the physical in the background. This balance can be achieved by feeling both bodies at the same time, as in my experience of February 22, 2006.

Just like an hourglass, we can move our essence from one part to another while maintaining the structure of the glass. This confirms that **no entity can take possession of our physical body**.

Working on your fears and hang-ups

Working on your fears opens the way to a more daring and fulfilling life.

- Susan Jeffers

1- Using your Inner Voice

Here's a little trick that's both amusing and surprising. I'd been experimenting with it before I read Robert Peterson's book; after reading it I had better understanding of the exercise, as his book gave me a great deal of insight about it. It's one of the few books on out-of-body experiences to go into such detail.

It involves talking to your subconscious. Theoretically, we can do this in any circumstance, but personally I do it when I'm walking alone in nature. You need to ask yourself a clear mental question and wait for an answer to come to you, remaining as neutral as possible. This can take the form of words, phrases, or images. Of course, we might wonder if we're not the ones doing this—if we just having a conversation with ourselves. The difference is that when we do this, we go deep into our minds to find answers. And it's often very surprising. Sometimes we sense that the answers don't come from us. It's hard to explain—you have to experience it—and it doesn't cost anything to try. On the contrary, you have everything to gain.

I remember walking through the Parc de la Grange in Geneva one morning. It must have been about 7 a.m., and I was alone in this vast and magnificent domain. It was springtime, the birds were singing, and it was the perfect moment for this exercise. I asked the question, "What is the key to out-of-body experiences?" and the answer that came to me was "Consciousness!" I didn't understand it at the time, and it surprised me because if I'd been thinking, I'd never have used that word. Then I wrote about my little experience in my journal. A few years later—without the memory of that moment in my head—I asked the question again during a meditation and the answer was the same: "Consciousness." I understood that consciousness is what we really are, and from the moment we become aware of our environment, of every moment of life, we do the same during the sleep of the physical body. This allows us to become aware that we are dreaming or out of body. Most of the time, we're in a state of semi-consciousness, overwhelmed by thoughts. Listening to your subconscious is what we now call "mindfulness." I won't dwell on the explanation as my aim is just to illustrate what I'm saying. Have fun with your Inner Voice. I advise you to supplement this with Robert Peterson's books, particularly his second one, "Lessons Out-of-the Body."

For fears or blockages, don't hesitate to use this little method. Ask your higher self—your subconscious (whatever you want to call it):

- Why do I have these fears?
- What can I do to destroy them?
- What are the obstacles holding me back in my experiments?

Write everything down in a small notebook and see how you can use it.

2- Affirmations

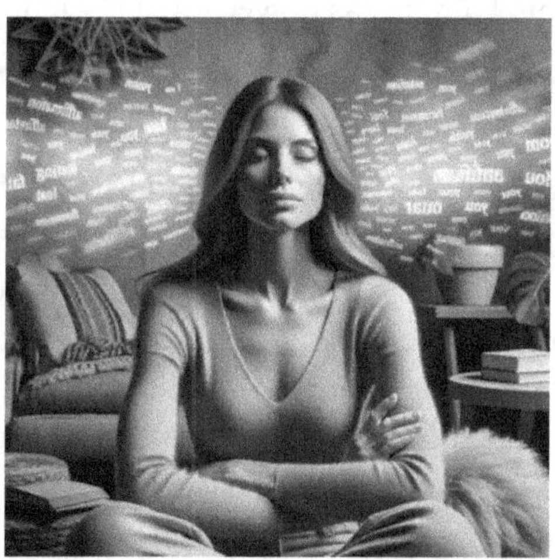

I've written about this before, but it's important to remind you that affirmations are extremely effective, not only for triggering experiences but also for personal reprogramming. One of the blocks that often comes up is doubt. Believing that we're incompetent—that out-of-body experiences are out of our reach or that an innate talent is required—can really limit our potential. In this case, you could repeat to yourself throughout the day, "It's easy for me to have out-of-body experiences!" or, "I induce out-of-body experiences with ease!" Add a visualization. See yourself performing an out-of-body experience with ease and feel the joy of having succeeded.

The subconscious doesn't differentiate between visualization and reality. By consistently showing your subconscious who you are—a person who can easily get out of his body—you convince it that this is so. Little by little, this will enable you to think differently and gain self-confidence. Bear in mind that dwelling on negativity acts as a kind of self-hypnosis, reinforcing the idea that you're stuck in your physical body.

Do the same for fears: "I am much more than a physical body and, as a soul, the afterlife is as much my home as it is for any entity. And because of this I am just as powerful!" Or, "Out of my body, I create my reality and I'm absolutely safe because part of my consciousness still resides in my physical body!"

The simplest and most effective method is to sit down, close your eyes, and relax for two minutes. Then think about the affirmation you're going to make. Your intention must be clear. It should be a command sent to the subconscious mind with an affirmative phrase like: "Subconscious mind, from now on I'll get out of my body very easily!" Once the sentence has been defined, visualize your subconscious as a double of yourself and repeat your affirmation three times with intention, i.e., with the certainty that the order has been heard and that changes are taking place. Then open your eyes and completely forget what you've just done.
You can repeat this several times during the day, but allow at least an hour to pass before practicing the exercise again.

This technique is inspired by an ancient Rosicrucian exercise.

3- Meditation Techniques

There are meditation techniques derived from Tibetan Buddhism and hypnosis that use the power of visualization to work on fears.

- One of them consists of visualizing your fears, your phobias, and your blockages as demons. Give them any shape you like, as close as possible to what you imagine they might look like. This allows you to materialize them and tell them: "I can see you now!" These demons feed on your fears; they need you to exist. Once the visualization is stable and clear, say to them: "You need me to feed you, so okay, go ahead and eat me!" In that instant, let go and see yourself melting and being swallowed up in the demon's mouth. By not resisting, you're demonstrating that it no longer has a hold on you, and that you're not afraid of it. Then watch it swell up more and more—as if it were swallowing you whole—until it bursts. As soon as it bursts, feel a sense of relief. Feel liberated from it; it's definitely disintegrated. Then regain consciousness by opening your eyes and enjoying the feeling of well-being inside you. Of course, if you feel that this meditation hasn't completely erased the fear or blockage, practice it again until you get a result.

- Another method consists of sitting down, relaxing and then imagining yourself stepping out of your body, then turning around to observe your physical body from the outside. See yourself with your fears and blockages, and imagine yourself correcting them by sending out a beam of white energy. Once you've done this, feel your new body, your new personality, as you would like it to be. As soon as you're sure you've made changes, re-enter your flesh body, become aware of every part of it, and feel it as a new form cleansed of all blockages and open your eyes. This is a method you can repeat several times if necessary.

Common errors and their solutions

- **Insufficient relaxation**

This is a very common mistake, and one that happens to even the most seasoned experimenters. If the body is not asleep then there is little chance that the exit can take place. If we start our technique too early and being too awake, we exhaust ourselves practicing. I've already talked about this, but this paragraph gives me another opportunity to stress the point. Give priority to relaxation—or to be more precise—to reaching the state of body asleep/mind awake, as this is in itself an exit method.

- **Lack of persistence, motivation**

One of the key factors for success is perseverance. Lucid dreaming and out-of-body experiences require daily work, with success sometimes taking a month, sometimes three months or even longer. Everything depends on your commitment, motivation, and perseverance despite failures and conscious or unconscious fears. Your patience may be sorely tested, but Rome wasn't built in a day. It took you time to learn to walk and ride a bike, and it will be the same here.

However, don't be discouraged by these words: it's perfectly possible to achieve results just a few days after starting a technique. Generally, success is achieved after three to four weeks of daily practice. And once the door has been opened—as Robert Monroe used to say—it never closes again. Indeed, even if you neglect your exercises for a period of your life, spontaneous experiences can still occur.

In any case, I've seen from my own trials and those of others that motivation is at its peak the first week; the second week we continue to practice fairly well, the third we start to lose heart, and then the difficulties begin. We feel frustrated, incapable while others succeed; in short, we give up most of the time. We forget to practice for a day or two and move on. When we give up after a month or more of effort, one of two things happens: either we give up completely, or by relaxing, we become the happy victims of a spontaneous experience. If there's one thing you need to remember from this chapter it's that the secret to success is perseverance. I know and have known some of the biggest names in out-of-body experiences. I've never heard of success without hard work—except on forums or Facebook, where people boast of being able to get out at will—on demand—and ask us to take their word for it.

What all these authors and successful experimenters have in common is that they have persevered, believed in their research, and braved their fears. They have all experienced good times and bad. They all have family and professional lives. They are not "chosen ones" or spiritual masters. But they have that gleam in their eyes that ancient navigators, seekers, and explorers must have had when they set off into unknown lands in search of knowledge. And when we reach our goal—the reward being beyond our expectations—we feel driven to continue practicing and it becomes a bit like an addiction.

However, there are several tools we can use to keep us motivated when the going gets tough.

- 1- <u>Books</u>

Reading literary works can be highly motivating—depending on the author—especially when they relate their trials, adventures, and experiences. In some books, the writer only describes what he or she has experienced, sharing extraordinary encounters and so on without giving us the keys, without explaining how he got there—sometimes even describing himself as possessing an extraordinary ability. In the end, he gives us a story worthy of a fantasy novel. You have to be very wary of this kind of story. In the bibliography at the end of the book, you'll find a non-exhaustive list of books I consider serious. It's up to you to decide which ones inspire you.

- 2- <u>Forums and Facebook groups</u>

Here too, you need to be wary and sort things out. But there are forums and groups out there that have a lot going for them and, above all, that are full of interesting information. Exchanges between practitioners, between beginners and the experienced, are very enriching. It's a great source of motivation and progress. Here's a short list you might want to research.

<u>Facebook groups</u>:

- William Buhlman's group:
http://www.facebook.com/groups/420183204661463

- Astral Projection group-Techniques:
  http://www.facebook.com/groups/495848321095643
- TMI (The Monroe Institute) group:
  http://www.facebook.com/groups/TMIOBE
- Out of Body Explorers group:
  http://www.facebook.com/groups/221196514607411
- The Lucid Dreaming group :
  http://www.facebook.com/groups/luciddreamingPLANIT

There are many other quality products on the market and they're easy to find.

- 3 - <u>Films</u>

The film industry is often inspired by the esoteric environment, popularizing it or using images to offer viewers certain subtleties that only the initiated can grasp. There are films that skillfully transcribe experiences of altered consciousness. What's more, with today's incredible level of special effects, we have access to virtual images of the utmost beauty that faithfully depict what certain subtle realities may look like. Here are a few inspiring works for your consideration:

- Inception (2010)
- Doctor Strange (2016)
- Vanilla Sky (2002)
- Matrix - the trilogy (1999)
- Ghost (1990)
- Interstellar (2014)
- Flatliners (1990)
- What Dreams May Come (1998)

- 4- <u>Interviews</u>

Youtube has a wealth of interviews with well-known authors. It's true that the most interesting and numerous are in English, but there are a few in French, such as a video with Akhena.

- 5- <u>Define a plan with a goal</u>

This is the first thing to do when you start your journal. Putting down on paper the organization of your daily practice and the goal you want to achieve will establish benchmarks that must be respected. Over time, this will become your routine, and once a habit is established—even when motivation drops—you'll stay on course. At first, we tend to overload our schedules thinking we'll get results faster. We put ourselves through sessions of meditation, energy work, relaxation, conditioning, multiple attempts at experimentation and so on. In the end, we create an internal tension, and not achieving results is a very unpleasant experience. You need to find the right balance between letting go/adopting a cool attitude and determination. The most important thing is to practice a technique every day before going to sleep. Whether it's during a nap, in the evening before going to sleep, or after waking up at night, practice every day.

And don't forget to write it all down in your journal. Keeping up this serious rhythm for one or two months will be fruitful. And if you can incorporate some meditation during the day and/or an energy method such as Qi Gong, Tai Chi, NEW, Reiki. etc., so much the better. We're talking about adopting a healthy lifestyle, which is a plus but not a necessity. It's up to you to decide what suits you best. But don't overdo it, as this will be more counter-productive than advantageous, whether your goal is to see a loved one again, visit another planet, fly in the sky, experience your soul, etc. Keep your goal in mind, repeating it mentally or verbally throughout the day. If you're using the affirmation method, include it in your sentence. When we have an experience, the moment is so unusual that we sometimes forget our goal. Repeating it to yourself often usually helps you remember it right away once you're on the other side.

Tip: To revitalize your motivation, listen to haunting music that stimulates your imagination and invites you to dream. For a more immersive experience, use headphones and visualize an out-of-body experience. Feel the vibrations of this imaginary outing and once you're "out there," head towards the goal you've set yourself. Music reinforces our imagination in much the same way as it immerses us in the world of a film. This simple and highly effective tip can be practiced regularly without moderation.

-   **Lack of concentration**

Lack of concentration is a common mistake. The fact is that in today's society we receive a heap of information every second, and we have to do and think about a thousand things in a day. As a result, our brains tend to scatter and focus very little on any one thing. We therefore need to practice centering exercises to learn to focus on one point for several minutes at a time. For out-of-body experiences, the methods themselves require concentration, and repeating them daily will increase your ability to do so.

But adding a little exercise like focusing on a candle flame or breathing will speed up the results. The aim is to be able to focus one's out-of-body intention for a fairly long period of time. However, we often find that either our motivation isn't strong enough to maintain our focus, or we're too tired to focus our intention on one point. As we saw earlier, there are solutions for low motivation. As far as fatigue is concerned, practice in the middle of the night, in the early morning, or during naptime and you'll have more energy for practice.

- **Restless mind**

Once your body is relaxed, you need to calm your mind to reach the ideal state of consciousness. This is where things sometimes get tricky. There's only one solution: the practice of meditation or, more precisely, contemplation.

Meditation

Meditation is a journey to the center of our being, a return to the source of our true nature.

- Deepak Chopra

The main cause of most of our ailments is mental. Most people have symptoms whose causes are often emotional (stress, anxiety, anguish, etc.). We function very much with our minds. Human beings are never focused where they are. We're constantly in thought, wherever we are…in the past dwelling on our mistakes or nostalgic moments or in the near or distant future wondering what we're going to do or what's going to happen.

Contemplating

Stopping to think—if only for a moment—is a bit like being stopped in a traffic jam and discovering an environment you've been driving past for over ten years. We take a step back and realize that we're constantly thinking instead of being awake and aware of life and ourselves, realizing that we ourselves create our situations of anxiety and stress. External stimuli only have value if we give them value—we alone are responsible for our lives and who we are. Today, science recognizes the impact of our thoughts on our lives and our health, and more and more teachings are being made available to the public.

Meditation is not just for the elite. I suggest several simple techniques. It's important to note is that it's more effective to practice 10 minutes every day than 60 minutes once a week. The ideal time for a session is around 20 minutes.

Here are a few tips to help you overcome any difficulties you may encounter.

- If you tend to fall asleep during meditation: practice with your eyes open, looking straight ahead with panoramic vision.
- If thoughts invade your mind despite the technique: observe them and label them; i.e., when a thought presents itself to you, mentally say, "Thought!" Recognizing it as such will make it disappear.
- If you feel any pain during practice, observe it and it will subside.
- If an external noise such as a jackhammer disturbs your sitting, concentrate on it and make it your practice support.

- <u>Meditation 1</u>: Breathing as support.

"Follow the path of the air as it enters through the base of the nose, which is cold, and travels down into the lungs, only to rise again, this time warm, and exit through the tip of the nose."

Sit comfortably, back straight, and take three deep breaths. Your hands are on your knees, palms turned downwards, your eyes open with a panoramic gaze, staring at nothing. If you find it difficult to meditate with your eyes open, you can close them.

Then turn your attention to your breathing. Don't modify it, just observe its natural rhythm. Follow the path of the cool air as it enters at the base of the nose, goes down to the lungs and then rises again, being warm this time, and exiting at the tip of the nose. With each exhalation you release all your tension, and with each exhalation you sink deeper and deeper into relaxation. You can also visualize positive energy—a white light—that enters on the inhale and exits on the exhale as a black smoke loaded with tension, stress, etc.

Do this little exercise for 10 to 20 minutes a day.

- <u>Meditation 2</u>: Counting the breath meditation.

"1 on inhale - 1 on exhale, 1 on inhale - 2 on exhale, 1 on inhale - 3 on exhale, 1 on inhale - 4 on exhale, etc. to 20"

Sit comfortably, back straight, and take three deep breaths. Your hands are on your knees, palms turned downwards, eyes open with a panoramic gaze, staring at nothing. If you find it difficult to meditate with your eyes open, you can close them.

Now you will associate breathing with counting:

Count 1 on inhale - 1 on exhale, 1 on inhale - 2 on exhale, 1 on inhale - 3 on exhale, 1 on inhale - 4 on exhale, etc. to 20. (Keep the number '1' for each inhalation.)

Of course, you can count in your head but the main thing is to focus your attention throughout. If a thought arises during the exercise, you must start again from the beginning. This allows you to gauge your mental activity. If you can't get past three, for example, you're pretty agitated.

- <u>Meditation 3</u>: Walking meditation

For this exercise, just observe the process of walking while you're walking. Analyze and break down every movement of the foot, leg, and knee. Be aware, too, of the different points of support so that you can focus your attention on one point and think of nothing else.

It's a simple exercise that can be done anywhere, and the benefits are significant.

Tip: There's a little-known but remarkably effective elixir for improving concentration and meditation. It's called "Meditation" and comes from Australian Bush Flower Essences. I've personally experienced its benefits and thought it would be interesting to share this discovery with you. The usual dosage is seven drops morning and evening, but it is also advisable to administer seven drops before a meditation exercise. You can usually find it on the Internet.

- **Falling asleep too quickly**

This usually happens when we're very tired, often in the evening at bedtime. However, some people tend to fall asleep very quickly anywhere, anytime. The solution is to bring a little discomfort to the physical body by lying on your back, or by wedging several cushions at the back so you're almost sitting upright. Another trick is to try to position your eyes behind closed eyelids as if you were looking straight ahead. When we start to fall asleep, our body relaxes and our eyes roll back due to a loss of muscle tension when we sleep. Straightening your gaze brings you back to consciousness. It's a great way to play with the hypnagogic state.

Tip: Robert Monroe advised us to keep our forearm raised so that when we start to drift off to sleep, it falls down and brings us back to consciousness. In this way, the hypnagogic state can be reached gradually.

- **Not being committed enough to your technique**

If life's worries or your lack of motivation are at the forefront, it's hard to be 100% committed to your practice; yet total commitment is one of the keys to success. When you visualize yourself strolling through your living room or garden, or when you concentrate on an affirmation with the intention of going out, you are trying to communicate to the subconscious your desire to leave your body. You're even trying to fool it into believing that you're already out of your body. But for this to happen, your whole being must be fully focused on the goal. If anything interferes with the process, nothing will happen. In this situation, it's essential to address your problems whenever possible; otherwise, don't hesitate to take a break.

Tip: Read a book on out-of-body experiences, preferably with a collection of adventure stories, just before your practice.

- **Not using the right method**

It's quite common for beginners to look for the best method promising quick results. And it's enough for them to read on a forum or newsgroup that a member has successfully exited on the first try with a specific technique for them to decide to use it, even if it doesn't suit them.

Take the time to try out different approaches to see which one you're most comfortable with and, above all, which one you enjoy the most. Then practice it for one or two months before changing methods. Don't be influenced by others because we're all different. You risk wasting more time than anything else.

-   **Practicing at the wrong time**

This is perhaps the most common mistake everyone makes. We all tend to concentrate on the out-of-body exercises at first, underestimating importance of the relaxation phase. We then exhaust ourselves concentrating on our visualization or affirmation, and lose effectiveness. Keep in mind that the most important thing is to reach the ideal state of consciousness, also known as the trance state. Once in deep relaxation, most of the work is done. Exit methods are just there to give the final push.

Another aspect of this mistake is practicing at the wrong time of day—at bedtime, for example. Now, this isn't true for everyone, and you'll have to test it to find out. But at bedtime, consciousness usually needs to rest just as much as the physical body, and it's difficult to induce an experience under these conditions. It is usually during the night—or even better during the early hours of the morning or at naptime—that is most conducive to practicing. It's up to you to make your own tests and find out when you feel most effective in your practice.

I made this mistake for a long time. The consequence was a low quantity of OBEs compared to the efforts made. I used to make my attempts at bedtime or around 3 - 4 a.m., thinking that was the ideal time. However, as someone who falls asleep quickly in the evening, this time slot didn't suit my profile. Like many people, I needed to be totally rested to have the energy I needed for good practice and concentration. Everything changed the day I realized that I naturally woke up every day around 5 - 5.30 a.m. with the feeling of having recovered well, and that this was therefore the best time to do my exercises. When you're tired, it's hard to focus your mind; it tends to go off in all directions. The body relaxes easily, but the intention is not strong and sustained enough.

Once the body and consciousness have been invigorated, it's still easy to relax the physical form since the night is not yet over but we still have enough energy to focus properly on the goal. It's important to take this into account, depending on your profile. For some, the ideal time is more likely to be at naptime—for others, at bedtime or at 9 a.m. Everyone's different. You'll need to experiment to find the ideal time for you to perform your technique.

If—despite your best efforts—you haven't achieved an out-of-body experience, evaluate your dreams. Are they unusual? Do you dream that you're flying, that you are in a classroom, or that you're having an out-of-body experience? If you answer 'yes' to any of these questions, it means you're on the right track. Now all you have to do is to persevere on a daily basis.

- **Overdoing it**

I have frequently observed this phenomenon in certain individuals who—eager to maximize their chances of success— devote their days and nights to practicing various methods. I've seen them practicing several hours of meditation a day, performing energy exercises in the morning and evening, attempting OBEs in the morning, at noon, in the evening, at bedtime, and during the night, etc. These people put so much pressure on themselves that they negate one of the most important aspects of the experience: letting go.

I'll say it again: enjoy yourself. If your wish is to have an out-of-body experience, it's better to practice an exercise at the right moment on a daily basis than to overdo it. It's essential to cultivate strong intention while maintaining low internal tension.

-   **Thinking that it's not for you, that you'll never succeed**

When we're just starting out, we're usually torn between the excitement of achieving such a feat and doubts about our abilities. It can seem so extraordinary that the goal sometimes seems unattainable. However, bear in mind that with the exception of a few atypical cases, everyone who has gone through these experiences started out like you. At one time or another, we've all had our doubts about our ability to succeed, including those who have already had out-of-body experiences but are encountering difficulties for various reasons.

Think about it: have you ever had dreams that seemed particularly real or experienced inexplicable moments in your childhood? I remain convinced that each of us—at some point in our lives—has experienced an out-of-body experience unconsciously, even if only a vague memory or impression remains. The main difference between those who succeed in consciously inducing these releases and those who don't is usually perseverance. So if you find yourself in this situation, don't be discouraged. Discussion groups and online communities are also valuable resources for support and encouragement. Keep exploring, learning, and practicing, and you'll increase your chances of success. As Robert Louis Stevenson famously said, *"It's not the destination that's important, it's the journey."*

-   **The empty passages**

Whether or not we are experienced in altered-consciousness experiences, we all go through periods of emptiness—in other words, moments when we lose interest or motivation to move away from physical reality. It's a bit like life is calling us back so we don't forget that we are here on earth to experience the trials of evolution.

These are usually moments when life's events and worries bring us back to Earth. They can last from a few days to a few years. As the biblical metaphor expresses it, they are similar to crossing the desert. It's essential to accept this and seize the opportunity to explore new areas of interest so as to avoid giving in to frustration.

I've been through several such periods, but one was particularly long. During this period, I completely turned my back on meditation, out-of-body experiences and lucid dreaming. I then embarked on an extreme sporting challenge: a long-distance road bike competition. For months I had to train hard, review my diet, work on my mental state and so on. In retrospect, this period enabled me to put down roots, to fully experience the material world and to face up to myself. When you ride alone for hours on end in the middle of nature, many emotions surface and you go from laughter to tears. After that, I naturally and gradually returned to my experiments in the subtle dimensions with a mind of steel. It's as if I'd needed to hit rock bottom to bounce back higher—to experience a brief sojourn of total immersion in physical reality—to learn from it and make an inner change to better prepare me for what's to come.

In my personal opinion, empty passages are necessary for our evolution. We build ourselves on our failures and trials, not on our successes. Knowing that these moments are common to all spiritual seekers and that you have to go through them, you can prepare for them and accept them as an event that testifies to a definite evolution of your soul.

Natural aids

Natural helps are the subtle signs of the caring hand of the universe, reminding us of the sacred connection between our being and the greater web of life.

- Eckhart Tolle

No human life is linear. Throughout our lives, we experience ups and downs. There are bad days and good days. As hard as we may try, disciplines such as meditation, prayer, concentration, lucid dreaming, and out-of-body experiences cannot be practiced optimally on a daily basis. Fatigue, lack of motivation, and unforeseen events sometimes sabotage our efforts. It is in these moments that certain natural aids can be useful to us.

In this part of the book, I share some of these aids with you:

1- <u>Binaural sounds:</u>

The principle is to use sound frequencies to train the brain to adopt the rhythm imposed on it. It's exactly the same principle as that of shamanic drumming. The idea came from the observation that train passengers tended to doze off, lulled by the regular sound of wheels on rails. Scientists hypothesized that the brain must be attuned to external rhythms. This was confirmed by electroencephalogram experiments in the laboratory. The frequencies emitted by the brain in different states of altered consciousness were then measured during sleep, deep relaxation, meditation, wakefulness, and so on. Then, once the tracings had been recorded, sounds were created to reproduce these frequencies in order to bring the guinea pig into the desired state of consciousness. The Monroe Institute is one of the pioneers in this field. The principle they have developed is to send sound waves of different frequencies into each ear; this synchronizes the two cerebral hemispheres, creating a third sound, known as binaural sound.

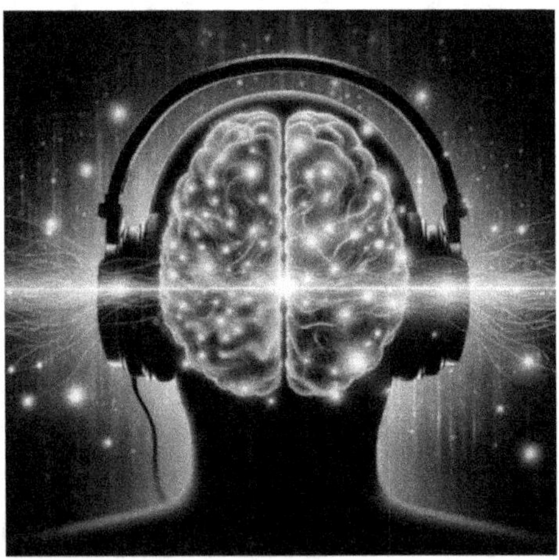

Illustration of brain synchronization

For example, if we use headphones to send a 100-Hz frequency to the right ear and a 104-Hz frequency to the left, the brain will produce a binaural sound with a frequency of 4 Hz, corresponding to the frequency of deep sleep.

It was from this discovery that the Monroe Institute developed its Hemi-Sync technology. Listening to these musical creations brings us into the desired states of consciousness efficiently, quickly, and safely. The interesting thing about using it is that it's a form of training. With repeated use, there comes a time when we can do without it because our brain can reach that state without Hemi-Sync assistance. On my return from my stay at the Monroe Institute, thanks to the intensive training I'd undergone with William I could very easily reach a state of deep relaxation in five minutes without Hemi-Sync support.

Here are a few titles I recommend:

- **Deep 10 Relaxation** - guided meditation (with Robert Monroe's voice) to achieve the famous Focus 10 state (body asleep, mind awake). This is the one to own and work on.

- **Spiral of Light** - Relaxation music with Hemi-Sync technology

- **Awakening Consciousness** - Relaxation music with Hemi-Sync technology

- **Ascension** - Relaxation music with Hemi-Sync technology

- **ARIA** - Relaxation music with Hemi-Sync technology

I will discuss the Hemi-Sync technology in more detail later in this chapter; now let's take a look at the connection between brainwaves and altered-state experiences.

The study of brainwaves and the analysis of different frequencies in different states of consciousness are exciting fields at the crossroads of neurology, psychology, and neuroscience. Hans Berger, a German psychiatrist, is renowned for his pioneering work in the 1920s developing electroencephalography (EEG), a revolutionary technique for non-invasively measuring the brain's electrical activity.

Not only did Berger discover that the brain generates electrical waves, but he also classified the first types of brain waves, called alpha waves and beta waves. These discoveries laid the foundations for future research into brain mechanisms.

Brainwaves are divided into several categories based on their frequency, expressed in hertz (Hz), and each category corresponds to different states of consciousness and mental processes. Here are the details:

1. <u>Delta waves (0.5 to 4 Hz)</u>: Associated with deep, dreamless sleep. In this state, the body rests and regenerates.

2. <u>Theta waves (4 to 8 Hz)</u>: Theta waves characterize states of light sleep, deep meditation, and daydreaming. They are also linked to creativity, intuition, and memory. These frequencies have also been observed in out-of-body experiences.

3. <u>Alpha waves (8 to 12 Hz)</u>: Present when awake but relaxed, with eyes closed. Alpha waves increase during meditation and deep relaxation.

4. <u>Beta waves (12 to 30 Hz)</u>: Dominant when we are awake, active, and engaged in mental tasks that require attention. Beta waves are associated with logical thinking, decision-making, and alertness.

5. <u>Gamma waves (over 30 Hz)</u>: Associated with sensory perception and acute consciousness. Gamma waves are important for learning, memory, and information processing.

Altered states of consciousness such as deep meditation, hypnosis, and psychedelic experiences can influence the frequency and type of brainwaves emitted. For example, it is common to observe an increase in alpha and theta waves during deep meditation, indicating a state of intense relaxation and expanded awareness.

Similarly, some studies indicate that psychedelic experiences can enhance the synchronization of gamma waves, thus improving brain connectivity and sensory perception. The study of brainwaves and their link with various states of consciousness remains a dynamic field of research that continues to illuminate our understanding of how the brain functions and interacts with our environment.

Beta waves characterize our usual waking state. When we're awake with our eyes open, we actively concentrate and direct our attention to the external environment. Whether at work or at home, our brains emit mainly beta waves, with frequencies generally varying between 14 and 40 Hz. These rhythms dominate our brain activity and are associated with functions such as active attention, arousal, concentration, and cognition. At higher levels, they can also be linked to fear and anxiety. This explains the influence of emotions on our ability to perform an out-of-body experience.

When we reduce the rhythm of our brain activity, we gradually enter a state of deep relaxation, focusing our attention inward. During the alpha state—where brainwave frequency varies between 8 and 13 Hz—these alpha waves dominate our brain activity, producing a sensation of tranquility often referred to as the alpha state. This state is typically associated with the onset of relaxation or mental neutrality, frequently observed in stress-free people. It's a state sought in meditation or certain types of yoga.

As we reach complete relaxation and approach light sleep, our brain switches to a slower but deeper state called theta, with frequencies oscillating between 4 and 8 Hz. It lies on the borderline between wakefulness and sleep—the hypnagogic state. During this phase, it is not uncommon to experience spontaneous mental images and lucid dreams, reflecting rich and diverse brain activity. The hypnagogic state is particularly popular with those seeking to induce an out-of-body experience. Theta waves also facilitate connection to the subconscious. However, maintaining this state can be arduous over a prolonged period, presenting a challenge for researchers.

When we are completely asleep, the dominant brain waves are delta waves. When we fall into a deep sleep, delta waves—which are even slower than theta waves and have a frequency of less than 4 Hz—become predominant. Nonetheless, when we practice out-of-body experiences, with practice we can still manage to keep our consciousness awake. It is by mastering this Ideal State of Consciousness (ISC) that we can trigger various transcendental experiences.

More about the Hemi-Sync process

After experimenting with several hundred frequencies, Robert Monroe and his team discovered a particular sound capable of keeping a person in a fluctuating state between wakefulness and sleep. The process was repeated, refined, and finally patented. They observed that most volunteers entered a state in which the body remained asleep while the mind remained alert, a state they arbitrarily named Focus 10.

A significant advance was made by adding beta frequencies—known to be linked to extrasensory perceptions—to the basic sound frequency. According to a physiological principle identified in the 1930s, like a tuning fork the brain tends to resonantly align itself with perceived frequencies. This discovery led to the development of the Hemi-Sync process, which enabled the two cerebral hemispheres to operate in sync.

The human brain is divided into two hemispheres—left and right, which are connected by the corpus callosum. Each hemisphere manages specific functions and has unique skills. The left hemisphere is often associated with logical, analytical, and detailed processing. It is considered dominant for language, processing grammar, and word production. The left brain is also involved in tasks related to mathematics, logic, and sequential thinking. It is often described as more detail- and structure-oriented.

The right hemisphere—on the other hand—is recognized for its ability to process information more holistically and intuitively. It is often linked to creativity, emotion, and global thinking. The right brain plays a key role in recognizing faces, interpreting emotions, and managing spatial perception. It is also associated with imagination and the ability to see things as a whole (the "big picture").

Take, for example, a musician who plays an instrument. Many aspects of the activity require close collaboration between the two hemispheres. The left hemisphere is responsible for interpreting the notes on the score, understanding rhythm, and decoding musical symbols, whereas emotional expression through music, improvisation, and the creation of a unique interpretation of the piece require more global and creative thinking, which is associated with the right brain.

Complete synchronization of the two hemispheres of the brain in the waking state is rather rare, as each hemisphere is often specialized in distinct functions and can operate relatively independently for certain tasks. However, a certain amount of coordination is necessary and occurs continuously for optimal overall functionality. We now know that meditation, relaxation, dreams, and out-of-body experiences have a direct relationship with this synchronization.

The Hemi-Sync process has enabled many people to access altered states of consciousness that would normally require years of practice to achieve. It's highly likely that many of them would never have been able to experience such things had it not been for the innovative research carried out by Robert Monroe and his team.

 *Tip: You'll find all these products on streaming platforms such as Spotify, Apple music, and Deezer. In the search bar, enter "Monroe products," "isochronic tones," "brainwave music," or "binaural frequencies."*

Bonus gift

To let you try out a binaural composition, along with my book I'm offering you a creation whose frequencies were arranged by me and whose music was composed by Christopher Lloyd Clarke.

Please scan the QR code below:

Or copy the link:

https://out-of-body.org/binaural-sounds-for-the-out-of-body-experience

The access code to the page is: **outofbody**

For any problems, please contact me: franck@out-of-body.org

2- Galantamine

The Snowdrop flower

Galantamine is a natural alkaloid extracted mainly from the bulbs and flowers of plants such as snowdrops, narcissus, and lycoris radiata. First discovered in the Soviet Union in the 1940s, it can be produced synthetically but is still extracted from natural sources for certain applications. It extends from the coasts of the Black Sea to the Pyrenees, and has the particular function of an insecticide within the plant. It blocks the nervous system of insects by inhibiting acetylcholine, a key neurotransmitter for memory and learning. In the pharmaceutical field, it is used in the treatment of Alzheimer's disease. Galantamine has a significant effect on improving memory and concentration. It optimizes relaxation and sleep. This substance is used in low doses to induce lucid dreams. It is then marketed as a dietary supplement, most often combined with choline, a micronutrient associated with the B-vitamin group.

The trick is to take 4 - 8mg of Galantamine after four or five hours of sleep during a WBTB. Of course, it's not a magic pill. It does work very well in inducing lucid dreams, but only if you're already practicing the techniques on a regular basis. If you're a beginner, it's unlikely to work. I won't go into more detail here nor will I give a brand name, because even though it's a natural supplement, it's best to ask your doctor's advice. Especially if you're on medication.

Tip: You won't find this product in France, but you can order it from Amazon.com.

3- Vitamin B6

Vitamin B6—also known as pyridoxine—plays a crucial role in the maintenance of various bodily functions, including metabolism, brain development during pregnancy and childhood, and the maintenance of immune function. It is present in many foods, including poultry, fish, potatoes, chickpeas, bananas, and certain non-citrus fruits. The influence of vitamin B6 on dreams has been the subject of research and studies, with results indicating that vitamin B6 supplementation could affect the vividness, clarity, and ability to recall dreams. This hypothesis is based on vitamin B6's role in the conversion of tryptophan to serotonin, a neurotransmitter that influences not only our moods and emotions but also our sleep cycles and dreams.

A study published in the journal *Perceptual and Motor Skills* examined the effect of vitamin B6 supplementation on dream vividness. Study participants who took vitamin B6 before bedtime reported an increase in the ability to recall their dreams compared with those who took a placebo. This suggests that vitamin B6 may play a role in improving dream clarity and the ability to recall dreams. The exact mechanisms by which vitamin B6 might affect dream content and vividness are not fully understood. Furthermore, as with any supplementation it's crucial not to exceed recommended doses, as too much vitamin B6 can lead to undesirable side effects including neurological disorders. Although preliminary evidence suggests that vitamin B6 may influence the vividness and recall of dreams, further research is needed to fully understand these effects and the underlying mechanisms. As always, consultation with a healthcare professional is recommended before starting any new supplement or diet.

4- Audiovisual stimulators

Like the Monroe Institute's Hemi-Sync tools, audiovisual stimulators facilitate the synchronization of cerebral hemispheres to achieve altered states of consciousness. However, these devices go a step further by combining binaural sounds with visual stimulation via small colored LEDs integrated into glasses, offering a doubly effective approach for a more pronounced effect.

A variety of models are available for both professional and private use. Among those for the general public, the best-known are the Proteus, Procyon, Laxman, Psio, and Kasina. For therapy professionals, the PandoraStar is particularly popular.

If you're thinking of adopting this type of technology, I strongly recommend that you try it out before making a purchase. While effective for many, dual stimulation can be poorly tolerated by some people. Testing the device will ensure its suitability for your needs and sensitivities.

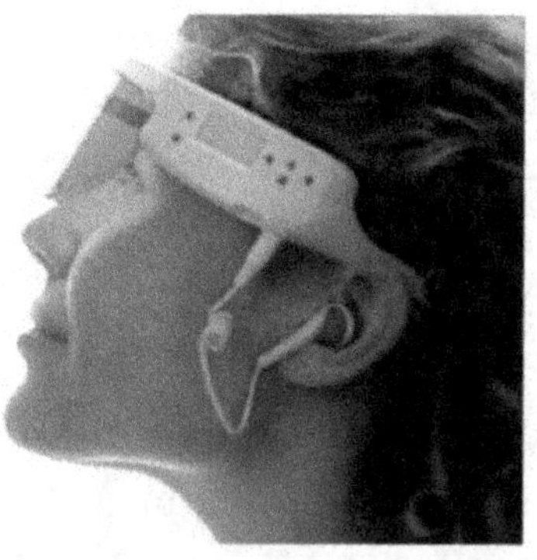

Psio

4- <u>Essential oils</u>

Essential oils are widely appreciated for their many properties, whether taken orally, applied locally, or inhaled. Although they are not often considered direct means of inducing altered states of consciousness, they can nevertheless enrich our "spiritual medicine kit." Some people use them like incense or candles—as part of rituals. In such cases, they serve to condition the mind, helping to imbue the subconscious with our intentions. Using essential oils in this way is entirely possible, and some possess notable therapeutic qualities. Here are just a few examples:

- <u>True lavender essential oil</u>:

Well known and perhaps even the most widely used, it has the virtue of soothing. Breathing it in conjunction with a relaxation method promotes faster, more sustained relaxation. It can be an invaluable aid at times when we find it difficult to relax.

- <u>Mugwort essential oil</u>:

It is generally used for its antispasmodic, anti-inflammatory action and for painful periods. In esotericism, it is considered protective. When inhaled directly just before sleep, it can be effective in provoking clear—even lucid—dreams.

- <u>Ylang Ylang essential oil</u>:

Renowned for its extremely relaxing properties, it is highly effective in inducing deep relaxation.

- <u>Olibanum essential oil</u>:

This is the essential oil for meditation par excellence. It promotes the expansion of consciousness, calms the mind, and soothes stress. As part of your meditation practice, use it with a diffuser.

There are many interesting essential oils, these being the most used in the field concerned. In all cases, the best is to use a diffuser or pour one or two drops on a handkerchief and inhale it.

6 - Self-Hypnosis

Self-hypnosis is a practice that enables a person to guide their own mind into a state of deep concentration and relaxation. This state is often compared to a form of trance similar to what can be experienced under professionally guided hypnosis, but here the individual uses techniques on their own to achieve it.

The aim of self-hypnosis is often to achieve personal change or improve some aspects of daily life. This can include managing stress, improving sleep, reducing anxiety, relieving pain, increasing self-confidence, or even working on specific habits such as quitting smoking or losing weight.

This method is particularly effective for overcoming obstacles such as fears and for strengthening our skills by reducing our doubts about our ability to experience altered states of consciousness such as OBEs.

The sensory spiral

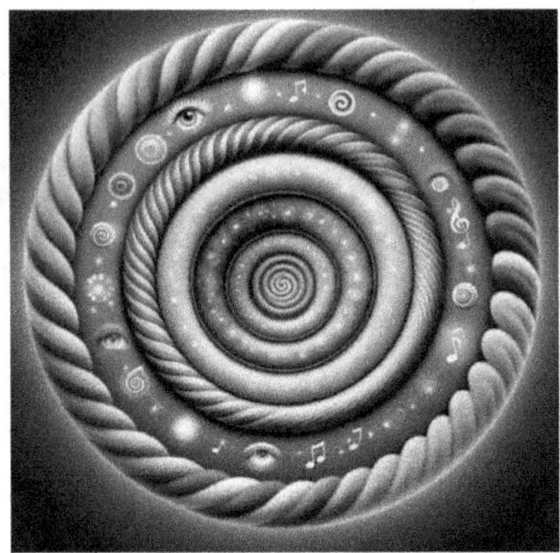

Self-hypnosis represents an extremely powerful tool for personal development, enabling individuals to take control of their own subconscious and actively work towards their personal goals and well-being. It would be a shame not to **exploit this potential in our exploration of altered states of consciousness.** The aim here is to overcome fears, doubts, and even to directly program an out-of-body experience.

There are a multitude of self-hypnotic induction techniques, but I've chosen to **concentrate on** the sensory spiral for two main reasons. Firstly, it's highly effective. **Correctly** practiced, you can reach the desired state long before the end of the exercise. The second reason is that **this technique can be particularly useful for putting the body to sleep while keeping the mind awake.** Whether **before falling asleep or after waking up at night,** you can do exactly the same thing with **the following suggestion:** "Every time I see (or hear, or feel) this, I become more and more aware, while my body falls deeper and deeper asleep!"

The hypnotic induction method known as "the sensory spiral"

was devised by Betty Erickson, daughter of the famous hypnotherapist Milton H Erickson. It's a technique that requires concentration on three senses: sight, hearing, and touch. Whether practiced on oneself (self-hypnosis) or with a patient, it involves focusing attention on a specific perception for each sense, such as an image, sound, smell, texture, or taste. For each sense, a relaxation suggestion is associated.

During the sensory spiral, you can start by concentrating on various visual elements, then listening to different sounds, and finally experiencing various tactile sensations. Each stage of the spiral can be enhanced with relaxation suggestions or affirmations to guide the subconscious mind towards the desired state.

In the following exercise, we'll use this exercise to help you enter the hypnotic state. Once you've reached your goal, you'll be able to formulate suggestions tailored to your own personal goals.

Here are just a few examples of affirmations you might use to assist you:

"I'm getting out of my body more and more easily!"
"The out-of-body experience is serene and safe!"
"Every time I dream, I become aware of my dream environment!"
"Tonight at 4:30 a.m., I consciously leave my body!"

The method:

To begin, make yourself comfortable and relax by taking three deep breaths, releasing tension with each exhalation. Then stare at a point in front of you—whatever the object of concentration—until your vision begins to blur and you feel the need to close your eyes.

Once relaxed with your eyes closed, begin the method by choosing four objects for reference.

- We start with the sense of vision. Mentally list what you perceive visually: for example, "I see the ceiling, it's [specify] color…I now notice the doorknob, it's [specify] shape and [specify] color…I contemplate the painting on the wall, it represents [specify]…Next to it, there's a lamp of [specify] color and [specify] size."

Then link these observations to the state you wish to achieve:

"Watching all this, I relax more and more. As I look at each of these objects, I am slowly, serenely approaching the hypnotic state."

- Continuing with the sense of hearing, mentally list what you can hear: e.g., "I can hear the wind outside lulling me to sleep…now I can hear my heartbeat gently slowing down…I can hear my breathing getting deeper and deeper…I can hear the neighbors outside talking."

Reinforce relaxation with these auditory perceptions:

"Hearing all this makes me relax more deeply. Each sound gently guides me into a hypnotic state."

- Then, finally, let's use our sense of touch. Concentrate mentally on what you can feel: e.g., "I can feel my clothes on my skin keeping me warm…now I can feel temperate air caressing my face and relaxing me…I can feel the weight of my body on my bed getting heavier and heavier…I can feel the temperature of the room gently relaxing me."

-

Deepen your relaxation by feeling:

"Feeling all this, I relax more and more deeply. Every sensation reinforces my hypnotic state."

Repeat this process, gradually reducing the number of objects of concentration for each sense: start again with three, then two, and finally one. It's not uncommon to reach the hypnotic state before the exercise is even finished. Feel free to personalize the method by changing the words or the order of the sensations. The important thing is to use the senses in association with a gradual immersion into hypnosis. Once you've reached your goal, you should feel your body become heavy or not feel it at all. Then start auto-suggestion with the affirmation of your choice. You can combine it with a visualization, which will be even more powerful.

<u>Coming out of the state of hypnosis:</u>

Once you've completed the exercise, **gradually** regain awareness of your body. Take three deep breaths and start **gently moving** your fingers, then your feet. **Stretch slowly and, when you feel ready, open your eyes.** The return to normal consciousness should be gradual, to avoid any discomfort.

<u>Tip</u>: When you reach the state of hypnosis, take a moment to fully savor the experience and—above all—commit it to memory. After two or three sessions of this exercise, you'll find that you don't need to go through all the initial steps; simply recalling that precise moment will automatically induce the hypnotic state. This method of recall facilitates rapid access to a deep hypnotic state using the strength of the memory associated with the experience.

Root yourself to fly better

It may seem contradictory, but to experience things beyond physical reality you need to be firmly rooted. More colloquially, we'd say you need to have your feet planted firmly on the ground. You need to be psychologically stable to approach the adventure with serenity. Being grounded simply means living life normally, but in a very present way. We have to stay involved in our daily lives without going off on imaginary flights of fancy. We're here in this physical dimension, and there's a reason for that. We must remember our responsibilities and put them first.

Rooting is also a way of reconnecting with the Earth, living in the present moment, and enhancing our connection with nature. To achieve this, there are a number of different practices, such as:

- Walking barefoot on grass or sand.
- Practicing contemplation.
- Visualizing roots coming out of your feet to connect with the center of the Earth.
- Using black tourmaline.

If you sometimes feel off-center following an experience of altered consciousness, don't hesitate to use these exercises; they will enable you to re-establish the imbalance.

CHAPTER 4

THE 3 KEYS TO SUCCESS

Intention, concentration, and relaxation

The three keys to success

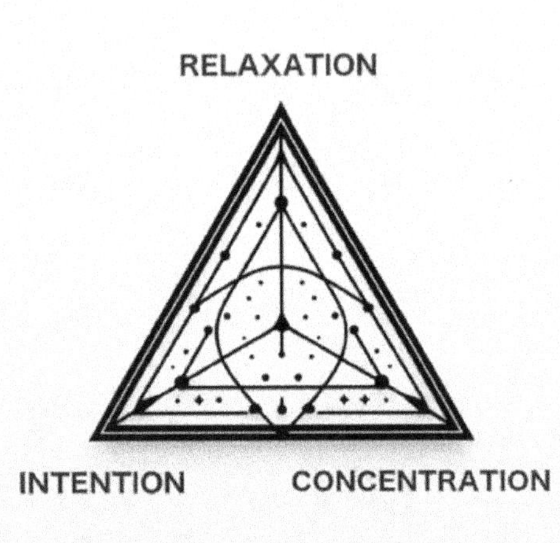

I hope I've adequately explained the importance/mechanics of these three key elements of successful altered-consciousness exploration, as they are often overlooked by both authors and aspiring explorers. Make no mistake about it: if you don't master these tools, you'll never reach your goal. Work on these indispensable keys—**intention, concentration, and relaxation**—and I assure you, you *will* succeed.

Concentration enables you to focus your awareness on a goal without deviating from it, without being distracted by anything else. **Intention** is the fuel that enables consciousness to leave the physical body. **Relaxation** eliminates the tensions that hold consciousness inside the body.

I therefore come back to these three critical aspects of the practice. You will find the appropriate exercises in Part 4 of this book but also in books such as those I cited in the bibliography.

1- Intention

As you've likely noticed, the word "intention" is omnipresent in this book. It refers to the goal or objective we set before carrying out an action. It is the essential mental state—the driving force—behind altered-consciousness experiences. When intention is sufficiently powerful, the method used to leave the body becomes secondary. Intention is not simply the desire to do something; it is also a conscious reflection on the means and consequences of these actions, forming a bridge between motivation, planning, and action.

To illustrate the necessary intensity of intention, imagine the following situation:

You've forgotten to set the handbrake on your car parked on a slope. The car starts to roll slowly. The slope is gentle and you have plenty of time to catch up and stop it. However, two people are holding you back. As you watch the vehicle gradually pick up speed, you become anxious about the damage it could cause. You struggle to break free of their grip. Despite your best efforts, the car pulls away. In a final burst of determination, you manage to free yourself. With intense rage, you finally manage to reach and stop your vehicle. It's this strength, this intensity of intention, that you need to channel to get out of your body.

We tend to identify with our physical form, therefore the intention to expel yourself from it must be stronger than anything else. The challenge lies in maintaining our relaxation while still concentrating on our desire.

Tip: It can be difficult to cultivate a powerful intention after waking up at night. To succeed, you need to play on your motivation. Have one or more inspiring stories of out-of-body experiences on your bedside table that particularly resonate with your own goals. These stories can come from books, articles, or even messages shared by friends in exchange groups on the subject. Reading captivating accounts of adventures like the one you want to have can rekindle your determination and strengthen your resolve to succeed in this experience whatever the cost.

2- Concentration

Tame the mind: the mind is a monkey.

Develop your concentration skills; focusing on an intention or image is an essential part of the practice. Buddhists compare our mind to a monkey that needs taming. Indeed, if your mind is too agitated, you'll find it very hard to concentrate. Think of your consciousness as a thread that has to pass through a pinhole to gain access to subtle dimensions. If it's agitated, it'll never make it through.

Do a test: sit down for a few seconds, relax, take three deep breaths, and release your tensions on each exhalation as if you were ejecting them from your body. Then fix your attention on one point. This could be your breathing, the movement of your belly, a mantra like "OM," or your heartbeat. Choose a single object of observation and see how long you can maintain your concentration without distraction. If you can't manage more than five minutes, then you're going to have to practice daily. Start with five minutes a day for a week, then increase to ten minutes, with a goal of twenty minutes. But if you master concentrating for just fifteen minutes a day, that's fine; not only will you reap the physical and mental health benefits but your practice of out-of-body experiences will be of higher quality and your results incomparable.

Practice regular exercises with your eyes closed and occasionally monitor the tension in your facial muscles, which tend to contract unconsciously when you focus your attention.

The nine stages of mental calm

In Tibetan Buddhism, the development of mental calm is often described in nine progressive stages. These stages are designed to help the practitioner develop deep, stable concentration. It's worth referring to them to assess your progress in this area. They are illustrated in the image above.

Here are the nine steps:

<u>1-Initial placement</u>: The ability to focus the mind on an object of meditation such as the breath, but the mind is still very distracted.

<u>2-Continuous placement</u>: The mind starts to stay on the object a little longer, even if distractions are frequent.

<u>3-Re-application</u>: The mind is able to return to the object of meditation whenever it is distracted from it.

<u>4-Close stabilization</u>: Distractions begin to diminish and the practitioner can keep his mind on the object with less effort.

<u>5-Taming</u>: The mind becomes more stable and emotional disturbances are less powerful.

<u>6-Pacification</u>: The mind is calmer and efforts to overcome subtle distractions become less necessary.

<u>7-Complete pacification</u>: The practitioner is able to maintain concentration without any conscious effort; subtle distractions are virtually eliminated.

<u>8-Simple unification</u>: The mind is completely absorbed in the object of meditation with great inner peace.

<u>9-Perfect equilibrium</u>: The final state in which the practitioner can maintain meditation for an extended period of time without effort and with perfect concentration.

These stages are not necessarily linear and may require time and practice to progress from one to the next.

<u>Tip</u>: To make learning to concentrate easier and faster, you can help yourself with a Hemi-Sync composition from the Monroe Institute called "Concentration." It features a combination of non-

verbally guided frequencies with no music whatsoever. Use it on low volume with headphones.

3- Deep relaxation

Deep relaxation is a state of intense relaxation in which the body and mind are freed from habitual tension and stress. This state goes beyond the mere absence of stress and involves a deep sense of well-being and inner peace. It can be beneficial to both mental and physical health, offering respite from the damaging effects of everyday stress.

Relaxation to induce an out-of-body experience or lucid dream must strike a balance between effort and relaxation. Too much effort can lead to tension and stress, while too little can lead to inertia or lethargy. The right balance allows you to maintain the energy of the practice while remaining relaxed and open.

Concentration is essential for achieving optimal balance, and relaxation plays a key role in facilitating concentration. It's important to recognize that these two elements are interdependent.

Remember, you're not looking to achieve simple relaxation, but rather to induce what we call a deep trance. The aim is to put the physical body to sleep, i.e., to relax the body to the point that you're unaware of it and dissociating yourself from physical reality. Consciousness needs to free itself from this vehicle to venture into subtle dimensions. In deep trance, the individual can experience a detachment from the physical environment and usual bodily sensations, entering a space where ordinary perceptions are altered or absent. Therefore it's crucial to practice daily to achieve the "body asleep/mind awake" state. Again, don't hesitate to use binaural sounds—they're a great help. Although it may take some effort and time at first, you should be able to reach the trance state you're seeking relatively quickly. What's more, the practice of deep relaxation is not only beneficial for isolated moments of relaxation but can also contribute to a healthier and more balanced lifestyle when regularly integrated into your daily routine.

Rosicrucian philosophy teaches that the soul enters the physical body at birth through the first breath and leaves it at death with its last breath. This is an interesting perspective, as it reflects the fact that consciousness is maintained inside of the vehicle of flesh through breathing and—by extension—the heartbeat. This explains why deep relaxation is fundamental. If we want to let go of our soul (consciousness), we have to reduce these vital functions. Some research has noted a drop in heart rate and a slowing of breathing in subjects in a state of deep relaxation or out-of-body experience. The next time you relax, pay special attention to your breathing. Understanding its importance can enrich and improve your practice.

Remember that one of the most common mistakes is insufficient relaxation. Today's society makes it very difficult for people to let go. You can't achieve total relaxation as long as mental tensions are present.

To conclude

I've intentionally devoted a section of this book to the three essential keys—**intention, concentration, and relaxation**—to emphasize their crucial importance. Very often I notice people who—despite their daily efforts—don't get any results and end up getting discouraged.

The cause frequently lies in weakness in one or more of these fundamental skills. It's critical to identify which skill needs more work and integrate specific exercises into your daily routine to strengthen it.

CONCLUSION

The conclusion of a book is like the last note of a melody, sealing the experience and leaving a lasting imprint on our hearts.

- Paulo Coelho

A few years ago, I had the privilege of crossing paths with Serge Toussaint, Grand Master of the French-speaking jurisdiction of The Rosicrucian Order. It was an unforgettable encounter. Mr. Toussaint is distinguished by his great humility and profound wisdom. Our discussions revolved around metaphysical experiences, in particular what Rosicrucians call *psychic projection*. I still remember his concluding words: "Metaphysical experiences, however fascinating they may be to explore, are secondary; the essential remains in spiritual alchemy." This spiritual alchemy is the process of transforming our flaws into qualities to become better people. This ties in with Gandhi's famous quote: "Be the change you want to see in the world." Experiences of altered consciousness should serve this purpose. They include meditation, prayer, contemplation, lucid dreaming, and out-of-body experiences. If these practices only lead to personal satisfaction, then we've missed the real purpose.

Be indulgent with yourself, start by recognizing your true values and don't be judgmental. As a lama of the Tibetan lineage taught me during a retreat in a Buddhist monastery: "If you think you've meditated well, then you've meditated badly!" In other words, as soon as self-criticism intrudes into the practice, it loses its depth and becomes a mere activity in the same way as relaxation or physical exercise.

In conclusion, out-of-body experiences plunge us into the deepest mysteries of human consciousness. Through our exploration of this fascinating phenomenon, we've discovered that the boundaries between physical reality and consciousness appear to be far more fluid than we ever imagined. In this book, we examined the various interpretations and perspectives on out-of-body experiences. We've explored my personal accounts, the scientific research that attempts to understand them, and the spiritual traditions that have interpreted them for centuries. It's clear that out-of-body experiences cannot be reduced to a simple explanation. They represent a complex blend of neurological, psychological, cultural, and spiritual phenomena. They challenge us to rethink our conceptions of consciousness, reality, and personal identity.

Yet—despite all our advances—many questions remain unanswered. Out-of-body experiences invite us to continue our exploration, to remain open to new perspectives and to keep pushing back the boundaries of our understanding.

Ultimately, whether you're a seeker, a spiritual practitioner or simply a curious individual, I encourage you to continue your quest for knowledge and understanding. Out-of-body experiences are an invitation to explore the depths of human consciousness, to embrace the diversity of human experience, and to remain open to the mysteries that surround us.

Thank you for accompanying me on this journey. May your own exploration of out-of-body experiences bring you wisdom, wonder, and a deeper understanding of the wonderful complexity of human existence.

APPENDIX

Summary of out-of-body experiences

Out-of-body experiences are not:

- The soul leaving the body
- Imaginary
- Dangerous
- Leaving an empty body behind
- Being bound with a silver cord that can break
- Limited to special persons
- A diabolical practice

Out-of-body experiences are:

- A natural phenomenon
- Expanding consciousness beyond the body
- Multidimensional exploration beyond the five senses
- A transformative experience
- Accessible to everyone
- A safe practice

Index 1: Example of a 30-day practice plan

Establishing a month-long practice plan for out-of-body experiences requires a gradual and steady approach. Structuring your approach helps you to organize your practice efficiently and give it a clear direction. Although your plan is designed for the next four weeks, it is possible to have an experience during the very first days of your practice. Customize it to your specific needs, targeting the areas where you want to improve.

Here's a four-step plan to guide you through the process:

Week 1 : Preparation

1-Keeping a journal

- Start by keeping a journal. Every morning, write down all the details of your dreams from the previous night. Use this notebook to record all your sensations, the energetic phenomena you experience, and your intention to strengthen your practice. For example, "Last night I consciously left my body!" Every day, write down the technique you use and the quality of your practice. It sometimes happens that you botch an exercise or skip it altogether because you're so tired. Make a note of it and add a resolution so you don't make the same mistake next time. In short, don't neglect your logbook; use it to fine-tune your practice and record all your experiences (dreams, signs of subconscious understanding, lucid dreaming, out-of-body experiences, etc.).

2-Practicing mindfulness

- Incorporate mindfulness practices into your daily routine. Take a few minutes each day to focus on your breathing, your body sensations, and your surroundings.

3-Practicing energy stimulation

- Though not obligatory, it improves the results and clarity of consciousness during experiments. Please refer to the section on preparation where you'll find various techniques for stimulating the chakras.

4-Out-of-body exit techniques

- Try out different techniques this week to see which one resonates most with you. Don't forget to relax beforehand. As explained in this book, achieving the ideal state of consciousness is the most important skill to master.

5-Defining your goal

- To boost your motivation, you need to set yourself a goal. Why do you want to go out of your body? To verify the immortality of your consciousness? To see a dead loved one again? To visit majestic places? Record the answer to this question in your journal. And above all, keep this goal in mind when you attempt to exit your body.

Week 2: Strengthening Concentration and Relaxation

1-Meditation and relaxation

- Practice meditation and relaxation every day. You need to reach that state where the body is asleep and the consciousness awake, all while maintaining mental calm.

2-Developing concentration

- Choose a concentration object such as a candle or your heartbeat, and practice concentrating on it for a few minutes every day. The aim is to develop your ability to maintain stable, focused concentration. You can also focus on your breathing while your eyes are closed, which remains the most recommended method for inducing an OBE.

3-Exit technique

- Once you've found your ideal out-of-body exit technique, keep using it and never change it until you've succeeded. Practice it daily in a state of deep relaxation, just before going to sleep. Apply yourself to bringing your intention into your sleep. And don't forget to write it all down in your journal.

Week 3: Exploring the Inner Dimension

1-Visualization

- Practice visualization to explore your inner world. Use audio recordings or create your own scenarios to guide you on imaginative and creative journeys. See yourself stepping out of your body and reaching your goal. Feel the joy of success. Do this regularly to reinforce your intention.

2-Boost your motivation

- By the third week of practice, if you still haven't managed an out-of-body exit, it's possible that your motivation is gradually giving way to frustration. Remember that very few people succeed in their early days of practice. It's no ordinary experience, so we need to alter our perspective. Blocks such as apprehension can also consciously or unconsciously hold us back. Don't hesitate to use the exercises provided in this book to get your practice back in gear.

Reread your journal to see if there are any areas for improvement. Is your relaxation sufficient? Is your intention strong enough? Program yourself using visualization as described above, repeating affirmations to yourself throughout the day: "Tonight at 4 a.m., I will consciously leave my body!"

Review your journal to see if you've notice any signs of evolution during these three weeks of practice. For example, have your dreams changed? It's not uncommon to dream of dead people, flying, or driving a car at high speed…or perhaps becoming aware that you're dreaming. These are all signs that things are moving in the right direction. That's why it's a good idea to write everything down in your journal. It allows you to see where you stand in your practice and to modify or improve what needs to be improved.

3-Read about out-of-body experiences

- If you haven't already done so, read (or listen to) other people's experiences in books or on the Internet. It's interesting to see how other experimenters practice, to read about their exhilarating adventures, and to see the mistakes they share. It's all very enriching and motivating. And don't hesitate to join a discussion group to share your problems or ask your questions. You'll always be well received and the members will be happy to help you.

Week 4: Integration and reflection

1-Integrating experience

- Continue to keep your dream journal and note any unusual experiences or sensations you may have during your practice sessions. Be alert for any signs of out-of-body experiences.

2-Reflection and adjustment

- Take time to reflect on your experiences and adjust your practice accordingly. Identify what works best for you and what you can improve.

3-Planning for the future

- Consider continuing to practice the techniques you have found most effective. Keep in mind that out-of-body experiences can take time and practice to develop fully.

Remember that patience, persistence, and open-mindedness are essential when exploring out-of-body experiences. Be kind to yourself and remember that every experience, every exercise you perform, is an opportunity for learning and growth.

Index 2: Simplified Daily Plan for OBE Practice

- <u>Morning (15 minutes)</u>: Concentration

  - Spend the first few minutes after waking up focusing on your intentions for the day.

- <u>Noon (20 minutes)</u>: Relaxation

  - Take a moment to relax fully, releasing the tensions accumulated during the morning. Use a binaural composition of your choice, the aim being to achieve a state of body asleep/ consciousness awake.

- <u>Evening</u> : Preparing for the Nocturnal Experience

  - Schedule your evening to prepare for a conscious experience during the night. Relax, visualize yourself performing an out-of-body experience, and affirm, "Tonight I will consciously step out of my body at 5 a.m!"

- Night : Conscious Sleep Cycle

  - About six hours after going to bed, wake up to practice the WBTB technique starting with relaxation and followed by your body exit technique.

- <u>During the day</u>: Autosuggestion

  - Practice autosuggestion—with or without visualization—by repeating the affirmation, "I get out of my body easily."

<u>Option</u>: Add an energy-boosting exercise during the day or just before practicing your out-of-body method.

Index 3 : Tribute to Akhena

I like to call Akhena "our French William Buhlman." I discovered Akhena on her website in 2007, but initially I wasn't convinced. Her content dealt with channeling the Egyptian pharaoh Akhenaton, and seemed too "new age" for my taste. However, my curiosity led me to read her first book, "Out of Body," and I quickly realized that she was truly an expert in the field of out-of-body experiences.

After having initially passed a harsh and hasty judgment on her, I wrote to her to tell her how much I liked her work. I then decided to take her online training course in early 2008. I received the seven CDs and instructions by email, and we regularly exchanged e-mails and phone calls. Akhena's approach was always caring and attentive, offering a truly personalized training experience.

It was during this online course that I had the most striking out-of-body experience of my life in which I met Akhena. I had not yet met her in real life. As far as I knew at the time, there were no photos of her on the Internet, and I didn't know what she looked like.

I recounted this OBE at the very beginning of this book under the heading, "My most unusual contact experience." Therefore I won't tell the story again. But because of the fact that Akhena and I eventually met and she confirmed that she had had almost the same experience, I know it's possible to meet living people during out-of-body experiences. I'm sure that our "remote relationship" via email, phone calls, and my participation in her workshop helped to strengthen our emotional connection and thus facilitate our astral meeting. It's an experience I'll never forget and it represents the pinnacle of my explorations in altered consciousness to date.

From the time that we met and compared notes on our shared experience, we became friends. I did her a few favors such as finding her a place in Valence to organize her workshop, translating the back cover of her second book into English, and so on. Of course, we also exchanged ideas about William because she admired him very much. I offered his book to the English-speaking community and gave it to Robert Peterson to read. He loved the book, wrote an article about it on his blog which—given the influence he has— helped to make William's book known to the English-speaking community.

In France, serious experimenters can be counted on the fingers of one hand, but Akhena was one of them, and I pay tribute to her for her work and her friendship. She was a simple woman, with no ego whatsoever, and was extremely kind.

FAQ

What has contributed most to improving your results?

The daily practice of concentration on my breathing and relaxation with the Monroe Institute CDs, in particular "Relaxation Reinforcement" from the "Journeys Out of the Body" album. The latter enabled me to quickly reach the ideal state of consciousness by counting from 1 to 10 (Focus 10).

Do you have out-of-body experiences on a daily basis?

That's a good question. We often wonder whether those who write on the subject frequently have such experiences. For me, the answer is no. I'm one of those people who needs to practice regularly to induce a release. While initial enthusiasm and the discovery of this unexplored universe multiplied my experiences, over time I've adopted a wiser approach, practicing according to periods and needs. Nonetheless, I do sometimes go on spontaneous outings.

What do you usually do during an OBE?

My first action is to get away from my physical body, then I venture out to explore. Most of the time, I like to let myself go wherever the wind takes me, but sometimes I have a specific goal for my outing.

What's the most common feature of your outings?

There's one phenomenon that accompanies most of my out-of-body experiences, and it's also what confirms that I'm on an astral journey, and that's the presence of a cool breeze on my face. To my knowledge, only Robert Bruce mentions this in his book Astral Dynamics.

Are you afraid you won't be able to return to your physical body, or that an entity will take over?

As I explained in this book, what we call out-of-body experience is actually a displacement of consciousness into other realities via different energy bodies. In no case is there an exit from the soul, and we don't leave an empty shell behind. The connection with the physical body remains unbroken for as long as the latter is alive, making the phenomenon of possession impossible. The real challenge lies in remaining out-of-body for as long as possible.

What's the difference between a lucid dream and an out-of-body experience?

This is not an easy question to answer. The ideal way to enjoy the difference is to transform a lucid dream into an out-of-body experience. In general, a lucid dream is characterized by the fact that one becomes aware of the phenomenon during the scenario, while in an OBE one experiences it from separation to reintegration into the physical body. The vision is also different. In a lucid dream, the environment is extremely realistic and clear, often very colorful. During an astral projection, the vision is often blurred or even dark when one is close to the physical body, and one must readjust one's consciousness to bring clarity. I also noticed a difference when interacting with the protagonists. When one wakes up in a dream world and interacts with the characters around us, they tend to freeze like lifeless dolls, staring into space. During an OBE, the encounters are completely different because the characters are entities in their own right, evolving with their own consciousness.

How have you benefited from out-of-body experiences?

The first benefit—and this is common to all experiencers—is the confirmation of the existence of consciousness independent of the physical body. This offers a new perspective on life after death. As a result, daily life takes on a new flavor, and we naturally adopt a certain detachment from the events of life. Knowing that we are much more than a body of flesh and bones contributes to a striking and transformative awareness. Beyond that, we remain the same people; we don't become wisemen or great masters.

When is the best time to practice?

Personally, I practice after waking up at night, between 4 a.m. and 5 a.m. In fact, this is the most common response when you ask people this question. For others it's naptime. However, the end of the night remains the ideal moment, as we've already had a good night's rest and are able to go back to sleep.

What's the best position in which to induce dissociation?

Based on a large number of testimonials and my own personal experience, I don't know of any one position that's better than another. I've been able to project myself on my back as well as lying on my side. I have also found that geographical orientation has no influence on success.

How long does it take to achieve an out-of-body experience?

The answer varies from person to person depending on age, gender, psychological conditioning, family, professional life, and so on. There are so many factors that our results vary. You may well experience an astral exit tonight or it may take you a year. However, as a general rule, a person who practices seriously on a daily basis will begin to witness changes within a week, particularly in their dreams and energetic sensations (such as small vibrations, for example). And quite often they will experience an out-of-body experience after twenty to thirty days of practice. Note here that perseverance is one of the keys to success, and that the journey is as enriching as the destination.

What's the most common mistake?

A mistake frequently made by practitioners is not allowing enough time for deep relaxation. It's not simply a question of relaxing the body, but of reaching a trance-like state where the body is asleep but consciousness is awake. Superficial relaxation is insufficient for this kind of experience; it's crucial to no longer be aware of your physical body. This is why I strongly recommend that you first master the ideal state of consciousness (ISC), which will make the following steps much easier.

Why do you do this type of experiment?

My interest in out-of-body experiences began at the age of ten, following an involuntary experience. It awakened in me the need to understand this phenomenon. My main motive, however, is a deep desire to discover who I am and where I come from—to explore the meaning of this life so that I can embrace it fully. Religious and spiritual texts are enriching, but experiencing it for myself offers me a deeper understanding than just "knowing;" I prefer to "see" for myself.

What is your practice?

I usually get ready in the evening before going to bed. I relax and program myself to have an out-of-body experience at around 5 a.m. while reminding myself of my goal. Then I practice the "Wake Back To Bed" method, which involves getting up for five to ten minutes then going to back to bed to perform my OBE method. I lie on my back, using this position not only because I'm practicing in bed but also to signal to my subconscious that the goal is not to sleep, but to achieve an astral exit. I count from one to ten according to Robert Monroe's relaxation method. This position makes it easier for me to stay awake. Then I practice a chakra-stimulation technique to focus my attention and improve my energy. Once I feel energized yet drowsy, I repeat my affirmation, "I'm out of the body now!" or, "I'm leaving my body now!" until I fall asleep or reach the vibrational state.

I've been trying for years and I still haven't succeeded. Why?

Ask yourself several questions: are you reaching the ideal state of consciousness, where the body is asleep and the mind is awake? Do you practice regularly? Is your desire for an out-of-body experience a priority, or do you have other major activities or projects? It may be worth adjusting your priorities, examining your fears, or changing your technique if you've been using the same one for a long time. Success depends on many factors, and it's not always easy to create the optimum conditions. If you're going through a period of fatigue or demotivation, consider starting with lucid dreaming, which represents a more accessible approach to inducing an out-of-body experience.

Can anyone have an out-of-body experience?

Theoretically, yes. However, some people seem more willing than others to succeed in these experiments. Interest in out-of-body experiences is already a good indicator. If only superficial or ephemeral attention is paid to this phenomenon, it is unlikely that significant results will be achieved. Personally, I believe that some people are specifically "called" to explore these states of consciousness—rather like a religious calling. We are all destined to achieve different things during our lives on Earth, and for some, out-of-body experiences are an integral part of that.

I have aphantasia; can I still have out-of-body experiences? And if so, do you think I'll be able to distinguish the astral environment?

For those who don't know, aphantasia is the inability to conjure a mental image; they can't visualize. That's why I advise you to use techniques that don't involve visualization, such as affirmations and internal movement. Once you're out of the body, you'll perceive the environment in the same way you perceive that of physical reality.

GLOSSARY

Temporal Anomaly: An experience in which the perception of time differs significantly from the goal measurement of time.

Affirmation: A positive phrase or statement that we repeat to ourselves regularly with the intention of modifying our subconscious thoughts and behaviors. The idea is that—through continual repetition—these affirmations can influence internal beliefs and—by extension the individual's actions and destiny.

The Soul: An ancient concept central to many philosophical, religious and spiritual traditions around the world. It is often regarded as the immaterial, eternal essence of an individual, distinct from his or her physical body.

Astral Body: A subtle component of the human being, able to travel to the astral plane during sleep, meditation or OBE.

Energy Body: The nonphysical vehicle of consciousness. We possess different energy bodies with different vibratory rates, enabling us to carry our souls into different dimensions.

Consciousness: A complex term that encompasses many aspects of human experience, and is often defined as the capacity to be aware of oneself and one's environment. It includes perception, thought, memory, and the subjective experience of sensations and emotions.

Splitting: The sensation of being separated from one's physical body, typical of out-of-body experiences.

Nonphysical Dimension: A plane of existence that transcends the physical world, including concepts such as the afterlife, the astral plane, and other levels of consciousness that are thought to exist beyond the limits of the material world.

State of Expanded Consciousness: A state in which consciousness exceeds habitual limits, achieved through spiritual practices.

Binaural Beat Frequency: An audio technique that induces altered states of consciousness through tones of different frequencies.

Hypnagogia: The transitional state between wakefulness and sleep, with visual and auditory phenomena.

Mental Imagery: The practice of actively visualizing images in the mind, used to induce lucid dreams or OBE.

Dream Lucidity: The ability to consciously recognize that one is dreaming.

Dream Memory: The ability to remember details of dreams after waking up.

NDE (Near Death Experience): An experience reported by people who have been close to death.

OBE (Out-of-body experience): The perception of oneself as separate from the physical body.

Sleep Paralysis: A state of immobility when falling asleep or waking up, often a gateway to OBE.

Exit Phenomenon: The sensations experienced when consciousness separates from the physical body.

Non-Ordinary Reality: Any state of consciousness—or experience—differing from everyday physical reality.

Induced Awakening: A technique for interrupting sleep to facilitate entry into a lucid dream.

Polyphasic Sleep: Dividing sleep into several short periods to increase the frequency of lucid dreams.

Guided Visualization: A meditative practice using narration to induce relaxation and altered states of consciousness.

Collective Consciousness: The notion that individuals share common beliefs and values at the level of a group or society.

Egregore: A thought-form or collective consciousness created by the beliefs and rituals of a group of people.

Rooting : A practice aimed at energetically connecting a person to the earth to improve physical and spiritual well-being.

Experiencer: A practitioner of altered-consciousness experiences

Chakra Harmonization: A practice aimed at balancing the body's energy centers to promote health and spiritual well-being.

Manifest Intention: The power of thought and conscious intention to influence the physical world and manifest desired realities.

Kundalini: In spiritual traditions, a cosmic force or energy located at the base of the spine, often associated with spiritual awakening.

Mediumship: The ability to perceive and communicate with spirits or entities from other dimensions.

Planes of Existence: The various levels or dimensions of reality, each having its own characteristics and inhabitants.

Lucid Dream: A dream in which the dreamer is aware that he or she is dreaming. In this state, the dreamer can often exercise a degree of control over his or her dream environment.

Physical Reality: Everything that is tangible and measurable in the universe, i.e., everything that can be observed, quantified, or experimentally confirmed in our environment. It encompasses material objects, forces, energy, and phenomena that obey the laws of physics.

Synchronicity: The significant coincidence of two or more events that are not causally linked, but whose relationship is meaningful to the person perceiving them.

Energetic Transmutation: The process of changing or converting one form of energy into another, often used in spiritual practices for healing or personal evolution.

Shamanic Journey: A kind of meditation or trance used in certain spiritual traditions to travel to spiritual worlds or to obtain answers and healings.

Spiritual Awakening: A process of profound personal transformation, often characterized by a heightened awareness of spiritual reality and self.

Archetypes : Universal symbols or motifs in collective psychology often encountered in dreams and visions.

Aura: An energy field said to surround living beings, often perceived by mediums and during certain spiritual experiences.

Clairvoyance: The ability to perceive events or obtain information by extrasensory means beyond normal perception.

Deja Vu: A strange and sometimes disconcerting feeling that you've already experienced a specific event, even if it's not possible.

Trance State: An altered state of consciousness characterized by deep relaxation and openness to outside influence or suggestion.

Spiritual Guides: Nonphysical entities believed to offer wisdom, protection, and guidance on an individual's spiritual journey.

Law of Attraction: The principle that positive thoughts attract positive results in a person's life, while negative thoughts attract negative results.

Prana: In Eastern traditions, the vital breath or life force that animates living beings.

Past-Life Regression: A therapeutic or spiritual technique intended to reveal experiences or memories from past lives.

Energy Care: Practices designed to manipulate or rebalance the flow of energy in the body for healing and well-being.

Telepathy: The communication of information from one mind to another by means other than the physical senses.

Fortune Telling: The ability to perceive information or predict future events without the use of the normal senses.

Visualization: A psychological technique that involves using the imagination to create specific, detailed mental images. This can be used for a variety of purposes, such as mental preparation, stress reduction, performance enhancement, and the manifestation of desired results.

BIBLIOGRAPHY

English books

- Adventures Beyond the Body - William Buhlman (HarperOne)

- The Secret of the Soul - William Buhlman (HarperOne)

- Adventures in the Afterlife - William Buhlman

- Higher Self Now! - Susan and William Buhlman

- Beyond The Astral - Susan and William Buhlman

- Journeys Out of The Body - Robert Monroe

- Far Journeys - Robert Monroe

- Ultimate Journey - Robert Monroe

- Out of Body Experiences - Akhena

- Hacking the Out of Body Experience - Robert Peterson

- Out of Body Experiences: How to Have Them and What to Expect - Robert Peterson

- Lessons Out of the Body - Robert Peterson

-Explorations in Consciousness - Frederick Aardema

- Astral Dynamics - Robert Bruce

- My Big TOE - Thomas Campbell

- Out-of-Body Adventures - Rick Stack

- Soul Traveler - Albert Taylor

- Multidimensional Man - Jurgen Ziewe

- The Art of Lucid Dreaming - Dr. Clare Johnson

- Llewellyn's Complete Book of Lucid Dreaming - Dr. Clare Johnson

- Advanced Lucid Dreaming: The Power of Supplements - Thomas Yuschak (ed. Lulu)

- Dreams of Awakening - Charlie Morley (ed. Hay House UK)
- Lucid Dreaming: Gateway to the Inner Self - Robert Waggoner

French books

- Voyage au-delà du corps, de William Buhlman (éd. AdA Inc)

- Le Secret de l'âme, de William Bulhman (éd. AdA Inc)

- Aventure dans l'au-delà, de William Buhlman (éd. AdA Inc)

- Sortir hors de son corps, 40 années d'expérience aujourd'hui partagées, de Akhena (éd. Channel Soleil)

- Sorties Hors-du-corps : Manuel pratique

- Le voyage hors du corps, de Robert A. Monroe

- Fantastiques expériences de Voyage Astral, de Robert A. Monroe

- Voyages ultimes, de Robert A. Monroe

- La projection du corps astral, de Sylvan Muldoon et Hereward Carrington

- Méthode de dédoublement personnel, de Charles Lancelin (éd. Fernand Lanore)

- Le médecin de l'âme , de Yram

- Voyager dans la lumière, de Paule Boucher (éd. Le Dauphin Blanc)

- Le voyage astral, de Jérôme Bourgine (éd. du Rocher)

- La vie de l'âme pendant le sommeil, de Peter Richelieu (éd. Vivez Soleil)

- Cell Cerc. Voyage Astral - Le Message de Lumière (Kindle)

- L'art de rêver, de Carlos Castaneda (éd. du Rocher)

- Yogas tibétains du rêve et du sommeil, de Tenzin Wangyal Rinpoché (éd. Claire Lumière)

- Rêve lucide, de Robert Waggoner et Caroline Mccready

Other

- Chakra Research for Access to Higher Consciousness - Dr Hiroshi Motoyama

- Chakra Manual - Shalila Sharamon & Bodo J.Baginski

- Energy Work - Robert Bruce

Websites

- Astralinfo.org - William Buhlman's website
- https://www.facebook.com/groups/420183204661463 - William Buhlman's Facebook group
- Robertpeterson.org - Robert Peterson's website
- www.levoyageastral.com - Akhena's website (French)
- https://hemi-sync.com - Online store of Hemi-Sync products

CDs

- Journeys Out of the Body - Relaxation Reinforcement - Hemi-Sync
- Pearl Moon - The Beginning - Hemi-Sync
- Ascension - Hemi-Sync
- Out-of-Body Techniques - William Buhlman - Hemi-Sync
- How to Have an Out of Body Experience: Transcend the Limits of Physical Form and Accelerate Your Spritual Evolution - William Buhlman - Sounds True
- Akhena's SHC CD on sale at www.levoyageastral.com

ACKNOWLEDGMENTS

I would like to take advantage of the publication of this book to express my gratitude to all those who have contributed significantly to the development of my research and experimentation on altered states of consciousness. All the individuals mentioned are friends or acquaintances who have left an indelible mark on my work and practice. I may have inadvertently omitted a few names, so I apologize in advance to those who may have been overlooked, as there are so many people who have contributed to my evolution.

First, I'd like to express my sincere gratitude to my wife, **Karen**, who has always supported me without any judgment and has been an essential pillar in my explorations beyond this reality. I would also like to thank my children, **Tom and Tina**, for the stimulating and enriching discussions we have shared on this subject. Their perspective has greatly contributed to my reflections and advancement.

I'd like to thank **my parents,** with whom I've been able to discuss this subject freely on several occasions. My father even took part in the first workshop led by William Buhlman that I organized in France in 2007. A special tribute to my mom, who was born in heaven in July 2018.

A special thanks to my dear friend **Amélie** for our enriching discussions about my book and the experiences it describes. And to my soul brother, **Franck**, with whom I share a solid fifty-year friendship, a true pillar in my life.

Thanks to **Jerry Kaywell**, an extraordinary priest, a true man of God with a deep heart, whom I had the good fortune to meet at the Monroe Institute and who was an immeasurable support. Jerry is a true friend. I invite you to listen to his superb albums "Field of Stars" and "Very Jerry."

And to **Robert Peterson**, an essential author on out-of-body experiences and a Facebook friend who has inspired me a lot through his books and his superb blog.

The experts :

- Todd Acamesis, Jade Shaw, Nick Barrett, Patty Avalon, Luigi Sciambarella, Thierry Cantara (spiritual son of Akhena), Ken Elliott, Mark Certo, Michel Borguignon (Nuevomouni), Karen Pearce, Nélson Abreu (The International Academy of Consciousness)

Facebook friends :

- Claudia Carlton Lambright, Lynn Stephens, Jaime Lundquist-Munoz, Hugues Marty (co-founder of Astralsight), Liliane Lambert, NelsonAndy Nagao, Eduardo Pinto, Arnaud Thuly.

Friends of the Monroe Institute:

- Masami Noro, <u>Lisa Ober</u>, <u>Daves NotHere</u>, <u>Nelida Rodriguez</u>, <u>Gary Blechingberg</u>, Faith Nouri, Junior Ivenso, Jerry Kaywell , Katie Wright Tarabochia, Sharon McGrath Sananda Kumara, Jalyn Noel, Bob Wood, Nancy Honeycutt McMoneagle (daughter-in-law of Robert Monroe and former president of the Monroe Institute), Denise Files (head of the Monroe Institute store)

I would also like to express my gratitude to all the members of the **astralsociety** and **astralsight** forums, whose exchanges were more than beneficial to the success of my experiments. These two forums unfortunately no longer exist, but most of the old members are on the Facebook groups.

A special thanks to the **members of William Buhlman's Facebook group,** of which I am administrator along with William and Claudia Carlton Lambright. It's a bit like a family and our discussions are always extremely enriching, all overseen by William of course.

I'd like to express my deep gratitude to **Maura Biryoukoff**. Without her crucial intervention—in particular her live translation— it would have been impossible to organize William's courses in France

Thank you, **Claudia Carlton Lambright**, cclediting@gmail.com, editor of my book, for your great editing skills and the thoughtful comments you provided. It was very helpful and very important for me to offer a well-written book for readers.

In conclusion I would like to express my deep gratitude to **William and Susan Buhlman** who proofread and corrected the English version of this book. Many thanks also for your valuable advice.

ABOUT THE AUTHOR

A native of Talence, near Bordeaux, in the Gironde region of France, Franck Labat's childhood experience would slowly shape the course of his life. At just 10 years of age, a spontaneous out-of-body experience opened the doors to a little-known universe, awakening a deep interest in altered states of consciousness.

This was just the beginning of a long journey of exploration and learning. For 13 years, Franck immersed himself in the study of Tibetan Buddhism, immersing himself in the teachings and spiritual practices that helped him forge a compassionate and understanding worldview.

Over time, his passion for healing and his interest in altered states of consciousness naturally led him to the practice of acupuncture. For the past 24 years, he has been offering his services in Valence, in the Drôme, humbly striving to bring well-being and balance to his patients through his knowledge and experience.

In a desire to share and make his knowledge accessible, Franck wrote and published a book in 2012 entitled "*Comprendre l'acupuncture*" (Understanding Acupuncture), published by Editions Ambre. The book aims to bridge the gap between the complexity of acupuncture and the curiosity of the general public, seeking to demystify this ancient practice and reveal its benefits and principles.

In addition to his daily commitment to his patients, Franck has also embraced the role of sponsor in France for William Buhlman, an American author and expert renowned for his work on out-of-body experiences. This responsibility illustrates his desire to humbly contribute to the dissemination of knowledge that can help others explore and understand the deeper dimensions of their being.

In every aspect of his life, Franck Labat seeks to learn and share, guided by an insatiable curiosity and a sincere desire to help. His approach is that of a humble and dedicated explorer, engaged in an ongoing journey of awakening and service.

Addresses

Author's email: franck@out-of-body.org
Author's website: www.out-of-body.org

out-of-body.org

9 782959 544705